ENTERTAIN YOUR BRAIN

Edited by

Ella Harris & Caroline Christin

Sterling Publishing Co., Inc.
New York

Library of Congress Cataloging-in-Publication Data Available

2 4 6 8 10 9 7 5 3

Published by Sterling Publishing Co., Inc.
387 Park Avenue South, New York, NY 10016
© 2007 by Sterling Publishing Co., Inc.

This book is comprised of material from the following Sterling titles:
BrainStrains™ Great Color Optical Illusions © 2002 by Keith Kay; *BrainStrains™ Sneaky Lateral Thinking Puzzles* © 2002 by Paul Sloane &
Des MacHale; *BrainStrains™ Clever Logic Puzzles* © 2002 by Norman D. Willis; *Critical Thinking Puzzles* ©1996 by Michael A. DiSpezio; *Great
Critical Thinking Puzzles* © 1997 by Michael A. DiSpezio; *Challenging Critical Thinking Puzzles* © 1998 by Michael A. DiSpezio; *Eye-Popping
Optical Illusions* © 2001 by Michael A. DiSpezio; *Quick-to-Solve Brainteasers* (English translation) © 1998 by Sterling Publishing Co., Inc.
Originally published under the titles *Para Resolver en el Autobús* and *Para Resolver en el Ascensor* © 1996 and 1997 by José Julián Mendoza
Fernandez; *Match Wits with American Mensa*® © 1999 by Peter Gordon; *Lateral MindTrap Puzzles* © 2000 by MindTrap® Games Inc.; *The
Little Giant*® *Book of Whodunits* © 1998 by Hy Conrad; *Hard-to-Solve Brainteasers* (English Translation) ©1998 by Sterling Publishing Co., Inc.
Originally published under the title *Cómo Jugar y Divertirse con su Inteligencia* © 1978 and 1996 by Jaime and Lea Poniachik; *Ingenious
Lateral Thinking Puzzles* © 1998 by Paul Sloane and Des MacHale; *Tricky Lateral Thinking Puzzles* © 1999 by Paul Sloane and Des MacHale;
Super Lateral Thinking Puzzles © 2000 by Paul Sloane and Des MacHale; *Tricky Optical Illusion Puzzles* (American edition) © 2001 Sterling
Publishing Co., Inc. Originally published in the Netherlands under the title *Optische illusies en andere Puzzels* by Bookman International, bv
Heideveldweg 12, 51 XN LAREN © 1995 Bookman International bv © Jerry Slocum & Jack Botermans English translation © 2000 by
Bookman International bv, Laren; *Cunning Mind-Bending Puzzles* © 2002 by Terry Stickels; *Devious Mind-Bending Puzzles* © 2002 by Terry
Stickels; *Mesmerizing Mind-Bending Puzzles* © 2002 by Terry Stickels; *Test Your Smarts: The Big Book of Self-Scoring IQ Tests* © 1998 by The
Twin Brothers; *Truly Baffling Optical Illusions* © 2003 by Diego Uribe; *Impossible Objects* © 2001 by J. Timothy Unruh

Designed by StarGraphics Studio

Manufactured in China
All rights reserved

Sterling ISBN-13: 978-1-4027-4794-6
ISBN-10: 1-4027-4794-2

For information about custom editions, special sales, premium and corporate purchases,
please contact Sterling Special Sales Department at 800-805-5489 or specialsales@sterlingpub.com.

CONTENTS

Introduction 4

Puzzles 9

Clues 195

Answers 200

Index of Puzzles 255

INTRODUCTION

Welcome to *Entertain Your Brain*! You have just opened up a trove of optical illusions, lateral and critical thinking puzzles, all sorts of brainteasers and mind-benders, Mensa® trivia questions, and math and number stumpers. Puzzle-solvers are always seeking challenges big and small, involving interesting quandaries to ponder—often with surprising resolutions. In one huge volume, *Entertain Your Brain* provides all of these elements along with the one truly priceless benefit: new ways of thinking.

The puzzles in this book may be attacked in a variety of ways. You can look in the Index of Puzzles (beginning on page 255) and note on which pages throughout the book a specific puzzle type appears. Or, if you favor a different approach, you may go through the book in a linear fashion, from the beginning to the end, and encounter a plethora of changing puzzle types. Think of it as training for a marathon—all the time you spend doing the puzzles will inevitably result in the strengthening and toning of your brain. Finally you will end up with the tools to approach not only puzzles with deftness and alacrity, but also your problem-solving skills with real-life obstacles and issues will be greatly enhanced.

ABOUT THE PUZZLES

Optical Illusions

Optical illusions of one kind or another have been part of the human experience throughout all of time. Whether you are gazing at the moon and a face appears or trekking through the desert and encounter a mirage, these experiences are at once familiar and fascinating. These tricks of the mind and eye certainly raised questions and got the imagination going. Ultimately, such elements were used to develop techniques in art, lighting, and architecture. Think of the shadows and play with colors that a painter employs to represent perspective. Look at the architecture of great buildings and how illusions are used to enhance their aesthetic.

Some of the optical illusions will be more straightforward than others. Some will ask questions about a picture just to encourage you to view it differently. Some will have answers to the questions asked and others will not.

The puzzles entitled "Impossible Objects" are a more unique strain of optical illusion. The technical training of our perception fundamentally lies in our ability to see real three-dimensional objects in a two-dimensional drawing or medium. Impossible Objects involve the manipulations of depth and perspective in these two-dimensional media. Impossible in the real three-dimensional world, they operate on misplaced perspective; depth inversions; misleading visual cues; discontinuity of planes; ambiguous coverings, shadings, and joinings; false and conflicting orientations and connections; altered vanishing points, and other "tricks" of the artist. All these techniques involve perspective, which is itself an illusion, because perspective involves nothing more than creating the appearance—or illusion—of depth in three-dimensional space. Looking at it this way, Impossible Objects are actually double illusions.

Impossible Objects work contrary to our fundamental notions of perception. For example, when we look at a figure in this book we first perceive a three-dimensional object, but then we sense that something is not quite right. A moment later we realize that the object is spatially impossible, yet we see clearly that it is obviously possible on paper. It is not the two-dimensional representation that is possible, but the three-dimensional one. In other words, impossible objects represent a sort of netherland of figures that can be imagined and fairly easily drawn, but not constructed in the real world.

Lateral Thinking Puzzles

A man was held in a high-security prison and closely watched. His wife sent him a letter in which she asked, "Should I plant the potatoes in the garden now?" He replied, "Do not plant anything in the garden. That is where I hide the guns." A little later he received another letter from his wife saying, "Many policemen came to our house. They dug up the garden but did not find anything." He wrote back, "Now is the time to plant the potatoes."

That man used a little lateral thinking to solve his wife's gardening problem—and so can we all. We need new and creative ways of problem solving, and more and more people see lateral thinking puzzles as a way to fire up this process. Trainers use these puzzles in management training courses to force managers to check their assumptions; teachers use them in class to stimulate and reward children. In all cases, one person knows the answer and he or she answers the question for the other players.

The lateral thinking puzzles in *Entertain Your Brain* are situation puzzles. They should be fun—but they also help to develop skills in questioning, deduction, logic, and lateral thinking. They are based on a statement of situation that you have to use as a starting point in order to arrive at a particular explanation or solution. Often there can be many possible scenarios that explain the puzzle, but you have to find the "right" answer. If you get stuck, look to the lateral thinking clues (page 195) for some hints. The aim is to arrive at the solution given in the Answer section, not simply to find a solution that satisfies the initial conditions.

As with most problems we face, it is best to start by testing your assumptions, and by asking broad questions that establish general conditions, motives, and actions. Don't narrow in on specific solutions until you have first established the broad parameters of what is going on.

Critical Thinking Puzzles

When we think critically we are engaging in intellectual strategies to probe the basic nature of a problem, situation, or puzzle. By these strategies, we mean making observations; predictions; generalizations; reasoning by assumptions; comparisons and contrasts; uncovering relationships between the parts to the whole; and looking for sequences.

Some of these critical thinking puzzles are old favorites that have entertained people for years. Several of them are presented in their time-tested way. Most of the standards, however, have a new twist or updated story added. Other puzzles require some inventive solutions, so don't be afraid to be creative and to think outside the box.

Some require inexpensive material that can probably be found around the house: a pair of scissors, markers, tape, toothpicks, and a yardstick. Even though some puzzles can be solved using algebra, they were selected for their ability to be visualized and figured out this way. Therefore, in addition to being fun to do, they offer an arena to practice even more thinking skills.

IQ Tests

In the book you will find two IQ tests. Many believe these tests provide a fairly accurate evaluation of a person's intelligence. These tests don't assess every possible form of human intelligence, but rather, they provide a means to measure intelligence in certain precise classifications and will permit test-takers to make a solid validation of their IQ.

Explanations are provided along with the answers to help you with questions that you were unable to answer or that you got wrong. So if you don't give much credence to the IQ scores, treat the tests as good mind exercises. By taking note of your thought processes and by studying your results, you will gain a better understanding of how your mind works and how to make it work better.

Before You Start: Measuring Intelligence

There are various methods to calculate IQ. In this case the fixed median is 100. The median equals approximately half the number of attempts. These tests measure each of the three most characteristic forms of intelligence, defined by modern psychology as: verbal intelligence, numeric intelligence, and spatial intelligence.

Taking the Tests

To answer the different types of questions to achieve a valid score:

Allow 40 minutes for each test.

Try to avoid any disturbances while taking the test.

The tests contain questions that you are supposed to think about. Don't look at the questions prior to taking the tests. Your results will be more accurate.

During the test, take time to read each question carefully, so as to not waste time on incorrect answers.

INTRODUCTION

Trivia Questions

The trivia questions that follow cover five different categories: Movies & Television; Music, Arts & Letters; Sports & Games; Travel & Geography; and History & Science. Every question was sent to forty members of American Mensa (the High IQ Society) who had expressed interest in trivia or puzzles. Their answers were graded, and the questions in each category are presented in order of difficulty (so as you delve further into the book the questions within each category get progressively harder).

You will find that the answers to the questions are each accompanied by a percentage. This number indicates what percentage of the Mensa members got each question correct. So now you can compare yourself to the "cream of the crop," based on a running total or on each question. For the purposes of scoring, each question counts for one point. To count as correct, all parts of the answer must be right. If the question asks for two names, both must be correct to score the point. There is no partial credit. For the names of real people, only the last name is required. For fictional names, either the first or last name is enough. For cities, you need only the city name, not the state or country where the city is found. Any portion of the answer in parentheses is there for clarification, and is not required for our answer to count as correct. There is no penalty for wrong answers.

The Mensa members had to work alone and were not allowed any references. You can seek as much "assistance" as you feel comfortable with.

Now you are ready to begin a colorful, stimulating, and challenging journey through these eye-popping, mind-bending, brain-teasing pages.

Enjoy!

OPTICAL ILLUSION

Stare at the yellow dot for about 30 seconds. Try not to blink. Now stare at a piece of white paper. What do you see?

Answer on page 200

BRAINTEASER

1 How many times can you subtract 6 from 30?

2 What number can you subtract half from to obtain a result that is zero?

3 How can half of 12 be 7?

4 Find two positive numbers that have a one-digit answer when multiplied and a two-digit answer when added.

5 Find two whole, positive numbers that have the same answer when multiplied together as when one is divided by the other.

Answers on page 206

LATERAL THINKING

Bertha's Travels

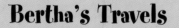

Every day Bertha travels 30 miles in the course of her work. She doesn't travel in a wheeled vehicle and never has problems with traffic, the police, weather, or airports. What does she do?

Clue on page 195
Answer on page 212

The Tracks of My Tires

The police found a murder victim and they noticed a pair of tire tracks leading to and from the body. They followed the tracks to a nearby farmhouse where two men and a woman were sitting on the porch. There was no car at the farmhouse and none of the three could drive. The police arrested the woman. Why?

Clue on page 195
Answer on page 212

OPTICAL ILLUSION

How many cubes can you see,
seven or eight?

Answer on page 200

BRAINTEASER

6 Find two positive numbers that have the same answer when multiplied together as when added together.

7 Find a two-digit number that equals two times the result of multiplying its digits.

8 Find three whole, positive numbers that have the same answer when multiplied together as when added together.

9 What two 2-digit numbers are each equal to their rightmost digit squared?

10 Find the highest number that can be written with three digits.

Answers on page 206

LATERAL THINKING

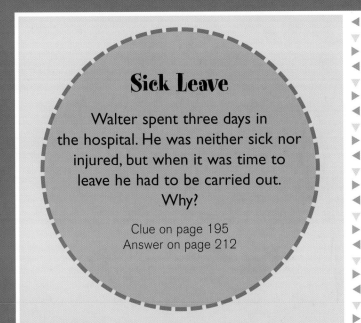

Sick Leave

Walter spent three days in the hospital. He was neither sick nor injured, but when it was time to leave he had to be carried out. Why?

Clue on page 195
Answer on page 212

The Upset Woman

When the woman saw him she was upset. Even though she had never seen him before, she had left some food for him because she knew he would be hungry. But he could not reach the food because he had an iron bar across his back. He died soon after and the woman was pleased. What's going on?

Clue on page 195
Answer on page 212

OPTICAL ILLUSION

This is a poster of vaudeville performer, T. Elder Hearn. He was a quick-change artist. What do you see in this publicity print?

Answer on page 200

BRAINTEASER

11 The ages of a father and a son add up to 55. The father's age is the son's age reversed. How old are they?

12 How much do 10 pieces of candy cost if one thousand pieces cost $10?

13 An outlet and a light bulb cost $1.20. We know that the outlet costs $1 more than the light bulb. How much does each cost?

14 If 75% of all women are tall, 75% are brunette, and 75% are pretty, what is the minimum percentage of tall, brunette, pretty women?

Answers on page 206

LATERAL THINKING

Top at Last

William was the least intelligent and laziest boy in a class of 30 students who took an examination. Yet when the results were announced, William's name was at the top of the list. How come?

Clue on page 195
Answer on page 212

In the Middle of the Night

A man wakes up at night in the pitch dark. He knows that on his bedside table are a razor, a watch, and a glass of water. How can he reach for the table and be sure to pick up the watch without touching either the razor or the glass of water?

Clue on page 195
Answer on page 212

OPTICAL ILLUSION

Magician Horace Goldin used this flyer to advertise his theater shows. Who looks taller, Goldin as a man or as a boy?

Answer on page 200

BRAINTEASER

15 Thirty-two students took a nationwide exam and all the students from New York passed it. If the students from New York made up exactly 5% of the total number of the students that passed the test, how many students passed it and how many students were from New York?

16 Of the 960 people in a theater, 17% tipped 5 cents to the usher, 50% of the remaining 83% tipped 10 cents, and the rest tipped nothing. How much did the usher get?

17 What must you do to make the equation below true?
$$81 \times 9 = 801$$

Answers on page 206

LATERAL THINKING

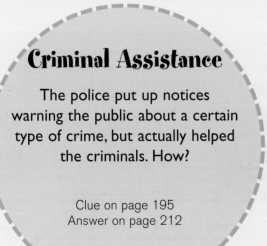

Criminal Assistance

The police put up notices warning the public about a certain type of crime, but actually helped the criminals. How?

Clue on page 195
Answer on page 212

Material Witness

In the fabric shop, the curtains are neatly arranged by style. The floral-patterned ones are in a section marked "Floral," the plain ones are in a section marked "Plain," and the striped ones are in a section marked "Striped." But one pair with vertical blue stripes is not in the "Striped" section. Why not?

Clue on page 195
Answer on page 212

CLOWNING AROUND

Clowns work in the circus.
Here's the clown. Where's the circus?

18 There are 100 buildings along a street. A sign maker is ordered to number the buildings from 1 to 100. How many "9's" will he need?

19 How many tickets with different points of origination and destination can be sold on a bus line that travels a loop of 25 stops?

20 We know that humans have up to 100,000 hairs. In a city with more than 200,000 people, would it be possible to find two or more people with the same number of hairs?

Answer on page 200

Answers on page 206

LATERAL THINKING

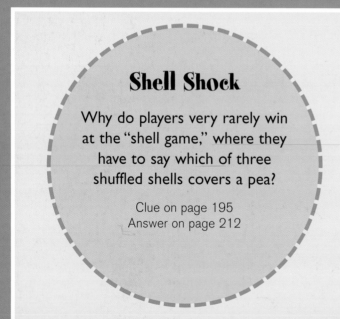

Shell Shock

Why do players very rarely win at the "shell game," where they have to say which of three shuffled shells covers a pea?

Clue on page 195
Answer on page 212

Plain and Simple

A boy who is three feet tall puts a nail into a tree at his exact height. He returns two years later when he has grown by six inches and the tree has grown by twelve inches. How much taller is the nail than the boy?

Clue on page 195
Answer on page 212

OPTICAL ILLUSION

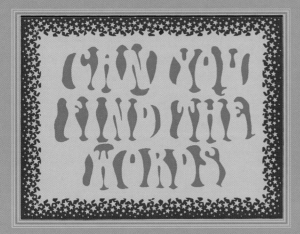

Can you find the hidden message?
What does it say?

Answer on page 200

BRAINTEASER

21 All my ties are red except two. All my ties are blue except two. All my ties are brown except two. How many ties do I have?

22 A street that's 30 yards long has a chestnut tree every 6 yards on both sides. How many chestnut trees are on the entire street?

23 A pet shop owner is in the country-side. If he says, "one bird per olive tree," there is one bird too many. However, if he says, "two birds per olive tree," there are no birds left over. How many birds and olive trees are there?

Answers on page 206

LATERAL THINKING

Wonderful Weather

A ship sank in perfect weather conditions. If the weather had been worse, the ship would probably not have sunk. What happened?

Clue on page 195
Answer on page 212

Rush Job

In 1849, a man went to the California gold rush hoping to make his fortune by selling tents to the miners. However, the weather was fine and the miners slept out in the open, so the man could sell no tents. But he made his fortune anyway and his name is famous to this day. How did he become rich and who is he?

Clue on page 195
Answer on page 212

OPTICAL ILLUSION

The hooded monk has a bizarre secret.
What is it?

Answer on page 200

BRAINTEASER

24 In a singles tennis tournament, 111 players participated. They used a new ball for each match. When a player lost one match, he was eliminated from the tournament. How many balls did they need?

25 Peter and John had a picnic. Peter had already eaten half of the muffins when John ate half of the remaining muffins plus three more. There were no muffins left. How many muffins did they take to the picnic?

Answers on pages 206 & 207

LATERAL THINKING

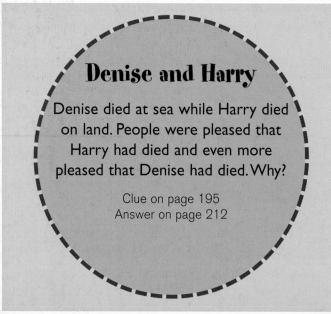

Denise and Harry

Denise died at sea while Harry died on land. People were pleased that Harry had died and even more pleased that Denise had died. Why?

Clue on page 195
Answer on page 212

The Office Job

A man applied for a job in an office. When he arrived at the busy, noisy office he was told by the receptionist to fill out a form and then wait until called. He completed the form and then sat and waited along with four other candidates who had arrived earlier. After a few minutes, he got up and went into an inner office and was subsequently given the job. The other candidates who had arrived earlier were angry. The manager explained why the man had been given the job. What was the reason?

Clue on page 195
Answer on page 212

OPTICAL ILLUSION

Can you figure out what this Victorian puzzle shows? Is it an animal, vegetable, or mineral? Try looking at it from different angles.

Answer on page 200

BRAINTEASER

26 A shepherd says to another, "If I give you one sheep, you will have twice the number of sheep that I have, but if you give me one, we will both have the same number of sheep." How many sheep did each shepherd have?

27 If I put in one canary per cage, I have one bird too many. However, if I put in two canaries per cage, I have one cage too many. How many cages and birds do I have?

28 If 1½ sardines cost 1½ dollars, how much would 7½ sardines cost?

Answers on page 207

LATERAL THINKING

Mechanical Advantage

A driver had a problem with his car in a remote area miles from the nearest garage. He stopped at a little candy store, where his problem was quickly solved. How?

Clue on page 196
Answer on page 212

Co-lateral Damage

During World War II, U.S. forces lost many bombers in raids over Germany due to antiaircraft fire. From the damage on returning bombers, they were able to build up a clear picture of which parts of the planes were hit most frequently and which weren't hit at all. How did they use this information to reduce losses?

Clue on page 196
Answer on page 212

OPTICAL ILLUSION

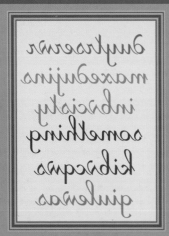

Only one of these sets of letters says
something when viewed in a mirror.
Can you figure out which one
it is before using the mirror?

Answer on page 200

BRAINTEASER

29 If a brick weighs 3 pounds plus $\frac{1}{2}$ a brick, what's the weight of $1\frac{1}{2}$ bricks?

30 If $1\frac{1}{2}$ dozen sardines costs $9\frac{1}{2}$ dollars, how much do 18 sardines cost?

31 If $1\frac{1}{2}$ men can eat $1\frac{1}{2}$ pies in $1\frac{1}{2}$ minutes, how many pies can 3 men eat in half an hour?

32 Yesterday afternoon, I went to visit my friend Albert, who is a painter. While I was watching him paint, I told him, "No wonder it takes you so long to finish a painting. Since I arrived, you have entered the studio twelve times." How many times did he leave the studio?

Answers on page 207

LATERAL THINKING

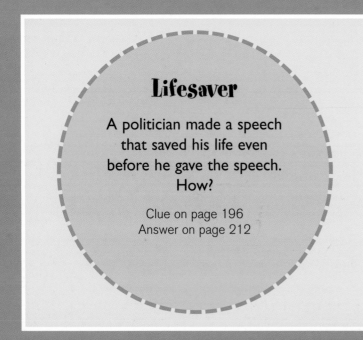

Lifesaver

A politician made a speech
that saved his life even
before he gave the speech.
How?

Clue on page 196
Answer on page 212

The Single Word

A woman whom I had never met before was introduced to me. I didn't say a word. She told me about herself, but I didn't say a word. She told me many more things about herself, but I didn't say a word. Eventually I said one word and she was very disappointed. What was the word?

Clue on page 196
Answer on page 212

OPTICAL ILLUSION

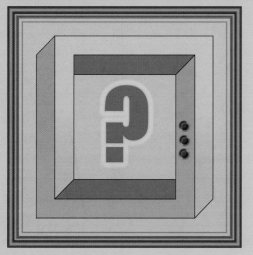

Are the three dots on the inside or the outside of this frame?

Answer on page 200

BRAINTEASER

33 If two ducks are swimming in front of another duck, two ducks are swimming behind another duck, and one duck is swimming between two other ducks, what is the minimum number of ducks?

34 Two people are flipping coins. Each time, they bet $1 apiece. At the end, one person won $3 and the other one won three times. How many games did they play?

35 If one nickel is worth five cents, how much is half of one half of a nickel worth?

Answers on page 207

LATERAL THINKING

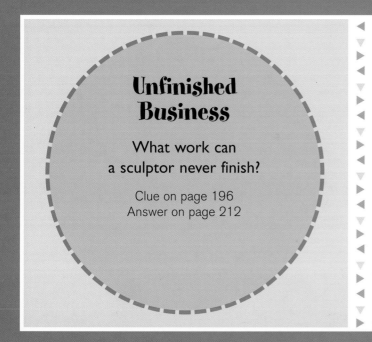

Unfinished Business

What work can a sculptor never finish?

Clue on page 196
Answer on page 212

Inheritance

In ancient Ireland, a king had two sons, each of whom wanted to inherit the kingdom. The king decreed that each should be put in a separate rowboat about one mile from shore and told to row in. The first to touch the shore would inherit the kingdom. The elder and stronger son rowed more quickly and was about to touch the shore with the younger son some 20 yards behind him and farther out to sea. How did the younger son inherit the kingdom?

Clue on page 196
Answer on page 213

This picture is based on what were known in Victorian times as "Fantasy Faces." What do you see?

Answer on page 200

36 A bottle with a cylindrical shape at the bottom and with an irregular shape at the top is filled halfway to the top with liquid. The cylindrical part contains approximately three-fourths of the capacity of the bottle and we wish to determine the exact percentage of liquid that the bottle contains. We cannot open it and we can only use a ruler. What must we do?

37 We put a spore in a test tube. Every hour the spore divides into three parts, all the same size as the original part. If we put it in at 3 P.M., at 9 P.M. the tube will be completely full. At what time will the tube be one-third full?

Answers on page 207

LATERAL THINKING

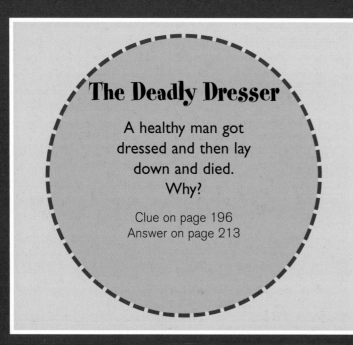

The Deadly Dresser

A healthy man got dressed and then lay down and died. Why?

Clue on page 196
Answer on page 213

Golf Bag

During a golf competition, Paul's ball ended up in a bunker inside a little brown paper bag that had blown onto the course. He was told that he must either play the ball in the bag or take the ball out of the bag and incur a one-stroke penalty. What did he do?

Clue on page 196
Answer on page 213

OPTICAL ILLUSION

Is there life after death?

Answer on page 200

BRAINTEASER

38 Two soldiers have been ordered to do the following chores:
1. Peel potatoes.
2. Do the dishes.
3. Mow the lawn.

Each of these chores, when done by one person, takes one hour. If they start at 8 A.M., what could they do to take as little time as possible if they have only one knife, one lawn mower, and one sink with room for one person?

39 How long is a rope that is 2 yards shorter than another rope that is three times the length of the first rope?

Answers on page 207

LATERAL THINKING

Landlubber

A man sailed single-handedly around the world in a small boat. Yet he was always in sight of land. How come?

Clue on page 196
Answer on page 213

Flipping Pages

Yesterday, I went through a book, which I had already read, in a peculiar manner. After I finished a page, I flipped to the next page, then rotated the book 180 degrees. After that page, I rotated the book 180 degrees and then flipped to the next page, rotated the book 180 degrees again, and continued in this fashion until I was done with the whole book. What was going on?

Clue on page 196
Answer on page 213

OPTICAL ILLUSION

This is the island of St. Helena.
Where is Napoleon?

Answer on page 200

BRAINTEASER

40 A spider spins its web in a window frame. Each day, it spins an area equal to that of the amount already completed. It takes 30 days to cover the entire window frame. How long would two spiders take? (In the case of two spiders, each of them spins an amount equal to the area of the existing part of the web made by that particular spider.)

41 If a post is 6 yards longer than half of its own length, how long is the post?

42 How much mud (measured in liters) is there in a rectangular hole 2 meters wide, 3 meters long, and 3 meters deep?

Answers on page 207

LATERAL THINKING

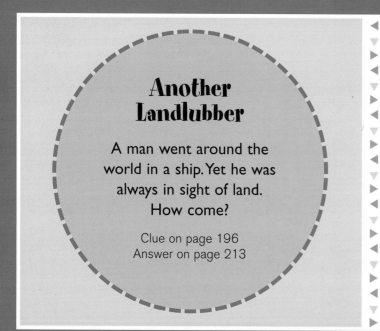

Another Landlubber

A man went around the world in a ship. Yet he was always in sight of land. How come?

Clue on page 196
Answer on page 213

The Test

The teacher gave Ben and Jerry a written test. Ben read the test, then folded his arms and answered none of the questions. Jerry carefully wrote out good answers to the questions. When the time was up, Ben handed in a blank sheet of paper while Jerry handed in his work. The teacher gave Ben an A and Jerry a C. Why?

Clue on page 196
Answer on page 213

OPTICAL ILLUSION

This old sketch is called
"Under the Mistletoe."
What's odd about this drawing?

Answer on page 200

BRAINTEASER

43 One mother gave 25 books to her daughter and another mother gave her daughter eight books. However, between both daughters they only increased their collection by 25 books. How can this be?

44 Emily is taller than Ann and shorter than Dolores. Who is the tallest of the three?

45 Rose is now as old as Joan was six years ago. Who is older?

46 If Emily speaks in a softer voice than Ann, and Dolores in a louder voice than Ann, does Emily speak louder or softer than Dolores?

Answers on page 207

LATERAL THINKING

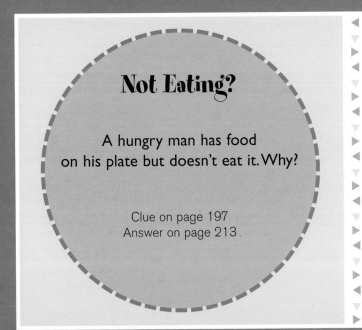

Not Eating?

A hungry man has food on his plate but doesn't eat it. Why?

Clue on page 197
Answer on page 213

Chimney Problem

An industrial archaeologist was examining an abandoned factory in a remote place with no one in sight or within earshot. He climbed to the top of an old 100-foot chimney by means of a rusty old ladder attached to the outside of the chimney. When he got to the top, the ladder fell away, leaving him stranded. How did he get down?

Clue on page 197
Answer on page 213

IT'S MAGIC!

96	11	89	68
88	69	91	16
61	86	18	99
19	98	66	81

What's so special about
this set of numbers?

Answer on page 200

47 James is sitting between John and Peter. Philip is sitting on Peter's right. Between whom is Peter sitting?

48 Which has more value—one pound of $10 gold coins or half a pound of $20 gold coins?

49 A sultan wanted to offer his daughter in marriage to the candidate whose horse would win the race. However, the rules of the race stated that the winner would be the one in last place. He didn't want the race to last forever, so he thought of a way to solve this. What was it?

Answers on page 207

LATERAL THINKING

Superior Knowledge

When the mother superior returned to the convent after a weekend away, she immediately noticed that a man had been there—and that was strictly against the rules. How did she know?

Clue on page 197
Answer on page 213

Alex Ferguson

In the early 1990s, Alex Ferguson was the coach of Manchester United, the most successful professional soccer team in England at that time. Previously he had been a very successful manager in Scotland. He would be a very successful manager of a soccer team anywhere in the world, except Singapore. Why is that?

Clue on page 197
Answer on page 213

OPTICAL ILLUSION

What happens when you rotate this page?

Answer on page 200

BRAINTEASER

50 A man went into a store and bought an umbrella for $10. He gave the salesperson a $50 bill. The salesperson went to the bank to get change. Two hours later, the bank teller went to the store claiming that the $50 bill was counterfeit, so the salesperson had to exchange it for a real one with the bank teller. Between the customer and the bank, how much did the store lose?

51 We have a scale and a set of weights in a field. The scale is not very accurate, but it is consistent in its inaccuracies. How can we know the exact weight of four apples?

Answers on page 208

LATERAL THINKING

The Engraving

A woman saw a color engraving of Queen Elizabeth II advertised for $1 and bought it. When it arrived, she had no cause for complaint, but she wasn't pleased. Why?

Clue on page 197
Answer on page 213

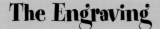

One Mile

If you go to your atlas and look at the western edge of the state of South Dakota where it borders Montana, you will see a straight line with a kink of about one mile. Everywhere else the border is a straight line. The kink does not benefit any local landowner, and no other states are involved. Why is the kink there?

Clue on page 197
Answer on page 213

What is unusual about
this sentence?

Answer on page 200

52 We have two pitchers—one with one quart of water and the other with one quart of wine. We take a tablespoon of the wine and mix it in the pitcher of water. Then we take a tablespoon from this pitcher and mix it into the pitcher with the wine. Is there more wine in the water pitcher or more water in the wine pitcher? What would have happened if after pouring a spoonful of wine into the water, we had not mixed it well?

53 Distribute nine marbles in four boxes so that each box contains an odd number of marbles, different from the three other boxes. You must use all nine.

Answers on page 208

LATERAL THINKING

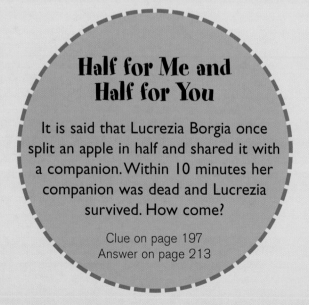

Half for Me and Half for You

It is said that Lucrezia Borgia once split an apple in half and shared it with a companion. Within 10 minutes her companion was dead and Lucrezia survived. How come?

Clue on page 197
Answer on page 213

Dali's Brother

Some time after Salvador Dali's death, his younger brother became famous as (believe it or not) a surrealist painter. This younger brother had great international success and the word "genius" was used to describe him. His name was Dali and he did not change it. Yet today, the world remembers only one Dali and few people even know that he had a brother. Why is this?

Clue on page 197
Answer on page 213

OPTICAL ILLUSION

This soldier is looking for his horse.
Do you have any idea where it is?

Answer on page 200

BRAINTEASER

54 On one side of a scale we have a partially filled fish bowl. When we put a fish in the bowl, the total weight of the bowl increases by exactly the same amount as the weight of the fish. However, if we hold the fish by the tail and partially introduce it into the water, will the total weight be greater than before introducing the fish?

55 A little bird weighing 5 ounces is sleeping in a cage. We put the cage on a scale and it weighs one pound. The bird then wakes up and starts flying all over the cage. What will the scale indicate while the bird is in the air?

Answers on page 208

LATERAL THINKING

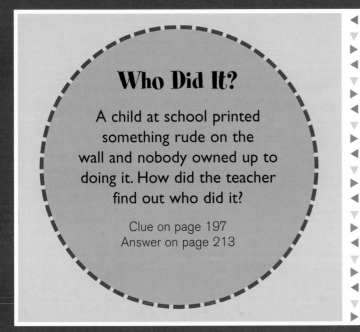

Who Did It?

A child at school printed something rude on the wall and nobody owned up to doing it. How did the teacher find out who did it?

Clue on page 197
Answer on page 213

Window Pain

A builder builds a house that has a square window. It is two feet high and two feet wide. It is not covered by anything. The person for whom the house is being built decides that the window does not give enough light. He tells the builder to change the window so that it gives twice the amount of light. It must be in the same wall, and it must be a square window that is two feet high and two feet wide. How does the builder accomplish this task?

Clue on page 197
Answer on page 213

OPTICAL ILLUSION

Can you discover why this old British colonial patriotic design is called
"The Glory of a Lion Is His Mane"?

Answer on page 200

BRAINTEASER

56 We have 10 sacks full of balls. All sacks contain balls weighing 10 ounces each, except one of the sacks, which contains balls weighing 9 ounces each. By weighing the balls, what would be the minimum number of weighings required (on a scale that gives weight readouts) to identify the sack containing the defective balls?

57 "And then I took out my sword and cut the thick chain that was linked to two posts into two pieces," said the samurai. "That is not true," said the monk. How did the monk know the samurai's story was untrue?

Answers on page 208

LATERAL THINKING

Lethal Relief

A famine-stricken Third World country was receiving food aid from the West, but this inadvertently led to the deaths of several people. How?

Clue on page 197
Answer on page 213

Nonconventional

In a convent, the novice nuns at the dinner table are not allowed to ask for anything such as the salt from the other end of the table. This is because they should be so aware of one another's needs that they should not need to ask. How do they get around this prohibition?

Clue on page 197
Answer on page 213

1

What number best completes the series?

4   7   10   13   .....

3

What two numbers complete this series?

8   11   10   9   12   7   ....

2

Complete the following analogy:

Man is to masculine as woman is to .....
(a) girl
(b) feminine
(c) wife
(d) lady

4

Which of the following figures does not belong?

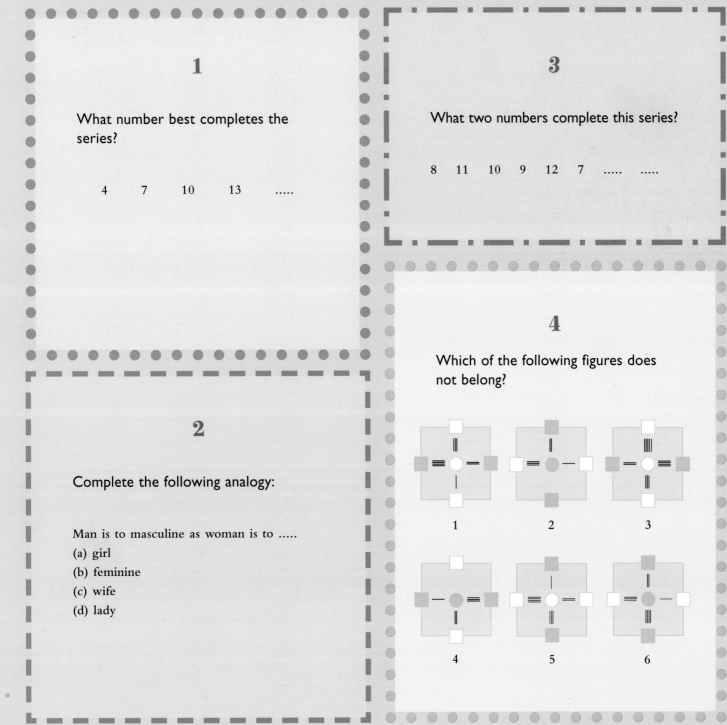

1   2   3

4   5   6

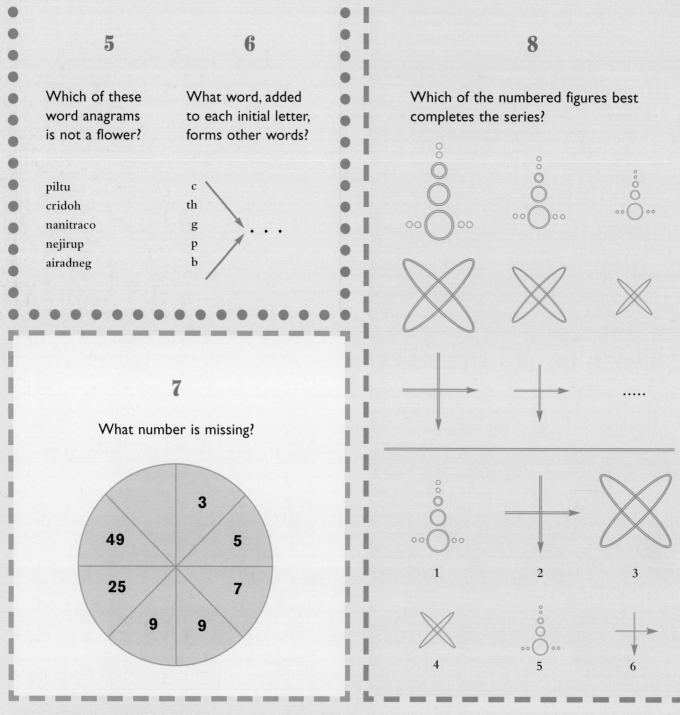

5

Which of these word anagrams is not a flower?

piltu
cridoh
nanitraco
nejirup
airadneg

6

What word, added to each initial letter, forms other words?

c
th
g
p
b

. . .

7

What number is missing?

49   3

25   5

     7

9   9

8

Which of the numbered figures best completes the series?

1

2

3

4

5

6

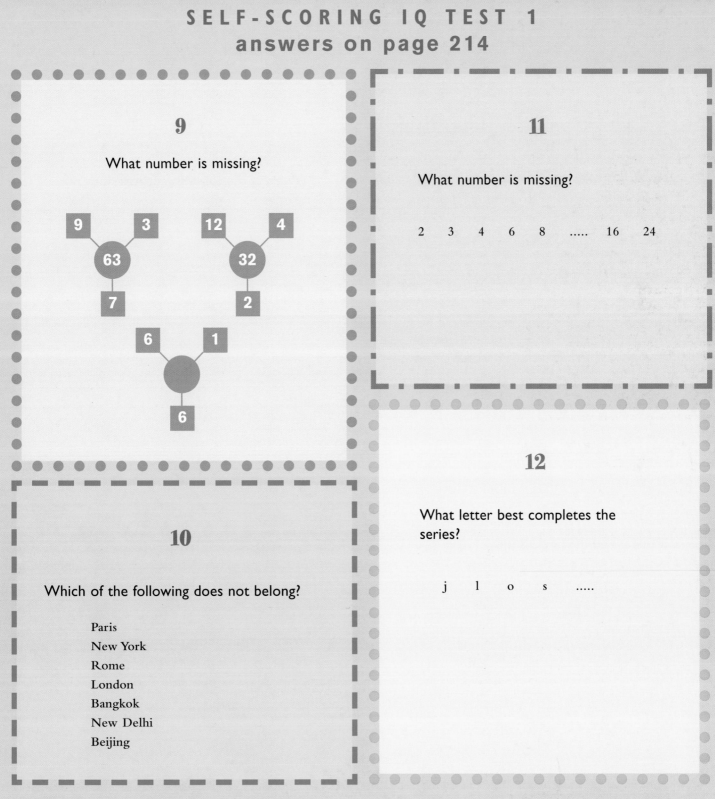

9

What number is missing?

9	3		12	4
63			32	
7			2	

6	1
( )	
6	

11

What number is missing?

2   3   4   6   8   16   24

10

Which of the following does not belong?

Paris
New York
Rome
London
Bangkok
New Delhi
Beijing

12

What letter best completes the series?

j   l   o   s   .....

13

Which of these word anagrams is not a U.S. city?

gronba
inhoxep
toditer
sangvelto
noterlam
dnartolp

14

What is the missing number?

3	6	6
4	9	12
2	3	.....

15

Which of the following figures does not belong?

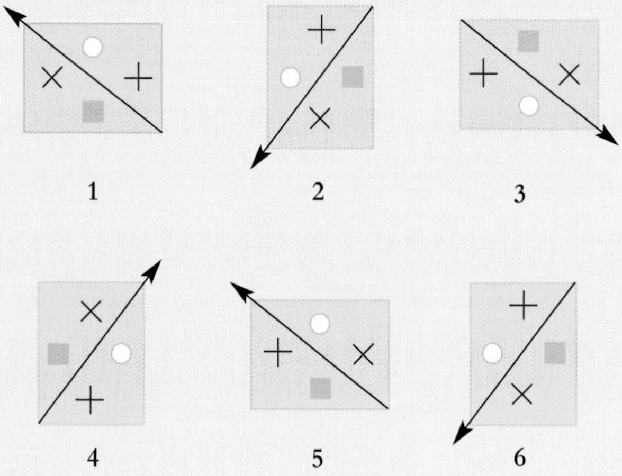

1   2   3

4   5   6

16

What number best completes the series?

2   3   7   13   27   .....

17

Which of these words does not belong?

queen
king
pawn
bishop
cardinal
castle

19

What are the missing numbers?

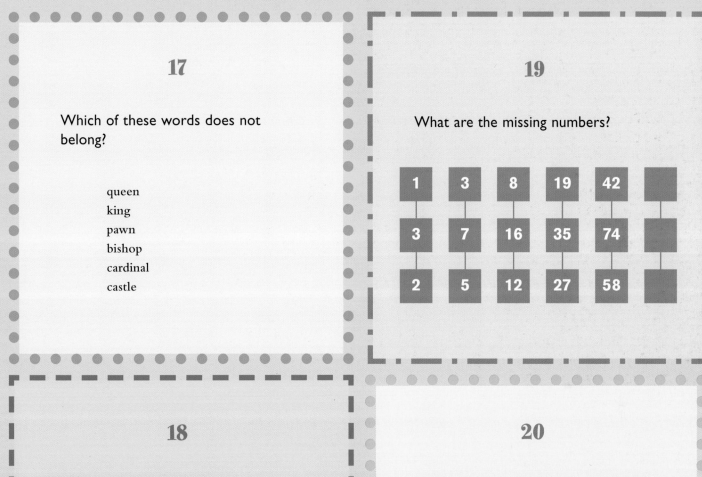

1	3	8	19	42	
3	7	16	35	74	
2	5	12	27	58	

18

What is the missing letter?

c   e   o
a   b   b
b   g   n
f   b   .....

20

Which two words are the most alike?

(a) match
(b) wheel
(c) hole
(d) iron
(e) blacksmith
(f) pencil

21

Which of the numbered figures best completes the series?

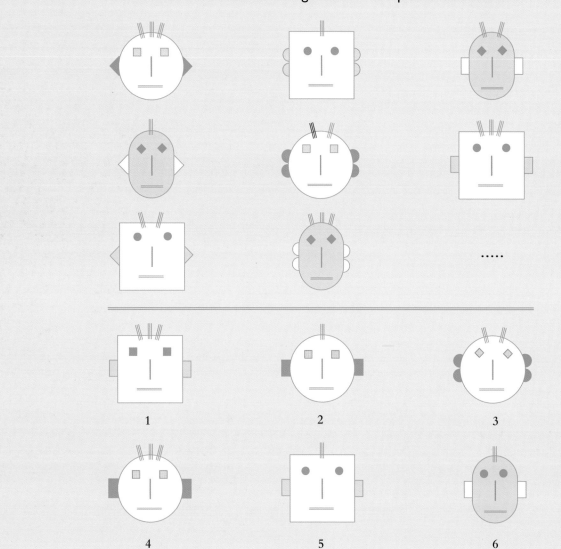

1

2

3

4

5

6

22

Choose the correct answer.

Ashley is bigger than Denise, but not as big as Fran. Sheila, Denise's friend, is shorter than her cousin Adria, but bigger than her sister Fran.

Who is the shortest?
(Ashley, Denise, Fran, Adria, Sheila)

24

Choose the correct answer.

Two parallel lines never intersect.
(a) Is always true
(b) Is never true
(c) Is sometimes true
(d) Is an opinion

23

What number is missing from the triangle?

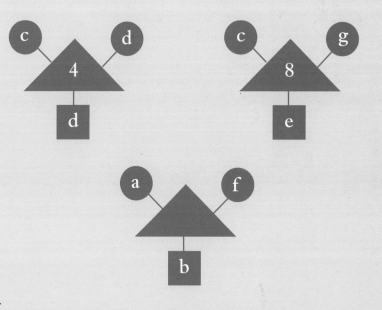

25

Which of the numbered figures best completes the series?

1

2

3

4

5

6

26

Complete the following analogy.

is to   as   is to

1   2   3   4

27

Which of these word anagrams does not belong?

honyvac
ottru
reghnir
adrisen
ahlew
askhr

29

What word best completes the series?

trombone   clarinet   tuba
oboe   saxophone

(a) tambourine
(b) harp
(c) bassoon
(d) viola

28

What are the missing numbers?

27	29	25	33	17	.....
25	23	27	19	35	.....
31	33	29	37	21	.....

30

What are the missing letters?

a	e	i
d	h	l
g	k	o
.....	.....	.....

31

Complete the following analogy.

165135 is to peace as 1215225 is to .....

32

Which of the numbered figures best completes the series?

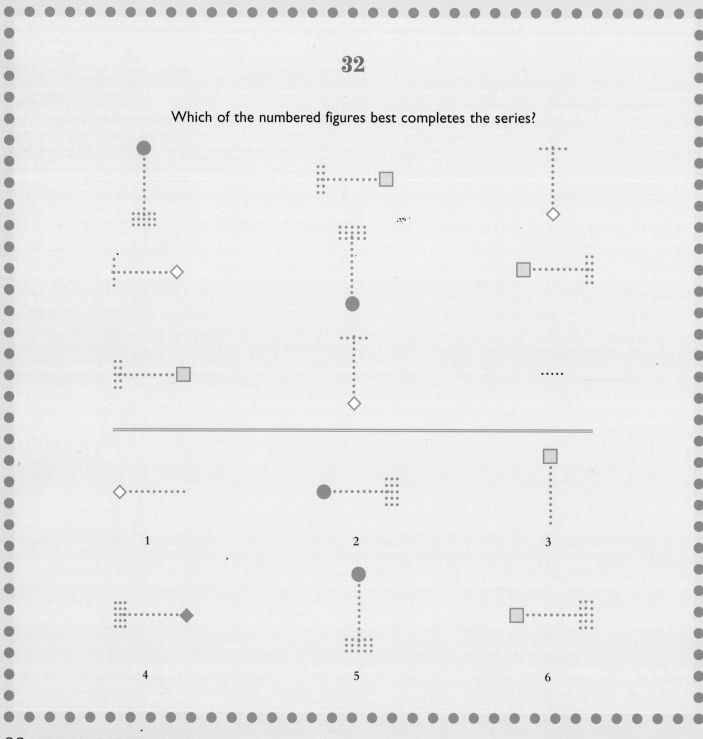

1

2

3

4

5

6

33

What numbers belong in the parentheses?

217 (266) 315
315 (.....) 413

314 (11) 111
213 (.....) 412

175 (16) 95
200 (.....) 125

35

What number best completes this series?

6   9   27   54   675   .....

34

What are the missing letters?

36

Which of the numbered figures best completes the series?

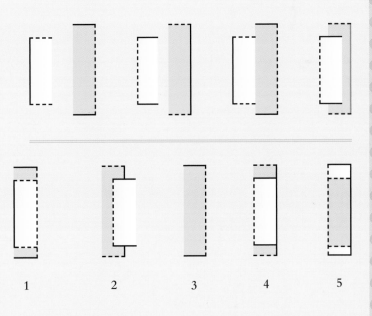

1   2   3   4   5

MIND-BENDER

1 Using only four numerals and any mathematical symbols that you choose, can you produce an equation that will yield the number 300?

2 Suppose all counting numbers were arranged in columns as shown below. Under what letter would the number 100 appear?

A	B	C	D	E	F	G
1	2	3	4	5	6	7
8	9	10	11	12	13	14
15	16	17	—	—	—	—

Answers on page 216

OPTICAL ILLUSION

WE SEE BUT WE WE DON'T OBSERVE.

Sherlock Holmes is reading a headline. What does it say? Are you sure?

Answer on page 200

TRIVIA

MOVIES & TELEVISION

1 What are the names of Donald Duck's three nephews?

2 What newspaper did Clark Kent and Lois Lane work for?

3 Kids' TV show host Bob Keeshan is better known by what name?

4 On *Star Trek*, what is the color of Mr. Spock's blood?

Answers on page 227

BRAINTEASER

58 Now we have 10 sacks that contain either 10-ounce balls or 9-ounce balls. Each sack has at least 1,000 balls, and all the balls in one sack are the same weight. However, we do not know how many sacks contain the 9-ounce balls or which ones they are. How can we identify these sacks by weighing the balls (on a scale that gives weight readouts) in the fewest number of tries?

59 Distribute ten marbles in three plastic cups so that every cup contains an odd number of marbles. You must use all ten.

Answers on page 208

MIND-BENDER

3 Nancy and Audrey set out to cover a certain distance by foot. Nancy walks half the distance and runs half the distance, but Audrey walks half the time and runs half the time. Nancy and Audrey walk and run at the same rate. Who will reach the destination first (or will it be a tie)?

4 The following seven numbers share a unique property. What is it?

1961   6889   6119   8008   8118   6699   6009

Answers on page 216

OPTICAL ILLUSION

Is the zebra black with white stripes or is it white with black stripes?

Answer on page 201

TRIVIA

MOVIES & TELEVISION

5 Tinky Winky, Laa-Laa, Po, and Dipsy are collectively known as what?

6 What TV series had, as a part of the plot, a TV show called *Tool Time*?

7 Which *60 Minutes* correspondent wears an earring?
a) Mike Wallace
b) Morley Safer
c) Ed Bradley
d) Andy Rooney

Answers on page 227

BRAINTEASER

60 I have six pieces of a chain, each piece made up of 4 links, and I want to make a single straight chain out of them. The blacksmith charges 10 cents for cutting each link and 50 cents for welding a link. How much will the chain cost?

61 We have six white marbles, four black marbles, and one red marble in a box. What would be the smallest number of marbles that we need to take out of the box to ensure that we get three of the same color?

Answers on page 209

MIND-BENDER

5 Find the hidden phrase or title.

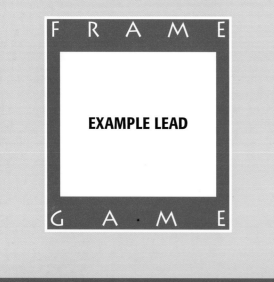

F R A M E

EXAMPLE LEAD

G A · M E

Answers on page 216

OPTICAL ILLUSION

The name of this old-time print is "Time Passes." Why do you think it was given this title?

Answer on page 201

TRIVIA

MOVIES & TELEVISION

8 What movie had a sequel entitled *Oliver's Story?*

9 What TV star of the 1960s had a valet named Rochester?

10 What regular from *The Bob Newhart Show* made a guest appearance in the final scene of the final episode of *Newhart?*

11 What actor was reelected mayor of Carmel, California, in 1988?

Answers on page 227

BRAINTEASER

62 A lady arrives at a hotel where rooms are $10 per night. When she checks in, she does not have enough money, but she offers to pay with a clasped gold bracelet. The bracelet has seven links, each valued at $10. What would be the fewest number of cuts necessary to let her stay for one week if she wants to pay one day at a time?

63 A clock gains half a minute every day. Another clock doesn't work. Which one will show the correct time more often?

Answers on page 209

MIND-BENDER

6 In the puzzle below, the numbers in the second row are determined by the relationships of the numbers in the first row. Likewise, the numbers in the third row are determined by the relationships of the numbers in the second row. Can you determine the relationships and find the missing number?

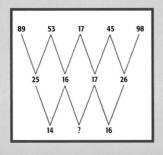

89   53   17   45   98

25   16   17   26

14   ?   16

Answers on page 216

OPTICAL ILLUSION

Can you figure out why this picture is titled "Before and After Marriage"?

Answer on page 201

TRIVIA

MOVIES & TELEVISION

12 What action star is nicknamed "Muscles from Brussels"?

13 What is Kramer's first name on *Seinfeld*?

14 What show's final episode was titled "Goodbye, Farewell, Amen"?

15 In an episode of what series did the character of Mork, later of *Mork & Mindy* fame, first appear?

Answers on page 227

BRAINTEASER

64 A criminal is sentenced to death. Before his execution, he is allowed to make a statement. If his statement is false, he will be hanged, and if his statement is true, he will be drowned. What should he say to confuse the jury and thus save his life?

65 We have 10 glasses sitting in a row. The first five are filled with water and the other five are empty. What would be the minimum number of glasses needed to move so that the full and the empty glasses alternate?

Answers on page 209

MIND-BENDER

7 A mathematician's will stated that his wife should get one-third of his estate, his son one-fifth, his older daughter one-sixth, and his younger daughter $9,000. Who received more, his older daughter or his younger daughter?

8 What single-digit number should go in the box with the question mark?

6	5	9	2	7
1	4	3	5	?
8	0	2	8	1

Answers on page 216

OPTICAL ILLUSION

This picture shows a young girl and her grandmother. Can you find both of them?

Answer on page 201

TRIVIA

MOVIES & TELEVISION

16 What Oscar-winning actress is sister to Warren Beatty?

17 What talk show host was once mayor of Cincinnati?

18 What Oscar-winning actress played Janet in *The Rocky Horror Picture Show*?

19 What state was the setting for the TV series *I Dream of Jeannie*?

Answers on page 227

BRAINTEASER

66 In five plastic cups there are five marbles, each of different colors: white, black, red, green, and blue. We mark each cup randomly with the initial of one of the colors. If the white, green, red, and blue marbles are in their respective cups, how likely is it that the black marble is in its cup?

67 A famous composer blew out 18 candles on his birthday cake and then died less than nine months later. He was 76 at the time of his death and had composed *The Barber of Seville*. How could this happen?

Answers on page 209

MIND-BENDER

9 In a store that sells clocks, I notice that most of them show different times. A grandfather clock reads 2:15, an alarm clock reads 2:35, a digital clock reads 2:00, and the store clock reads 2:23. The store clerk says that a clock in the corner has just been set correctly. It reads 2:17. What is the average number of minutes, fast or slow, that these five clocks are off?

10 Find the missing number in the following series:

$$2/3 \quad 7/12 \quad 1/2 \quad 5/12 \quad 1/3 \quad 1/4 \quad 1/6 \quad ?$$

Answers on pages 216 & 217

OPTICAL ILLUSION

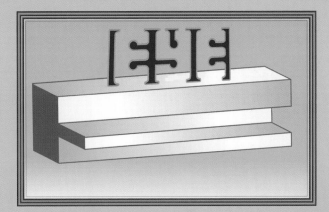

Can you figure out the meaning of
the shapes on the top shelf?
And what's unusual about the structure?

Answer on page 201

TRIVIA

MOVIES & TELEVISION

20 Who is the title character in *The Fugitive?*

21 Name the character played by Flip Wilson in drag whose boyfriend was named Killer.

22 What actress won the 1997 Oscar for Best Actress and the 1996–97 Emmy for Best Actress in a Comedy Series?

Answers on page 227

BRAINTEASER

68 We have 8 pairs of white socks and 10 pairs of black socks in a box. What would be the minimum number of socks that we need to take out of the box to ensure that we get one pair of the same color? (Imagine that you cannot see the color when you are picking them from the box.)

69 When I gave Albert a ride home, I noticed that the clock in his living room took 7 seconds to strike 8. I immediately asked him, "How long do I have to wait to hear it strike 12?"

Answers on page 209

MIND-BENDER

11 Find the hidden phrase or title.

Answer on page 217

OPTICAL ILLUSION

Slowly rotate this page in a circular motion.
What happens to the clown's drum?
What's unusual about the word "rotator"?

Answer on page 201

TRIVIA

MOVIES & TELEVISION

23 What was the movie shown that day in 1968 when NBC cut away from a football game between the Oakland Raiders and New York Jets with 50 seconds to go, and the Raiders took the lead by scoring two touchdowns?

24 What is the name of the first sound cartoon film featuring Mickey Mouse?

25 On the series *M*A*S*H*, what is Radar's favorite drink?

Answers on page 227

BRAINTEASER

70 We have 8 pairs of white socks, 9 pairs of black socks and 11 pairs of blue socks in a box. What would be the minimum number of socks that we need to take out of the box to ensure that we get one pair of the same color? (Imagine that you cannot see the color when you are picking them from the box.)

71 If you can speak properly, you will be able to answer the following question. Which is correct—"The yolk of an egg is white" or "The yolk of an egg are white"?

Answers on page 209

MIND-BENDER

12 While reading a newspaper you notice that four pages of one section are missing. One of the missing pages is page 5. The back page of this section is page 24. What are the other three missing pages?

13 Suppose a, b, and c represent three positive whole numbers. If $a + b = 13$, $b + c = 22$, and $a + c = 19$, what is the value of c?

Answers on page 217

OPTICAL ILLUSION

Stare at the red dot for about 30 seconds. Try not to blink. Then look at a blank wall or a sheet of white paper. You will see a famous lady. Who is she?

Answer on page 201

TRIVIA

MOVIES & TELEVISION

26 What Scottish actor represented Scotland in 1950 at London's Mr. Universe competition?

27 What actor changed his name from Archibald Leach?

28 Name the six children on *The Brady Bunch*.

29 What noted director is well known for playing clarinet in a Dixie jazz band Monday nights in Manhattan?

Answers on page 227

BRAINTEASER

72 We have 6 pairs of white gloves and 6 pairs of black gloves in a box. What would be the minimum number of gloves that we need to take out of the box to ensure that we get one pair? (Imagine that you cannot see the color when you are picking them from the box.)

73 On March 15, a friend was telling me, "Every day I have a cup of coffee. I drank 31 cups in January, 28 in February and 15 in March. So far, I drank 74 cups of coffee. Do you know how many cups I would have drunk thus far if it had been a leap year?"

Answers on page 209

MIND-BENDER

14

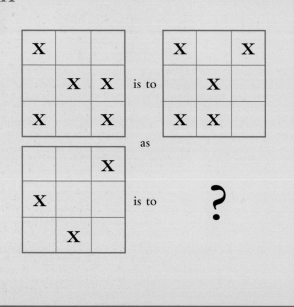

is to

as

is to

?

Answer on page 217

OPTICAL ILLUSION

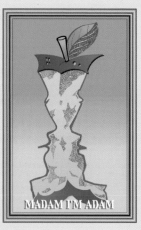

MADAM I'M ADAM

Do you notice anything unusual about this eaten apple? The clue is in the phrase. What's unusual about the phrase?

Answer on page 201

TRIVIA

MOVIES & TELEVISION

30 What was the name of the doorman on *Rhoda*?

31 Who is Gwyneth Paltrow's mother?

32 What was the first movie sequel to win the Oscar for Best Picture?

33 What was the first name of Norm's wife on *Cheers*?

34 What was Lucy Ricardo's maiden name on *I Love Lucy*?

Answers on page 227

BRAINTEASER

74 We have three boxes. One contains two black marbles, the second box contains two white marbles, and the third box contains one black and one white marble. The boxes are marked BB, WW, BW. However, no code corresponds to the marbles in its box. What would be the smallest number of marbles that must be randomly picked, from one or several boxes, to identify their contents?

75 What time is it when a clock strikes 13 times?

Answers on page 209

MIND-BENDER

15 At right is a "trickle-down" word game. Change one letter and one letter only on each line to arrive at the word on the last line:

MOVE
—
—
—
BARK

16 Sarah is older than Julie and Maggie. Maggie is older than Paula. Ann is younger than Julie, but older than Paula. Ann is younger than Maggie. Sarah is younger than Liz. Who is the second oldest woman in this group?

17 What is the missing number in the following series?

13 7 18 10 5 ? 9 1 12 6

Answers on page 217

OPTICAL ILLUSION

This attractive landscape print holds a secret. Can you find the landlord?

Answer on page 201

TRIVIA

MOVIES & TELEVISION

35 What special feature, designed for the movie *Earthquake*, allowed viewers to "feel" the vibrations?

36 Who was originally cast as Catwoman in *Batman Returns* but lost the role when she got pregnant?
a) Elisabeth Shue
b) Annette Bening
c) Sigourney Weaver
d) Geena Davis

Answers on page 227

BRAINTEASER

76 A schoolteacher uses a five-hour hourglass to keep track of class time. One day, he sets the hourglass at 9 a.m. and while he is teaching his class, a student inadvertently inverts the hourglass. Another student, who notices this, sets the hourglass to its initial position at 11:30 a.m. In this way, the class ends at 3 p.m. At what time did the first student invert the hourglass?

77 In a conventional clock, how many times does the minute hand pass the hour hand between noon and midnight?

Answers on pages 209 & 210

MIND-BENDER

18 Find the hidden phrase or title.

Answer on page 217

OPTICAL ILLUSION

Place a pencil along the line of the two arrows. What happens to the color of the circle?

Answer on page 201

TRIVIA

MOVIES & TELEVISION

37 What was the name of the souped-up Dodge Charger in *The Dukes of Hazzard*?

38 Who speaks the only word in Mel Brooks's 1976 comedy *Silent Movie*?

39 What three TV series were spun off from *The Mary Tyler Moore Show*?

40 Who directed the PBS documentary *The Civil War*?

Answers on page 227

BRAINTEASER

78 If a clock takes two seconds to strike 2, how long will it take to strike 3?

79 A clock takes five seconds when striking 6. How long will it take when striking 12?

80 A Roman was born the first day of the 30th year before Christ and died the first day of the 30th year after Christ. How many years did he live?

81 What is the opposite of "I AM NOT LEAVING"?

Answers on page 210

MIND-BENDER

19 How many triangles of any size are in the figure below?

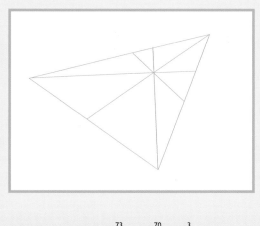

20 Which is larger: 2^{73} or $2^{70} + 2^{3}$?

Answers on page 217

OPTICAL ILLUSION

How can you get the bee
to move closer to the flower?

Answer on page 201

TRIVIA

MOVIES & TELEVISION

41 Who won an Oscar for Best Director in his directorial debut, *Ordinary People*?

42 What movie begins with Annie Savoy saying, as the first line of the script, "I believe in the Church of Baseball"?

43 What actor on the original TV show *The Love Boat* was elected to the U.S. Congress?

Answers on page 227

BRAINTEASER

82 If yesterday had been Wednesday's tomorrow and tomorrow is Sunday's yesterday, what day would today be?

83 Mrs. Smith left on a trip the day after the day before yesterday and she will be back the eve of the day after tomorrow. How many days is she away?

84 A man was telling me on a particular occasion, "The day before yesterday I was 35 years old and next year I will turn 38." How can this be?

Answers on page 210

MIND-BENDER

21 Find the hidden phrase or title.

Answer on page 217

OPTICAL ILLUSION

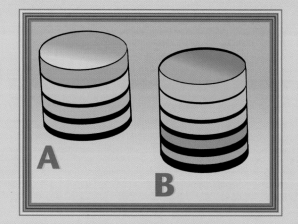

Which pile of disks
has the same height and width?

Answer on page 201

TRIVIA

MOVIES & TELEVISION

44 What are the names of the Blues Brothers?

45 Who is Jane Pauley's husband?

46 Who gave Elizabeth Taylor away at her marriage to Larry Fortensky?

47 What actress bought the town of Braselton, Georgia, for $20 million in 1989?

Answers on page 227

BRAINTEASER

85 Find a commonly used word that ends in T, contains the letters VEN, and starts with IN.

86 What 11-letter word is pronounced incorrectly by more than 99% of Ivy League graduates?

87 What 7-letter word becomes longer when the third letter is removed?

88 Five times four twenty, plus two, equals twenty-three. Is this true?

Answers on page 210

CRITICAL THINKING

Pretend you have five cards: a ten, a jack, a queen, a king, and an ace. In your mind's eye, shuffle these five cards together and put the pile facedown. If you were to select four cards, returning each card and reshuffling the deck after each pick, what kind of hand would you more likely draw: four aces or a straight picked in sequence? Can you explain why?

Answer on page 236

TRIVIA

MUSIC, ARTS & LETTERS

48 What are the last names of the feuding families in *Romeo and Juliet*?

49 What is the final word of "The Raven"?

50 How many keys are on a standard piano?

51 According to song, what train leaves from track 29 at Pennsylvania Station at about a quarter to four?

52 What Shakespearean play features the character Shylock, a moneylender?

Answers on pages 227 & 228

MIND-BENDER

22 Which of the following is the smallest?

a. $\dfrac{\sqrt{10}}{10}$

b. $\dfrac{1}{10}$

c. $\sqrt{10}$

d. $\dfrac{1}{\sqrt{10}}$

e. $\dfrac{1}{10\sqrt{10}}$

23 There are four colored pencils—two blue, one green, and one yellow. If you took two pencils from a drawer and you knew that one was blue, what would be the likelihood that the other pencil was also blue?

Answers on page 217

OPTICAL ILLUSION

What is this a picture of?

Answer on page 201

CRITICAL THINKING

Our planet spins counterclockwise on its axis. It also has a counterclockwise revolution around the sun. Suppose both motions now go clockwise. How would this affect the apparent direction of sunrise and sunset?

Answer on page 236

TRIVIA

MUSIC, ARTS & LETTERS

53 What's the name of the title character in *The Hunchback of Notre Dame*?

54 In ballet, what is the bending-of-the-knees movement?

55 What is the slogan of *The New York Times* (it appears in the upper left corner of every front page)?

56 What singer was named Robert Zimmerman at birth?

Answers on page 228

MIND-BENDER

24 Find the hidden phrase or title.

Answer on page 217

OPTICAL ILLUSION

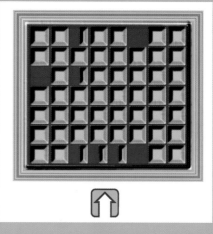

Can you discover the secret word that has been concealed in this design?

Answer on page 201

CRITICAL THINKING

Suppose ten billiard balls are placed in the standard triangular rack. If additional billiard balls are placed on top of this pattern, some balls will roll into the gullies to form a smaller, stable triangle (forget about the balls which roll off the stack). If you add more layers, you'll eventually build a billiard ball pyramid. How many billiard balls and levels would the pyramid contain?

Answer on page 236

TRIVIA

MUSIC, ARTS & LETTERS

57 What are the two cities in *A Tale of Two Cities?*

58 Who wrote *The Andromeda Strain?*

59 What three famous singers died in an airplane crash on February 3, 1959?

60 What is the third book of the Bible?

61 What musical period came between the Renaissance and Classical periods?

62 Who read the poem "I Shall Not Be Moved" at Bill Clinton's first inauguration?

Answers on pages 228

MIND-BENDER

25 Unscramble this word:

KISDTYCRA

26 A certain blend of grass seed is made by mixing brand A ($8 a pound) with brand B ($5 a pound). If the blend is worth $6 a pound, how many pounds of brand A are needed to make 50 pounds of the blend?

Answers on page 217

OPTICAL ILLUSION

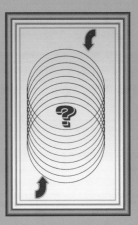

You can look through this coil from either end. Keep staring at it and what happens?

Answer on page 201

CRITICAL THINKING

Four couples enter a restaurant. How many ways can they be seated at a round table so that the men and women alternate and no husband and wife sit next to each other?

Answer on page 236

TRIVIA

MUSIC, ARTS & LETTERS

63 What singer changed his name from Reginald Dwight?

64 What war is depicted in Pablo Picasso's *Guernica*?

65 Which of the following titles is not a line from Shakespeare?
a) *The Catcher in the Rye* by J.D. Salinger
b) *Brave New World* by Aldous Huxley
c) *Something Wicked This Way Comes* by Ray Bradbury
d) *The Winter of Our Discontent* by John Steinbeck

Answers on page 228

MIND-BENDER

27 Find the hidden phrase or title.

Answer on page 218

OPTICAL ILLUSION

This mathematical problem is wrong. How can you correct it?

Answer on page 201

CRITICAL THINKING

An ancient Greek was said to have lived one fourth of his life as a boy, one-fifth as a youth, one third as a man, and to have spent the last 13 years as an elderly gent. How old was he when he died?

Answer on page 236

TRIVIA

MUSIC, ARTS & LETTERS

66 Simon Legree is the villain in what novel?

67 What best-selling author sometimes writes under the pseudonym Richard Bachman?

68 What musical is based on the story of Christopher Isherwood's *Goodbye to Berlin*?

69 What is the longest-running play in London?

70 Prior to 2006, what was the longest-running show on Broadway?

Answers on pages 228

MIND-BENDER

28 If you wrote down all the numbers from 1 to 100, how many times would you write the number 3?

29 Each of the following three words can have another three-letter word added to its beginning to form new words. Can you find at least one three-letter word to make this happen?

Ear   Less   Anger

30 What is $3/4$ of $1/2$ of 4^2 minus $1/2$ of that result?

Answers on page 218

OPTICAL ILLUSION

What do you see in this strange picture?

Answer on page 201

CRITICAL THINKING

Kristin wants to remodel her home. To save money, she decides to move a carpet from one hallway to another. The carpet currently covers a passageway that is 3 x 12 feet. She wishes to cut the carpet into two sections that can be joined together to fit a long and narrow hallway that is 2 x 18 feet. What does her cut look like?

Answer on page 236

TRIVIA

MUSIC, ARTS & LETTERS

71 How many syllables are typically in a haiku?

72 The mythical creature called the griffin is made up of what two animals?

73 What singer led the Mothers of Invention?

74 Which three U.S. states are titles of books by James A. Michener?

75 Who painted *Impression: Sunrise*, the painting that gave impressionism its name?

Answers on page 228

MIND-BENDER

31 Below are six discs stacked on a peg. The object is to reassemble the discs, one by one, in the same order on another peg, using the smallest number of moves. No larger disc can be placed on a smaller disc. How many moves will it take?

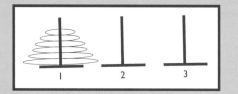

32 From the word "service," see if you can create 15 new words.

Answers on page 218

OPTICAL ILLUSION

Can you find this baby's mother?

Answer on page 201

CRITICAL THINKING

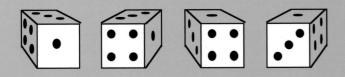

Which die is unlike the other three?

Answer on page 236

TRIVIA

MUSIC, ARTS & LETTERS

76 What rock star died in a bathtub in Paris on July 3, 1971?

77 Who painted *American Gothic*?

78 Who holds the record for being on the most covers of *People*?

79 What is Tom Sawyer's aunt's name?

80 What singing group had Fabrice Morvan and Rob Pilatus as its members?

81 What mythological figure is condemned to roll a huge stone up a hill, only to have it roll down again each time?

Answers on pages 228

MIND-BENDER

33 Below is a list of numbers with accompanying codes. Can you decipher the code and determine the number on the last line?

Number	Code Number
589	521
724	386
1346	9764
?	485

34 Which is greater, a single discount of 12 percent or two successive discounts of 6 percent—or are they the same?

Answers on page 218

OPTICAL ILLUSION

The soldier is pointing his finger straight at you. Move your head from left to right. What appears to happen?

Answer on page 201

CRITICAL THINKING

Emily can click a mouse ten times in 10 seconds. Buzzy can click a mouse twenty times in 20 seconds. Anthony can click a mouse five times in 5 seconds. Assume that the timing period begins with the first mouse click and ends with the final click. Which one of these computer users would be the first to complete forty clicks?

Answer on page 236

TRIVIA

MUSIC, ARTS & LETTERS

82 Georges Seurat's *Sunday Afternoon on the Island of La Grande Jatte* is one of the best-known examples of what painting style?

83 What was the name of the town through which Lady Godiva rode naked?

84 What magazine has regular departments that include "Letters and Tomatoes" and "Joke and Dagger"?

85 Who is the author of the *Goosebumps* series of children's books?

Answers on page 228

MIND-BENDER

35 Find the hidden phrase or title.

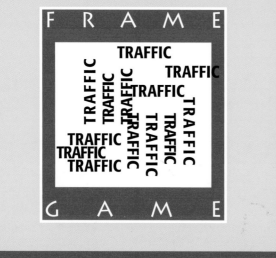

Answer on page 218

OPTICAL ILLUSION

Otto is holding a cake. One slice is missing. Can you find it? There is also something odd about the name "Otto." What is it?

Answer on page 201

CRITICAL THINKING

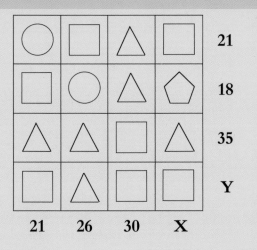

○	□	△	□	21
□	○	△	⬠	18
△	△	□	△	35
□	△	□	□	Y
21	26	30	X	

Use the pattern above to determine the value for X and Y.

Answer on page 236

TRIVIA

MUSIC, ARTS & LETTERS

86 What science fiction story features the Morlocks and the Eloi?

87 Who created Sam Spade?

88 What city is home to the Uffizi Gallery?

89 What author set many of his novels in fictional Yoknapatawpha County?

90 Name the four other original "spices" besides Ginger Spice in the Spice Girls?

91 Who was the third tenor, besides Luciano Pavarotti and Placido Domingo, on the Three Tenors album?

Answers on pages 228

MIND-BENDER

36 Here's a fun and challenging puzzle for those who remember their algebra. Solve the following:

$$\frac{x + y}{x^2 + y^2} \times \frac{x}{x - y} \div \frac{(x + y)^2}{x^4 - y^4}$$

37 Below is a sentence based on moving the letters of the alphabet in a consistent manner. See if you can crack the code and come up with the right answer.

BRX DUH D JHQLXV.

Answers on page 218

OPTICAL ILLUSION

Does this sign say "knowledge" or does it say "ignorance"?

Answer on page 201

SHREWD CHALLENGE

Monte Carlo

The famous playboy Hystrix Tardigradus explained to a beautiful woman his system for playing roulette:

"In each round, I always bet half of the money I have at the time on red. Yesterday, I counted and I had won as many rounds as I had lost."

Over the course of the night, did Hystrix win, lose, or break even?

Answer on page 249

TRIVIA

MUSIC, ARTS & LETTERS

92 What opera is the musical *Rent* based on?

93 In the Gustave Flaubert novel, what is the first name of *Madame Bovary*?

94 Mitch McDeere is the main character in what best-selling novel?

95 Who wrote the book *Chitty Chitty Bang Bang*?

96 What is the more commonly known name of Franz Schubert's *Symphony No. 8 in B minor*?

Answers on page 228

MIND-BENDER

38 This geometric figure can be divided with one straight line into two parts that will fit together to make a perfect square. Draw that line by connecting two of the numbers.

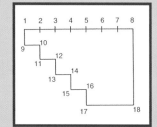

39 The number six is considered a "perfect" number because its factors add up exactly to the number itself (3 + 2 + 1 = 6). What is the next perfect number?

Answers on page 218

OPTICAL ILLUSION

How can you get the boy to take a spoonful of his medicine?

Answer on page 202

SHREWD CHALLENGE

The Harem

The story goes that the harem of the Great Tamerlane was protected by a door with many locks. A vizier and four slaves were in charge of guarding this door.

Knowledgeable of the weaknesses of men, the Great Tamerlan had distributed the keys in such a way that the vizier could only open the door if he was with any one of the slaves, and the slaves could only open it if three of them worked together.

How many locks did the door have?

Answer on page 249

TRIVIA

MUSIC, ARTS & LETTERS

97 The words "or the Modern Prometheus" are usually dropped from the title when discussing what 1818 novel?

98 What was the name of the dictatorial pig that ruled in *Animal Farm*?

99 What famous reporter wrote *Wired*, the biography of John Belushi?

100 What Russian writer died at the small railway junction of Astapovo during a train journey?

Answers on pages 228

MIND-BENDER

40 Find the hidden phrase or title.

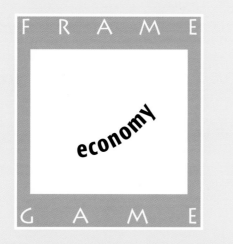

Answer on page 218

OPTICAL ILLUSION

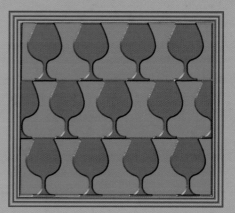

What do you see, purple glasses or green vases?

Answer on page 202

The Dividing End

My ID number is quite remarkable. It's a nine-digit number with each of the digits from 1 to 9 appearing once. The whole number is divisible by 9. If you remove the rightmost digit, the remaining eight-digit number is divisible by 8. Removing the next rightmost digit leaves a seven-digit number that is divisible by 7. This property continues all the way down to one digit. What is my ID number?

Answer on page 249

MUSIC, ARTS & LETTERS

101 What modern dancer died when her scarf got caught in the tire of a moving car?

102 In what complex of buildings is the Metropolitan Opera located?

103 What is the *Mona Lisa* called in Italian?

104 What's the name of the town in Thornton Wilder's *Our Town*?

105 What novelist features the fictional writer Kilgore Trout in several of his novels?

Answers on pages 228 & 229

41 Some pibs are dals.
All dals are zons.
Some zons are rews.
Some rews are dals.
Therefore, some pibs are definitely rews.
Is the above conclusion true or false?

42 The *Genesee Flyer* leaves the station at 60 miles per hour. After three hours, the *Seneca Streamer* leaves the same station at 75 miles per hour, moving in the same direction on an adjacent track. Both trains depart the station at milepost 0. At what milepost will the *Streamer* draw even with the *Flyer*?

Answers on page 218

Will the girl ever get to the bottom step on this flight of stairs?

Answer on page 202

The Island and the Englishmen

On a deserted island (except for a small group of Englishmen) there are four clubs.

The membership lists reveal that:

a) Each Englishman is a member of two clubs.

b) Every set of two clubs has only one member in common.

How many Englishmen are there on the island?

Answer on page 249

MUSIC, ARTS & LETTERS

106 Who is the composer of *Pictures at an Exhibition?*

107 What was the London street address of Sherlock Holmes?

108 In the Sherlock Holmes stories, what is Dr. Watson's first name?

109 What musical opens with the song "Six Months out of Every Year"?

110 What are the names of King Lear's three daughters?

Answers on pages 229

43 Which is larger: one-third times one-third of a dozen dozen, or one-third dozen halved and cubed?

44 A cyclist can ride four different routes from East Klopper to Wickly. There are eight different routes from Wickly to Ganzoon. From Ganzoon to Poscatool, there are three different routes. How many different combinations of routes from East Klopper to Poscatool can the cyclist take? (Do not consider going directly from East Klopper to Poscatool: all routes pass through Wickly, Ganzoon, and Poscatool.)

Answers on page 218

Are these two painted stripes exactly the same size, or is one bigger than the other?

Answer on page 202

SHREWD CHALLENGE

A Warm Farewell

At a train station, the Porter family is saying good-bye to the Robinson family. We don't know who is leaving and who is staying.

Each of the members of the Porter family says farewell to each of the members of the Robinson family. To say good-bye, two men shake hands, and both a man and a woman and two women kiss once on the cheek.

An eyewitness to the event counted 21 handshakes and 34 kisses.

How many men and how many women were saying good-bye?

Answer on page 249

CLEVER MIND

Lazy Days of Summer

The digits 1, 2, 3, and 4 can be arranged to form 24 different four-digit numbers. What is the sum of those 24 numbers? (There is a shortcut, in case you don't want to write them all down and add them all up!)

Answer on page 231

CRITICAL THINKING

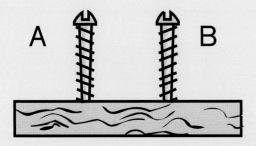

Take a close look at the two screws above. Suppose they were both turned in a counter-clockwise rotation. What will happen to each screw?

Answer on page 236

OPTICAL ILLUSION

What bird do you see here, a hawk or a goose?

Answer on page 202

The Ant and the Clock

Precisely when the big hand of the clock passes 12, an ant begins crawling counter-clockwise around the clock from the 6 mark at a consistent speed.

When reaching the big hand of the clock, the ant turns around and, at the same speed, starts marching around the clock in the opposite direction.

Exactly 45 minutes after the first meeting, the ant crosses the big hand for the second time and dies.

How long has the ant been walking?

Answer on page 249

Pieces of Eight

Suppose a wooden cube measures eight units on a side. If you cut the cube into eight identical smaller cubes, how long is a side of one of the smaller cubes?

Answer on page 231

Two cyclists race along a straight course. The faster of the pair maintains an average speed of 30 mph. The slower cyclist averages 25 miles per hour. When the race ends, the judges announce that the faster cyclist crossed the finish line one hour before the slower racer. How many miles long was the racing course?

Answer on page 236

Can you figure out what these shapes represent?

Answer on page 202

Mister Digit Face

Place each of the digits 1 to 9, one digit per blank, so that the product of the two eyes equals the number above the head, and the product of each eye and the mouth equals the number on the respective side of the face.

Answer on page 250

Something Is Missing

In the array of numbers below, what number should go where the question mark is?

3	11	21	41	91
6	14	15	23	53
3	5	6	8	?

Answer on page 231

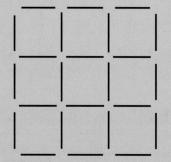

This arrangement of toothpicks forms fourteen different squares of various sizes. Can you remove six toothpicks and leave only three squares behind?

Answer on page 236

BACCHUS

This is a picture of the Roman god Bacchus. If you look very carefully you will also see a picture of Romeo and Juliet. Can you find them?

Answer on page 202

Digit Tree

Using each digit from 1 to 9 once, make seven numbers so that each number is equal to the sum of the numbers in the circles that are connected to it from below. (The numbers can be more than one digit.) There are two slightly different answers.

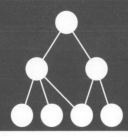

Answer on page 250

Seeing Spots

A regular six-faced die has 21 spots altogether. Without looking at any dice you might have lying around, how many of these spots are in the center of one of the faces? How many are at one corner or another? How many are somewhere else?

Answer on page 231

A computer and its monitor weigh a total of 48 pounds. If the monitor weighs twice as much as the computer, how much does each piece of hardware weigh?

Answer on page 236

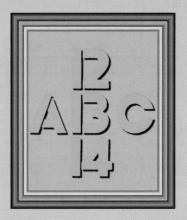

What do you see in the middle of the frame? Is it the letter B or the number 13?

Answer on page 202

New Race

Two cars start traveling from two different points and in opposite directions in a circuit race at a constant speed. The cars cross for the first time at point A. The second time is at point B. The third time is at point C, and the fourth one is again at point A.

How much faster is one car going than the other?

Answer on page 250

Fill in the Blanks

Fill in each box below with either +, −, ×, or ÷ to produce a valid equation:

12 ☐ 2 ☐ 7 ☐ 4 = 9

Answer on page 231

In order to win a free visit to the dentist, students had to guess the exact number of gumballs in a fish bowl. The students guessed 45, 41, 55, 50, and 43, but no one won. The guesses were off by 3, 7, 5, 7, and 2 (in no given order). From this information, determine the number of gumballs in the bowl.

Answer on page 237

The brown shapes may seem unrelated, but they form a figure. It is an example of a "closure." Can you see what the figure is?

Answer on page 202

How Far?

The number 907 is prime: it has no factors other than itself and 1. To prove that 907 is prime, you must check to see that it is not divisible by any prime number, beginning with 2, 3, 5, and so on. The question is, how far do you need to go before you can conclude that 907 is in fact prime?

Answer on page 231

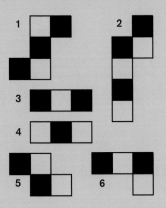

The six sections above are parts of a 5 x 5 checkerboard grid. Can you piece them back together to form the original pattern?

Answer on page 237

Logic Apples

Four perfect logicians, who all knew each other from being members of the Perfect Logicians' Club, sat around a table that had a dish with 11 apples in it. The chat was intense, and they ended up eating all the apples. Everybody had at least one apple, and everyone knew that fact, and each logician knew the number of apples that he ate. They didn't know how many apples each of the others ate, though. They agreed to ask only questions that they didn't know the answers to:

Alonso: "Did you eat more apples than I did, Bertrand?"

Bertrand: "I don't know. Did you, George, eat more apples than I did?"

George: "I don't know."

Kurt: "Aha!"

Kurt figured out how many apples each person ate. Can you do the same?

Answer on page 250

On All Fours

What is the smallest whole number that, when multiplied by 3, gives an answer consisting of all 4's?

Answer on page 232

Divide the face of a watch into three sections. The sum of the numbers included on each section must equal the sum of the numbers on either of the other two sections. Let's not waste any time—the clock is ticking.

Answer on page 237

Added Corners

Using the numbers from 1 to 8, place one in each shape with one condition: The number in each square has to be the sum of its two neighboring circles.

Answer on page 250

Don't Leave Me Out

The junior high school basketball team consists of just seven kids. From that group of seven, it is possible to create 21 different starting teams of five players. Suppose one of the team members is named Jerry. How many of the 21 possible starting teams include Jerry?

Answer on page 232

CRITICAL THINKING

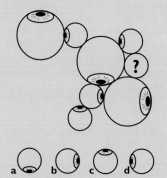

Note the direction in which each eye looks. Can you uncover the pattern? Good. Now find the empty eye. In which direction should this eye be looking?

Answer on page 237

Rectangles

The vertical rectangle (solid line) has an area of 40 square inches.

Find out in a quick way the area of the inclined rectangle (dotted line).

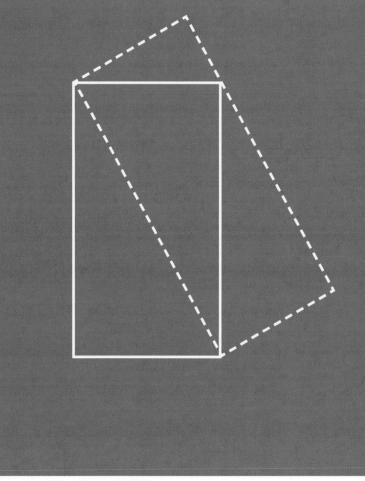

Answer on page 250

So Far, Yet So Close

By adding just one line to the equation below, form a correct equation. And in case you were wondering, you cannot use the line to convert the equal sign into an inequality!

5+5+5=550

Answer on page 232

CRITICAL THINKING

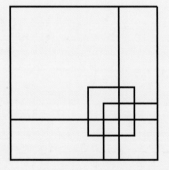

How many squares can you uncover in the pattern above? Don't forget to count the outer border as one of your answers!

Answer on page 237

Figures to Cut in Two

Each one of the following figures can be divided into two equal parts (that may be mirror images of each other). The dividing lines can follow the grid or not. The grid is only to provide proportion to the figures.

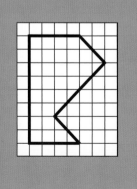

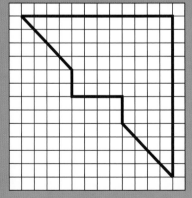

Answer on page 250

MINDTRAP

◆ "Listen, Shadow, Sally's life is on the line. They aren't bluffing," stammered Chip Dawson. "Is that Silicon Sally that's running your office?" inquired Shadow. "That was Sally," replied Chip. "Ain't she something?" "Well, I can certainly see how she came by her nickname," said Shadow as he read the ransom note:

"Dawson—You'll pay us $1 million in seven days or your beloved Sally is a goner. We know everything about her. We'll be in touch."

"See," said an ashen-faced Chip Dawson, "Sally's life is hanging in midair. I must have a couple of officers protecting her 24 hours a day. I count on her for everything. She basically runs my company." "I wish I could help you," replied Shadow, "but I'm afraid protecting Sally's life isn't in my jurisdiction. I have to run along because the Crabtree Pet Store was robbed last night and that's really a priority." Why would Sally's life rank below a simple pet-store robbery?

Answer on page 247

CRITICAL THINKING

A grocer has a large cube of cheese that she wishes to divide into twenty-seven smaller and equal-sized cubes. To cut out the twenty-seven blocks, she uses two cuts to divide the cube into three slices. She stacks these slices atop of each other and makes two more cuts. Finally, she rotates the cube a quarter-turn and makes the final cut. The result is twenty-seven identical cubes made with six cuts. Is it possible to get the twenty-seven cubes with fewer cuts? If so, how?

Answer on page 237

CLEVER MIND

Wagering Aboveboard

Two men play some games of chess for the stakes of one dollar per game. (This means that each player puts in a dollar and the winner of the game receives both dollars.) When the games are completed, the first man has won three games and the second has won three dollars. Assuming that none of the games ended in a draw, how many games did they play?

Answer on page 232

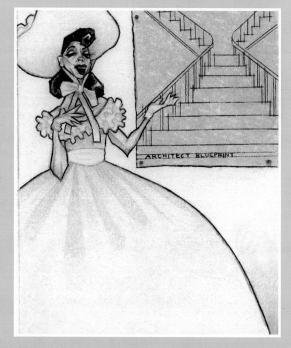

◆ Miss Scarlet O'Hara was a wealthy widow who could easily be described as eccentric. She believed herself to be the incarnation of the famous character in the novel *Gone With the Wind*, and as a result, she tried to imitate her in every way. As strange as this fixation could be, in addition, everything she owned had to be white. Miss Scarlet instructed an architect to build her a huge white bungalow that had no less than twelve white bedrooms and twelve white bathrooms. Her stables were all to be painted white to match both the white house and the white garage. The principal feature of her home was naturally the grand staircase. With all things being equal, what color would Miss Scarlet have instructed her painters to paint the grand staircase?

Answer on page 247

CRITICAL THINKING

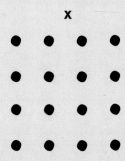

Without lifting your pencil from the paper, draw six straight lines that connect all sixteen of the dots above. To make things more of a challenge, the line pattern that you create must begin at the "x".

Answer on page 237

CLEVER MIND

All in the Neighborhood

Sarah is a little baby, only 27 days old. But she's not even the youngest in her neighborhood. Little Melanie across the street is only three days old. Sarah is nine times as old as Melanie!

How many days will it be before Sarah is *four* times as old as Melanie?

Answer on page 232

◆ Ms. Tittle was in tears as she placed the little hamster cage on Dr. Probe's examining table. "I've taken Goldie to four veterinarians, and they've all told me that Goldie is simply dying of old age." Dr. Probe peered into the cage to see the little hamster looking the worse for wear. "Look, Dr. Probe, I'm a very wealthy lady. Please make her well; money is no object." At that, Dr. Probe stood up and said, "Well, Ms. Tittle, I've been experimenting with an aging remedy. The cure is expensive and risky, and I must admit that I haven't attempted it so far." "If that's Goldie's only chance . . . ," blubbered Tittle.

Several days later, Tittle returned to find Goldie in good health. "Goldie took well to my treatment," agreed Dr. Probe, "but I fear that you're going to feel ill when you get my bill." How could Dr. Probe cure Goldie of the effects of old age?

Answer on page 247

CRITICAL THINKING

To move their armies, the Romans built over 50,000 miles of roads. Imagine driving all those miles! Now imagine driving those miles in the first gasoline-driven car that has only three wheels and could reach a top speed of about 10 miles per hour.

For safety's sake, let's bring along a spare tire. As you drive the 50,000 miles, you rotate the spare with the other tires so that all four tires get the same amount of wear. Can you figure out how many miles of wear each tire accumulates?

Answer on page 237

CLEVER MIND

Through the Looking Glass

Every once in a while a calendar year will be a palindrome, which means it reads the same way forward and backward. Starting with the year 10 A.D., can you come up with a pair of palindrome years that are

A) 110 years apart?
B) 11 years apart?
C) 10 years apart?
D) 2 years apart?

Answer on page 233

◆ Whenever Dee Septor, the world famous magician, went to a dinner party, and he sensed the hostess was just about to die of embarrassment because the party was as flat as her soufflé, it was a given that Dee, the party saver, would pull out the old knife-and-glass trick. "The task is this," challenged Dee. "Form an equilateral triangle with three identical glasses so that they are just slightly further apart than the length of three identical dinner knives. Now, using just the knives, and without moving the glasses, make a bridge between the three glasses that is strong enough to support a fourth glass full of water." How can this be done?

Answer on page 247

CLEVER MIND

Head Start

Chris and Jean play a game of flipping a coin. It's a simple game—the first person to flip a "heads" wins! If Chris goes first and the two alternate flips after that, what is the probability that Chris will win the game?

Answer on page 233

MIND-BENDER

45 The ratio of $3/7$ to $4/9$ is which of the following:

a. $\dfrac{8}{9}$

b. $\dfrac{35}{36}$

c. $\dfrac{3}{4}$

d. $\dfrac{27}{28}$

e. 1 to 1

Answer on page 218

◆ "Gentlemen," began Professor Beaker, "my new discovery will revolutionize the world. I've found a completely natural way to enhance growth, whether it's for plants, insects, or humans. So far, I've only experimented on plants and insects, but the results speak for themselves. On the left you'll notice huge grains and kernels—not to mention the extraordinarily large house fly. On the right you can see a fly, wheat, and corn, which are anemic in comparison. Example: when the two flies emerged from the pupae, neither of them was bigger than the head of a small nail. Two weeks after ingesting my invention, the fly on the left has grown twice as fast as the fly on the right, which has eaten nothing but...well you know what flies like best." "I know what flies like best," interrupted Quantum, "and Beaker, you're full of it!" Why would Quantum say this?

Answer on page 247

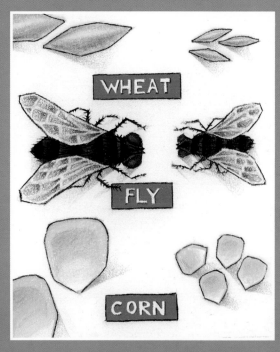

CLEVER MIND

Playing the Triangle

An isosceles triangle is a triangle in which two of the sides have the same length. Suppose you have a triangle and you know that two of the sides have lengths 17 and 8. If that triangle is isosceles, how long is the third side?

Answer on page 233

MIND-BENDER

46 Find the hidden phrase or title.

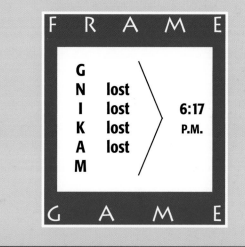

Answer on page 218

Full of Hot Air

Three balloons—one red, one blue, and one yellow—escaped into the air. The combined height of the red and blue balloons was 140 meters. The combined height of the blue and yellow balloons was 135 meters. The combined height of the red and yellow balloons was 155 meters.

Which balloon was the highest of the three?

Answer on page 233

47 Kelsey has flipped a penny 17 times in a row, and every time it has landed on heads. What are the chances that the next throw will land on heads?

48 Can you place a symbol between the two numbers below to create a number greater than 4, but less than 5?

4   5

Answers on page 218

IMPOSSIBLE OBJECT

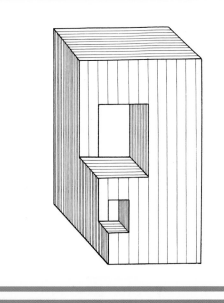

ESCALATING CUBE

While ambiguous depth-reversal figures throw the mind into a state of indecision, impossible cubes take us a step further into befuddlement. The concept of the impossible cube has now been telescoped into the intriguing figure dubbed the Escalating Cube, which has expanding or reducing possibilities.

In this figure, downsized cubes are developed into one entity. A thin wall on the left and a massive wall on the right share a common plane at the left and bottom, but not at the right and top. Tucked between them are ever-smaller cubes that demonstrate the same properties. The process of using still smaller cubes, or larger for that matter, could go on forever. Another name for this object, therefore, could be the Infinity Cube.

My Three Sons

A man has three sons. The oldest is three years older than the middle son, and the middle son is three years older than the youngest. Altogether, the three sons' ages add up to 57. How old are the three sons?

49 Below is a teeter-totter with a 5-pound weight placed 10 feet from the fulcrum and a 6-pound weight placed 5 feet from the fulcrum. On the right side of the fulcrum is a 16-pound weight that needs to be placed in order to balance the weights on the left side. How many feet from the fulcrum should the 16-pound weight be placed?

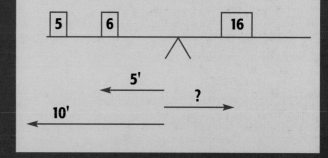

Answer on page 234

Answer on page 219

IMPOSSIBLE OBJECT

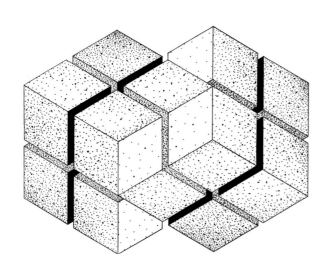

INTEGRAL CUBICLE

The Integral Cubicle shown opposite is another variation on the cube theme. At first glance, you seem to see two distinct clusters of cubes as if they were fused together. Then, on second glance, a curious discontinuity becomes evident. The right-side face of one set of cubes suddenly becomes the left-side face of the other set of cubes. Your mind cannot decide which concept to adopt.

CLEVER MIND

The A&P

Can you come up with a rectangle whose sides are whole numbers and whose area (A) is numerically equal to its perimeter (P)? There are two solutions.

Answer on page 234

MIND-BENDER

50 The probability of drawing the Ace of Spades from a deck of 52 playing cards is 1 in 52. What is the probability of drawing the Ace, King, and Queen of Spades on three consecutive draws?

51 Sometimes things that are mathematically or scientifically true seem impossible. You may think this is one of them. Can you guess what a cubic yard of water weights?

17 pounds

170 pounds

1,700 pounds

500 pounds

98.8 pounds

Answers on page 219

IMPOSSIBLE OBJECT

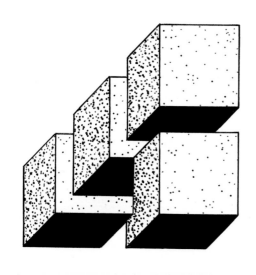

CUBES IN LIMBO

The figure to the left seems to be, at first glance, an acceptable arrangement of cubes. But, after a closer look you realize that there is something decidedly wrong. If you count the cubes they add up to four, yet the cube at the lower right is both a rear cube and a front cube at the same time. Check it out.

CLEVER MIND

Missed One!

Of the ten decades that made up the 20th century, only one of them had no year that was divisible by 11. Which decade was that? (Here it is understood that a decade begins with the year ending in 0, so that the '20s consist of 1920 through 1929, and so on.)

Answer on page 234

MIND-BENDER

52 If a team wins 60 percent of its games in the first third of a season, what percentage of the remaining games must it win to finish the season having won 80 percent of the games?

53 Given the initial letters of the missing words, complete the following sentence.

There are 50 S in the U S F.

Answers on page 219

IMPOSSIBLE OBJECT

TWO-STORY CUBE

The object featured on the left is another innovative variation of the basic impossible cube. In this figure we see what appears to be, at first glance, a structure consisting of four vertical members with cross-members at mid-height. But it does not take long to see that there is something very unusual about this object. The cross-members at mid-height are connected to the structure in an impossible way. They extend from the left and right verticals back to a rear vertical, which is, in reality, the front vertical—if you look at the top and bottom. In this figure we encounter an illusion similar to that found in The Space Fork (page 165)—confusion about the status of the middle member. If it is either the front or rear vertical, then where is the fourth vertical support? According to our view through the window at the top, there is no rear vertical. Yet, what we see at mid-height tells us that there has to be a rear vertical. The odd horizontals of this two-story cube seem to turn it wrong-side out—without bending it or deforming it—not even one inch!

◆ Charles Pompuss stopped off at the Soul-Ace Hotel for coffee. Always wanting to make an impression, Charles ordered coffee in his most debonair tone. "Monsieur, un café au lait, s'il vous plaît." "Listen, Mack," said the waiter, "we speak American here, so try again. What'll you have?" "A coffee with cream. Or a cappuccino, my good man!" said Charles, rolling his eyes at the boorish waiter. "Listen, young man," continued Charles, "you should be grateful to people such as myself who could teach you a few things about culture. I speak five languages fluently. I learned Polish while spending two years there; then I moved to Holland for 6 months and learned Dutch. From there I learned Belgian while in that country, and just recently I returned from France where I became fluent in French." "Nice try, blowhard," replied the waiter, "but you're a bald-faced liar!" Why would he say that?

Answer on page 247

CLEVER MIND

Six-Shooter

Suppose n is a whole number. Can you explain why the number $n(n + 1)(2n + 1)$ must be divisible by 6?

Let's try a couple of examples. If we let $n = 3$, we get the value $3 \times 4 \times 7 = 84$. If $n = 8$, then we get $8 \times 9 \times 17 = 1{,}224$. Both 84 and 1,224 are divisible by 6. There are no exceptions. Your job is to figure out why!

Answer on page 234

TRIVIA

TRAVEL & GEOGRAPHY

111 What city is home to the United States Naval Academy?

112 Queensland is a state in what country?

113 Halifax is the capital of what province?

114 What Pennsylvania town is famous for its Groundhog Day celebration?

115 What city was formerly called Byzantium and Constantinople?

Answers on page 229

◆ "Gentlemen," began Art Bragg, "I've been in Brazil for the past two years and I've discovered the proverbial goose that lays the golden egg. These eggs are none other than banana plants. True to my genius, I've developed a strain of plant that grows wild, particularly where tropical forests have been felled. For pennies per acre I can purchase freshly cleared rain-forest land and plant my strain of cuttings. They grow faster than weeds and require no care. We simply pick 'em and ship 'em in specially designed containers. I purchased 20 acres of land, and I've harvested two crops since. This picture shows me and a couple of locals picking the second crop, which was snapped up by the U.S. markets. With $1 million invested now I can guarantee a return of 300% in one year!" It was then that Ari Gant declared, "Bragg, both you and your picture are obvious frauds." Why?

Answer on page 247

CLEVER MIND

Look Before You Leap

If each of the two dimensions of a rectangle is increased by 100%, by what percentage is the area increased?

Answer on page 235

TRIVIA

TRAVEL & GEOGRAPHY

116 What city does the "D" mint mark on pennies stand for?

117 What state elected former wrestler Jesse "The Body" Ventura as its governor?

118 What is the German name for Germany?

119 On what Hawaiian island is Honolulu located?

120 What university do Rhodes scholars attend?

Answers on page 229

◆ Art Bragg, Colonel Blackhead, and Dr. Prod were swapping war stories at the Soul-Ace Hotel. Art loved to recall how he won his medal when he and one of his carrier pigeons saved a platoon from certain ambush. "As you may or may not know," began Art, "carrier pigeons are able to fly in excess of 70 kilometers per hour for a number of hours. As it happens, I was at our temporary headquarters when we intercepted an enemy transmission about an imminent ambush on our advancing troops. Immediately I attached the warning message to my prize carrier and sent him off to warn the platoon. Within hours, my carrier returned with a message that the troops would hold their position until reinforcements arrived." "What a cock-and-bull story that is," snorted Colonel Blackhead. Why?

Answer on page 247

CLEVER MIND

Strange Sequence

What number completes the following eight-term sequence?

19   5   17   21   5   14   3   ?

Answer on page 235

TRIVIA

TRAVEL & GEOGRAPHY

121 What is the highest mountain in Africa?

122 What strait separates Spain from Morocco?

123 What 500,000-square-mile desert lies on the border of southeast Mongolia and northern China?

124 What state is home to Pikes Peak?

125 What city do people on hajjes head for?

Answers on page 229

MINDTRAP

◆ This was Gloria Goody's second date with Charles Pompuss, and she swore it would be her last. "For our third date, Gloria," began Charles, "I think we'll go camping with my family. I'm a natural outdoorsman, you know." "Charles, I would love to, but the last time I went camping I had a horrible experience. First, I was eaten alive by mosquitoes and a bear attacked my tent while I was attempting to sleep. Panicking, I ran through the woods only to cross the path of a porcupine and her young. As I tried to back away, she fired 5 or 6 quills into my stomach. The pain was excruciating. By now, I was ready to go back to the tent to face the bear. I found my keys and drove to the nearest hospital, vowing to never go camping again." "If you don't want to go camping, just say so. You don't have to make up a phony story," replied Charles. What didn't he believe?

Answer on page 248

CLEVER MIND

Small But Powerful

What is the smallest integer greater than 1 that is both a perfect square and a perfect cube? What is the next largest number to have the same property?

Answer on page 235

TRIVIA

TRAVEL & GEOGRAPHY

126 What is the name of the imaginary line that runs around the Earth at 23°27' south of the equator?

127 What country has "Hatikvah" as its national anthem?

128 In what state is Zion National Park?

129 Godwin Austen, the second highest mountain in the world, is also known by what letter-number combination?

Answers on page 229

MINDTRAP

◆ The early settlers on the Isle of Begile were a rather conservative group who established the island's bylaws. One of the first laws passed was that all the men were to be clean-shaven, and furthermore, no man was allowed to shave himself. To make matters even more trying, the bylaws stipulated that all men had to be shaved by a licensed barber. For whatever reason, the Isle only issued one barber's license, and that was to an elder who was nearing eighty years of age. Strangely enough, everything seemed to work, until an immigrant lawyer arrived on the scene and asked the overlooked question, "If no man is allowed to shave himself, who then shaves the barber?" How did the Begilers avoid this paradox?

Answer on page 248

CLEVER MIND

Be Perfectly Frank

A hot dog vendor at a soccer game sells one-half of his supply of hot dogs during the first half of the game. During the intermission he sells a total of five hot dogs. During the second half he sells three-eighths of his original supply. He is left with only four hot dogs. How many did he have to start with?

Answer on page 235

TRIVIA

TRAVEL & GEOGRAPHY

130 What river does the Hoover Dam dam?

131 What world capital is divided into 20 *arrondissements*?

132 What four U.S. states meet at a single point called Four Corners?

133 What is the capital of Kansas?

134 What state has "Live free or die" on its license plates?

Answers on page 229

MINDTRAP

◆ Since it was Snorri's last night of bachelorhood, his friends Jon, Halldor, and Thorfin decided to take him downtown to Reykjavik, Iceland, to celebrate. Unfortunately for Snorri, he had a bit too much schnapps and eventually passed out. Seizing the moment, Halldor, an airplane pilot, decided to send him on a flight bound for Greece. Unlike Snorri's head, the night was perfectly clear. Not long after the plane had taken off, a bleary-eyed Snorri woke up to hear the pilot announce their destination—Greece! Still gathering his senses, Snorri gazed blankly out of the window to see a large city below. Instantly, he knew he was flying over London. How could he have known it was London?

Answer on page 248

CLEVER MIND

Making the Grade

A class of fewer than 30 students took a test. The results were mixed. One-third of the class received a "B," one-fourth received a "C," one-sixth received a "D," and one-eighth of the class flunked. Everyone else got an "A."

How many students in the class got an "A" on the test?

Answer on page 235

TRIVIA

TRAVEL & GEOGRAPHY

135 What state encompasses most of Yellowstone National Park?

136 What two countries make up the island of Hispaniola?

137 What country is divided into cantons that include Uri and Zug?

138 In the 1990s, what state allowed car drivers on its interstate highways during daylight hours to go any speed that was "reasonable and prudent"?

Answers on page 229

MIND-BENDER

54 If $\frac{1}{2}$ of 24 were 8, what would $\frac{1}{3}$ of 18 be?

55 In this "trickle down" puzzle, you must change one letter of each succeeding word, starting at the top, to arrive at the word at the bottom. There may be more than one way to solve this—use your creativity!

P A R T
_____
_____
_____
W I N E

Answers on page 219

OPTICAL ILLUSION

Turn the page upside down and you will see that the year 1961 still says 1961. When was the last "upside-down" year, and when will the next one occur?

Answer on page 202

SHREWD CHALLENGE

Twins

Peter and Paul are twin brothers. One of them (we don't know which) always lies. The other one always tells the truth. I ask one of them:
"Is Paul the one that lies?"
"Yes," he answers.
Did I speak to Peter or Paul?

Answer on page 250

CRITICAL THINKING

Suppose two boys and three girls go to the movie theater and they all sit in the same row. If the row has only five seats:

1. How many different ways can the two boys and three girls be seated in this row?

2. What are the chances that the two children at the ends of the row are both boys?

3. What are the chances that the two children at the ends of the row are both girls?

Answer on page 237

MIND-BENDER

56 Find the hidden phrase or title.

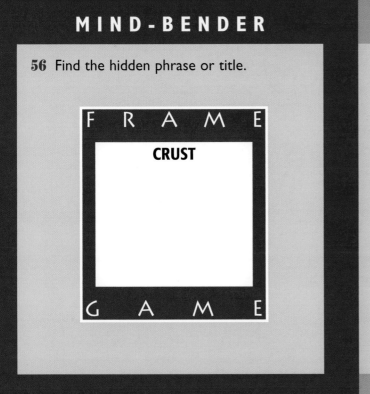

F R A M E

CRUST

G A M E

Answer on page 219

OPTICAL ILLUSION

What do you see in this picture?

Answer on page 202

SHREWD CHALLENGE

Twin Statistics

Suppose that 3% of births give rise to twins. What percentage of the population is a twin: 3%, less than 3%, or more than 3%?

Answer on page 251

CRITICAL THINKING

A pet store owner is counting the birds and lizards that Tarzan has delivered to her store. For some odd reason, she decides to tally only the heads and scaly legs of these animals. When she has finished, she has counted thirty heads and seventy legs. How many birds and how many lizards are there?

Answer on page 237

MIND-BENDER

57 Solve this puzzle without using a pencil or calculator:

$$1\ 3\ 1 = 1$$
$$11\ 3\ 11 = 121$$
$$111\ 3\ 111 = 12{,}321$$
$$1{,}111\ 3\ 1{,}111 = ?$$

58 There are six murks in a bop, eight bops in a farg, and three fargs in a yump. What is the number of murks in a yump divided by the number of bops in a yump?

Answers on page 219

OPTICAL ILLUSION

Read the words in the hat very slowly.
What do they say?

Answer on page 202

SHREWD CHALLENGE

The Professor and His Friend

Professor Zizoloziz puts 40 matches on the table and explains a game to his friend Kathy.

Each player in turn takes 1, 3, or 5 matches. The winner is the one who takes the last match. Kathy chooses to go first and takes 3 matches.

Who do you think will win this game, Kathy or the professor?

Answer on page 251

CRITICAL THINKING

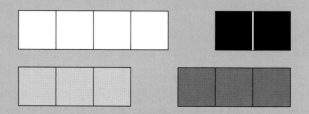

Make a copy of these four rectangles. Cut out the shapes and then arrange them to form a perfect square.

Answer on page 237

MIND-BENDER

59 Find the hidden phrase or title.

Answer on page 219

OPTICAL ILLUSION

FINISHED FILES ARE THE RES-
ULTS OF YEARS OF SCIENT-
IFIC STUDY COMBINED WITH
THE EXPERIENCE OF YEARS.

Using only your eyes, count the number of F's in the above sentence. How many are there?

Answer on page 202

SHREWD CHALLENGE

Economical Progression

Below are four terms in an arithmetical progression (a series in which the difference between terms is constant, in this case 50):
5, 55, 105, 155

Notice how the four terms use only three different digits: 0, 1, and 5.

Can you find six terms in an arithmetic progression that use only three different digits?

Answer on page 251

CRITICAL THINKING

Let's pick up an ant and place it on one corner of a sugar cube. This cube has sides all measuring 1 centimeter. If the ant can only walk along the edges of the cube, what is the total distance it can travel without retracing any part of its path?

Answer on page 237

MIND-BENDER

60 What is the missing number in the triangle on the right?

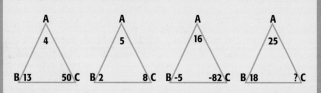

61 If the volume of a cube is 729 cubic feet, how many cubic yards is it?

62 If three pears and four oranges cost $.39 and four pears and three oranges cost $.38, how much does one pear cost?

Answers on page 219

OPTICAL ILLUSION

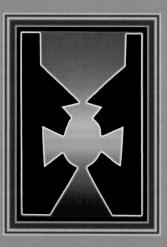

What do you see in this picture?

Answer on page 202

SHREWD CHALLENGE

Up and Down

This morning I had to take the stairs because the elevator was out of service. I had already gone down seven steps when I saw Professor Zizoloziz on the ground floor coming up. I continued descending at my usual pace, greeted the professor when we passed, and was surprised to see that when I still had four more steps to go, the professor had gone up the whole flight. "When I go down one step, he goes up two," I thought.

How many steps does the staircase have?

Answer on page 251

CRITICAL THINKING

There are six players on a coed volleyball team. After an exhausting game, each girl drinks 4 cups of water. Each boy drinks 7 cups of water. The coach drinks 9 cups.

A total of 43 cups of water is consumed by everyone. How many boys and how many girls are on the team?

Answer on page 237

63 What is the missing number in this grid?

15	81	168
23	111	?
5	27	56

64 If I quadrupled one-fifth of a fraction and multiplied it by that fraction, I would get one-fifth. What is the original fraction? (Hint: There are two answers.)

Answers on pages 219 & 220

Napoleon's supporters used to wear violets as a sign of their allegiance. This print hides the faces of Napoleon, Maria Louisa, and the young king of Rome. Can you find them?

Answer on page 202

What Month–I

A month begins on a Friday and ends on a Friday, too. What month is it?

What Month–II

The result of adding the date of the last Monday of last month and the date of the first Thursday of next month is 38. If both dates are of the same year, what is the current month?

Answers on page 251

Take a look at the pattern above. These symbols have a logical order. Can you draw the next symbol in the sequence?

HINT: A little reflection may help you solve this puzzle.

Answer on page 237

65 A six-piece band has agreed that the entire band will be paid $1,225 per gig. But the leader of the band is paid twice as much as each of the other five musicians. How much does the leader earn each gig?

66 What's the missing number next to the letter "E"?

P7   H4   O6   N6   E?

Answers on page 220

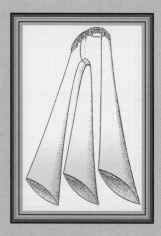

Can you see what's wrong with this pair of bell-bottoms?

Answer on page 202

Soccer Scores—I

A soccer tournament has just ended. Five teams participated, and each one played once against each of the other teams. The winner of a match received 2 points, the losing team 0 points, and each team received 1 point for a tie. The final results were:

Lions	6 points
Tigers	5 points
Bears	3 points
Orioles	1 point

We are missing one team, the Eagles. What was their point total?

Answer on page 251

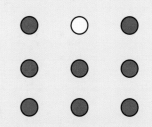

Starting at the top center dot, can you connect all of the other nine dots with only four straight lines? The four lines must all be connected, and your pencil can't leave the paper while drawing the answer.

Answer on page 238

MIND-BENDER

67 Find the hidden phrase or title.

Answer on page 220

OPTICAL ILLUSION

Observe this cow very carefully.
Do you notice anything unusual about it?

Answer on page 202

SHREWD CHALLENGE

Soccer Scores–II

In a three-team tournament, each team played once against each of the two other teams. Each team scored one goal.

The final results were:

Lions	3 points
Tigers	2 points
Bears	1 point

What was the score in each match?

Answer on page 251

CRITICAL THINKING

Look into a mirror and who do you see? You? Perhaps, but it's not the same you that everyone else sees. It's a right-left reversed image. The ear that appears on your left side is seen by others on your right side.

Suppose you want to see yourself exactly as others see you. How can you set up two small mirrors so that your reflection isn't reversed?

Answer on page 238

MIND-BENDER

68 Find the hidden phrase or title.

Answer on page 220

OPTICAL ILLUSION

Can you read this secret message?
Tilt the page to eye level and
look in the direction of the arrows
with one eye closed.

Answer on page 202

SHREWD CHALLENGE

What Time Is It–I

I'm looking at my watch. From this moment on, the hour hand will take exactly twice as long as the minute hand to reach the number six. What time is it?

What Time Is It–II

I'm looking at my watch. From this moment on, the hour hand will take exactly three times longer than the minute hand to reach the number six. What time is it?

Answers on page 251

CRITICAL THINKING

A gold bar balances with $9/10$ of 1 pound and $9/10$ of a similar gold bar. How much does each gold bar weigh?

Answer on page 238

69 In a foreign language, *fol birta klar* means "shine red apples." *Pirt klar farn* means "big red bicycles," and *obirts fol pirt* means "shine bicycles often." How would you say "big apples" in this language?

70 Find three consecutive numbers such that the sum of the first number and the third number is 124.

71 If $16_a = 20$ and $36_a = 32$, what does 26_a equal?

Answer on page 220

A farmer put up this sign. Can you understand what he was trying to say?

Answer on page 202

What Time Is It—III

I'm looking at my watch. The hour hand is on one mark and the minute hand is on the next one. (By marks, we mean minute marks.) What time is it?

What Time Is It—IV

I'm looking at my watch. The hour hand is on one mark and the minute hand is on the previous one. (By marks, we mean minute marks.) What time is it?

Answers on page 251

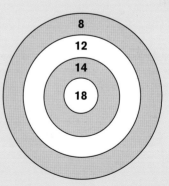

Ten arrows are shot at the target above. One of them misses the target completely. The others all strike it. If the total sum of points is one hundred, in which part of the target did each arrow strike?

Answer on page 238

MIND-BENDER

72 Find the hidden phrase or title.

F R A M E

over...over

G A M E

Answer on page 220

OPTICAL ILLUSION

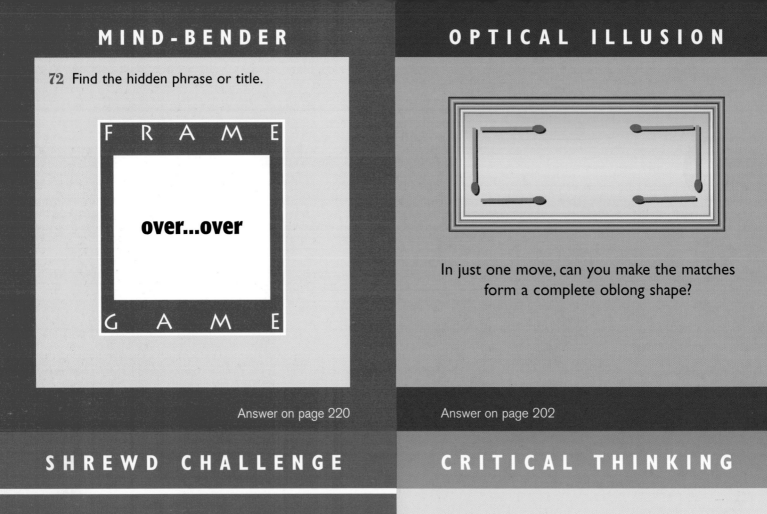

In just one move, can you make the matches form a complete oblong shape?

Answer on page 202

SHREWD CHALLENGE

Prohibited Connection

Using the numbers 1, 2, 3, 4, 5, and 6, put each of them in a circle. There is only one condition. The circles connected by a line cannot have consecutive numbers. For example, 4 cannot be connected to 3 or 5.

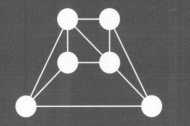

Answer on page 251

CRITICAL THINKING

A medium-size jet has a wingspan of 120 feet. An albatross is a bird with a wingspan of about 12 feet. At what altitude would each object have to fly in order to cast shadows of equal size?

Answer on page 238

MIND-BENDER

73 What nine-letter word is written in the square below? You may start at any letter and go in any direction, but don't go back over any letter.

```
T   E   M
R   C   O
I   G   E
```

74 Decipher the following cryptogram:

SALTS LA ELLG

Answers on page 220

OPTICAL ILLUSION

Can you see what's wrong
with this poster?

Answer on page 202

SHREWD CHALLENGE

Concentric

The big square has an area of 60 square inches. Is there a fast way to figure out what the area of the small square is?

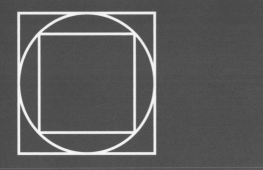

Answer on page 252

CRITICAL THINKING

At a certain time of day, a 25-foot telephone pole casts a 10-foot shadow. At that same time, how high would a tree have to be in order to cast a 25-foot shadow?

Answer on page 238

1

Which of these anagrams does not belong?

slotec
hoccu
sidtnagnht
uerabu
pabrededs
arhic

3

What word, added to the parentheses, completes one word and starts the second?

as (.....) cil
ma (.....) age

2

What are the missing numbers?

2   3   5   8   12   .....
23   18   14   11   9   .....

4

What are the missing letters?

c   l   a
e   n   c
g   p   e
....

5

Complete the following analogy.

Short is to 1811010 as skinny is to .....

7

What number is missing from the center square?

5	4	1
3		3
2	2	6

6

What numbers belong in the parentheses?

98 (33) 79
23 (.....) 55

12 (26) 13
11 (.....) 6

125 (21) 20
70 (.....) 35

8

What number best completes the series?

2   8   3   27   4   .....

9

Which of the numbered figures best completes the series?

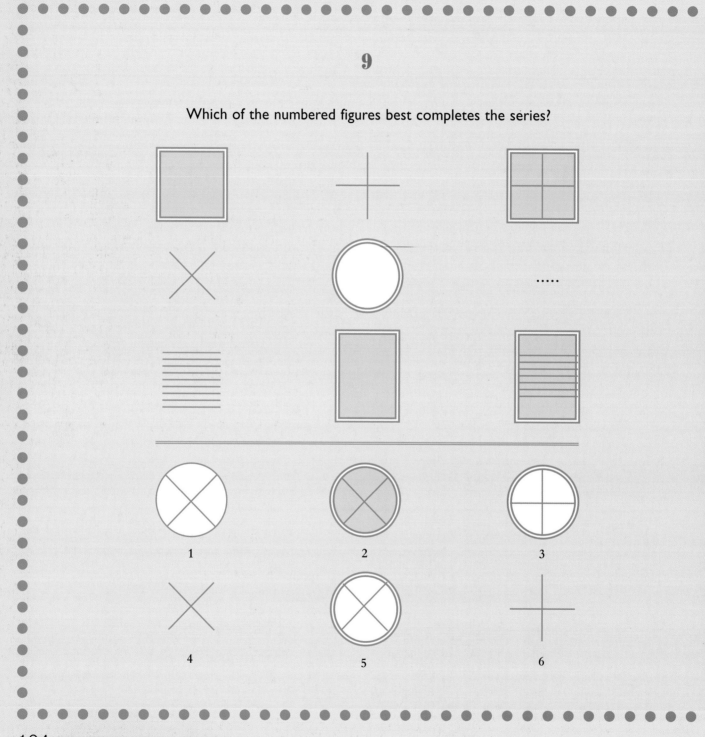

1

2

3

4

5

6

10

Complete the following analogies.

Auto is to steering wheel as bicycle is to .....
(a) wheel
(b) saddle
(c) handlebars
(d) moped

Eye is to sight as nose is to .....
(a) touch
(b) sense
(c) smell
(d) hearing

Chicago is to Illinois as Montreal is to .....
(a) Canada
(b) province
(c) Quebec
(d) Toronto

11

What number is missing from the triangle?

12

Choose the correct answer.

All animals are mammals.
(a) Is always true
(b) Is never true
(c) Is sometimes true
(d) Is an opinion

13

Which numbered figure comes next in the series?

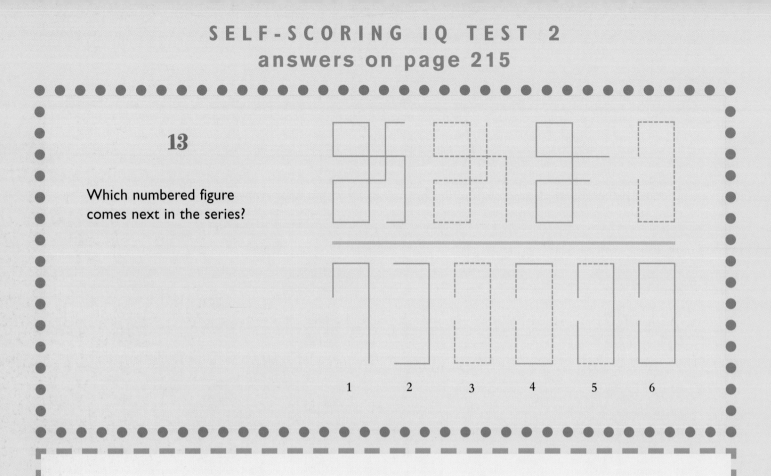

1   2   3   4   5   6

14

Which numbered figure completes the analogy?

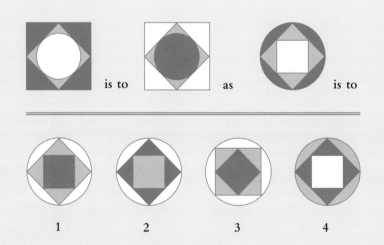

is to   as   is to

1   2   3   4

15

Which of the numbered figures best completes the series?

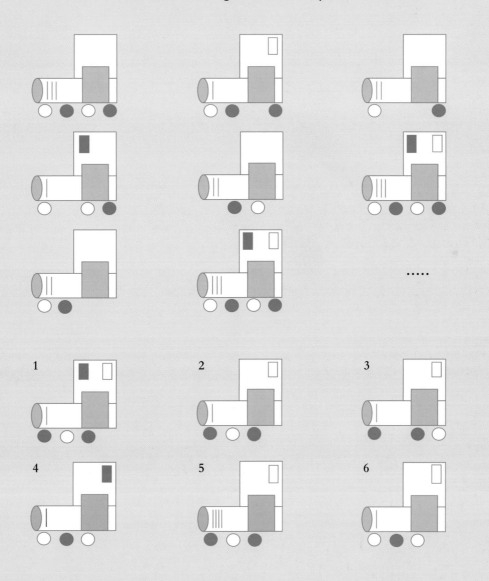

16

What number best completes the series?

3   8   6   11   9   .....

18

Which of the word choices best completes the series?

McKinley   Popocatepetl   Shasta
Rainier   .....

(a) Everest
(b) volcano
(c) Whitney
(d) mountain

17

Which of the following does not belong?

Oslo
Paris
Rome
Barcelona
Beijing
Frankfurt
Prague

19

What are the missing numbers?

13	14	12	16	8	
17	16	18	14	22	
21	22	20	24	16	

20

Which of the following does not belong?

icicle
nail
cone
fork
horseshoe
arrow

22

What word, added to the initial letters, forms other words?

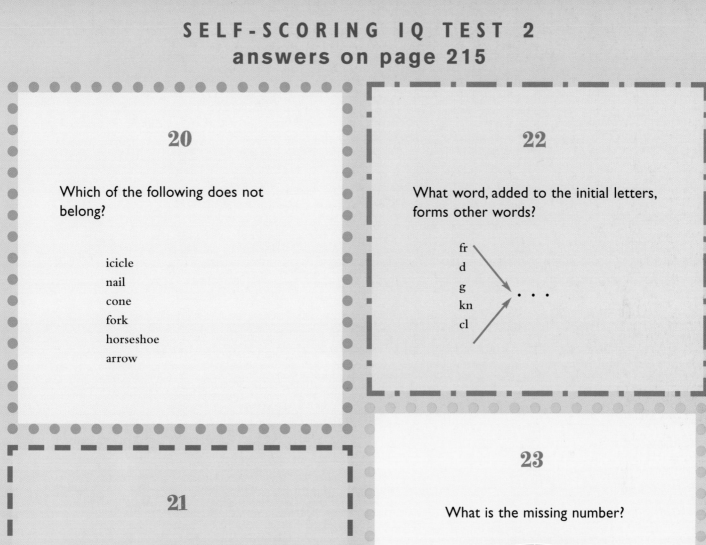

fr
d
g
kn
cl

. . .

21

Which of these word anagrams is not a sport?

luncigr
bigbacer
roascsel
lwstnrieg
gyubr
ceryarh

23

What is the missing number?

2
46
3
28
6
17
10

24

Which of the numbered figures best completes the series?

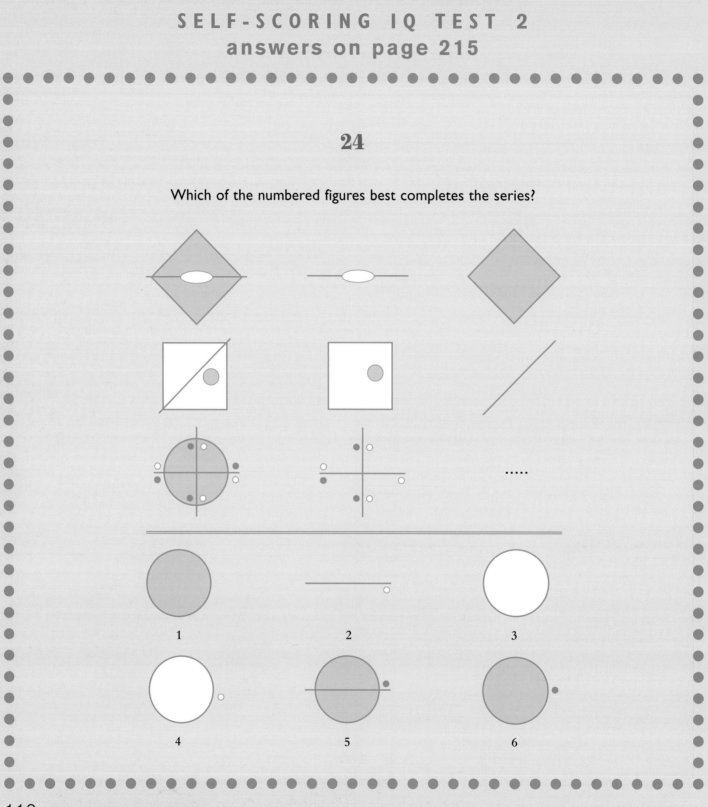

1 2 3

4 5 6

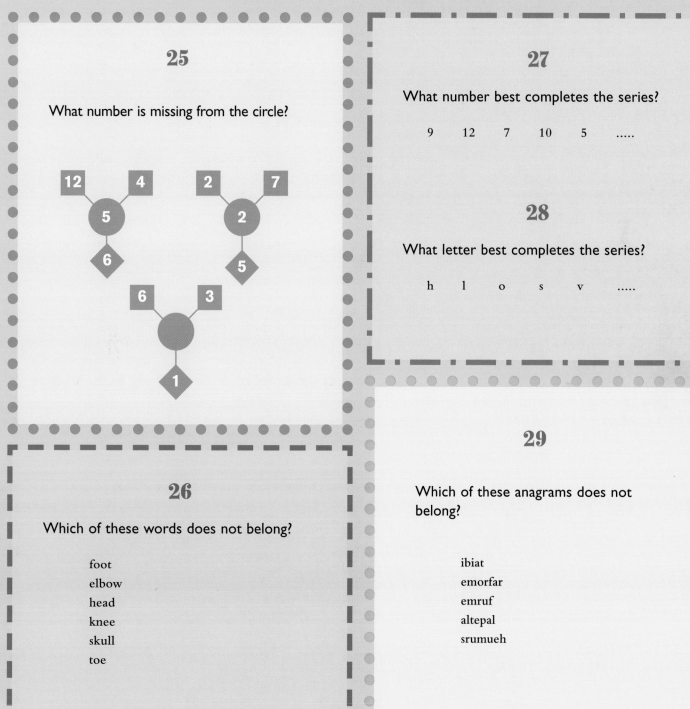

25

What number is missing from the circle?

27

What number best completes the series?

9   12   7   10   5   .....

28

What letter best completes the series?

h   l   o   s   v   .....

26

Which of these words does not belong?

foot
elbow
head
knee
skull
toe

29

Which of these anagrams does not belong?

ibiat
emorfar
emruf
altepal
srumueh

30

What is the missing number?

3   2   12
1   4   8
2   4   .....

31

Which of the following figures does not belong?

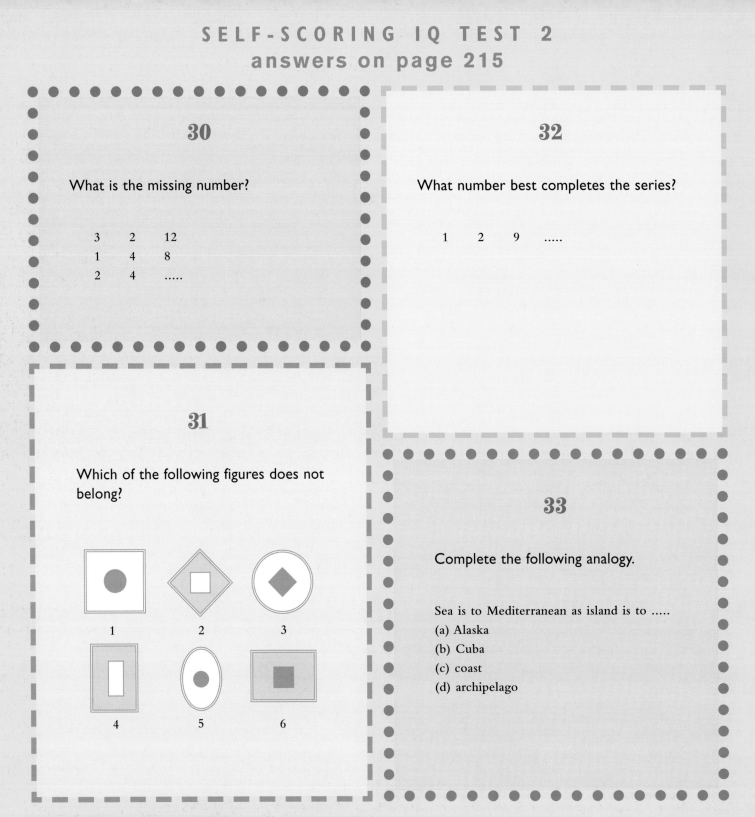

1   2   3

4   5   6

32

What number best completes the series?

1   2   9   .....

33

Complete the following analogy.

Sea is to Mediterranean as island is to .....
(a) Alaska
(b) Cuba
(c) coast
(d) archipelago

34

What number best completes the series?

2   3   3   6   15   .....

35

Which of the following figures does not belong?

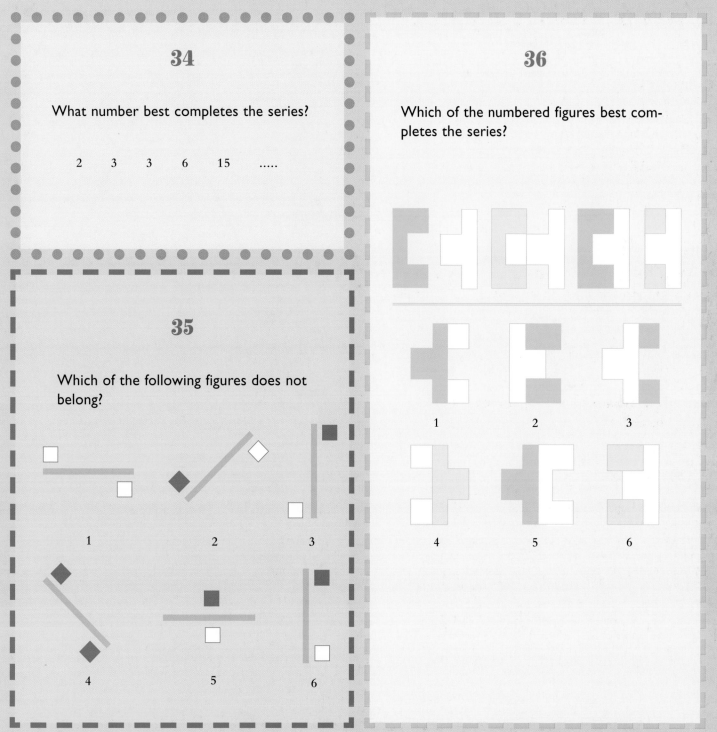

1   2   3

4   5   6

36

Which of the numbered figures best completes the series?

1   2   3

4   5   6

Agent Brown's Shining Moment

A black Cadillac tore around the busy street corner, barely slowing as it approached the steps of the courthouse. The tinted, passenger-side window rolled down and a semi-automatic handgun poked its barrel out.

Pauly Gillespie, mob informant and federally protected witness, stood frozen in his tracks, his worst fears looking like a definite possibility. Pauly's FBI bodyguards threw themselves on top of him, but not before two shots erupted and Pauly had taken a bullet in the shoulder.

The Cadillac screeched across two lanes of traffic. But it  made the mistake of turning left down an alley and getting stuck behind a double-parked delivery van. The two hit men scrambled out and raced away—right into the arms of four off-duty officers. Having heard the shots and the sirens, the officers grabbed the running men and held on until the FBI caught up.

Special Agent Brown was new to this unit and was always given the boring, inconsequential jobs. In this case, he was told to clear the Cadillac out of the alley so that normal traffic could resume. Brown adjusted the rearview mirror, backed the car out, and drove it around to where his colleagues were reading Miranda rights to their suspects.

Brown stood and watched. One of the handcuffed men was tall, lean, and sullen. The other was a good five inches shorter, Agent Brown's height. Large but short. He spoke animatedly, gesturing freely with his hands.

Agent Fordney, director of the unit, seemed exasperated. "They ditched the gun back in the alley," Fordney growled. "They ditched their gloves back there, too. All right, boys, I'm going to ask you again. Which one of you was the shooter?"

"Not me," said the large, short man.

"Not me," said the lean, sullen one.

Agent Brown smiled. Here was his chance to impress his boss. "I know who the shooter was," he said softly.

Who was the shooter and how did Agent Brown know?

Answer on page 240

Here's an easy question: Is the dot placed halfway up the triangle? If not, by how much is it off?

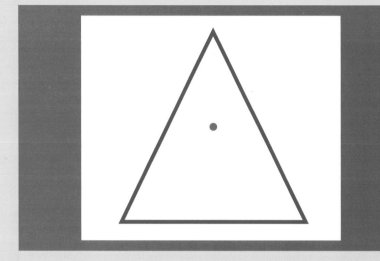

You may need a ruler to check this out, but that dot is exactly at the center. It appears, however, to be placed slightly higher than the middle.

TRIVIA

HISTORY & SCIENCE

139 What is the familiar term for nitrous oxide?

140 What is the name of the group of megaliths on Salisbury Plain in Wiltshire, England?

141 Pure gold is how many karats?

142 What is the first day of Lent called?

143 What do the letters SCUBA stand for?

Answers on page 229

Super Bowl Madness

Vince McCormick was a big, angry slug of a man just a month shy of retirement. On Super Bowl Sunday, his two sons, Vince Junior and Sonny, came over as usual to watch the game.

As kick-off time approached, the boys were in the kitchen, helping their mother prepare the snacks. Junior heated up nachos in the microwave while Sonny poured the bags of potato chips and pretzels into bowls. Marie McCormick was mixing the ice and ginger ale and rye together in tall glasses.

"Make sure mine is strong enough," came her husband's growl from the living room.

Junior saw the bruise on his mother's arm. "Did he do that to you?" he asked. Marie didn't answer.

"What'll you do when he retires and hangs around all day?" Sonny asked. "It'll only get worse."

"No one in our family gets divorced," Marie said firmly. "Oh, dear. I forgot which is your father's. Taste the highballs, Sonny."

Sonny tasted the drinks, nearly choking on the third one. "It's about twice as strong as the others."

"Give it to me." Vince was suddenly standing right behind them, grabbing for his drink. "Making me come in here," he muttered dangerously. Sonny carried in the snack bowls while Junior took in the nachos, just in time for the kick-off. Marie followed with the other drinks.

All four sat around the T.V., munching on the snacks and sipping their drinks. It was near the end of the first quarter when Vince Senior held up his empty glass. "Get me another," he bellowed.

Marie was in the kitchen working on the refill when she heard a gasp, then a moan. She returned to find her husband crumpled in his easy chair, dying.

"A strong, fast-acting poison," the homicide detective said. "Two to five minutes. And yet they all claimed to be eating the same things. They're obviously lying, covering up for each other."

"Not necessarily," a sergeant ventured. "It could've happened just the way they said."

How could Vince have been poisoned? And who could have done it?

Answer on page 240

Patterns and shapes that surround an object can create all sorts of effects. As you've seen, twists and turns can produce a spiral when there is no spiral. They can also change the way a person appears.

Take a look at these two people. Which one is looking at you? Which isn't? Are you sure?

Both of them are looking at the same place. Their eyes are identical! If you don't believe it, just cover up everything except the eyes and you'll see that their gaze is the same. It's the other cues, such as shadows and face angles, that affect how we perceive the direction of their gaze.

TRIVIA

HISTORY & SCIENCE

144 What constellation is known as the Winged Horse?

145 Ascorbic acid is another name for what vitamin?

146 Camp David is named after the grandson of what president?

147 What was the name of the cat in the White House during Bill Clinton's presidency?

Answers on page 229

Death of a Deceiver

Mona Fisher turned and gazed at Jerry, sleeping next to her on the plane. Her eyes wandered down to his wedding band. She still couldn't believe she was married to such a catch.

Their flight from Acapulco landed late that night. The next morning, February 10, Jerry Fisher shoveled the snow from the driveway, kissed Mona good-bye, and headed off to work.

At seven that evening, a cleaning woman entered the law offices of Fisher & Dyce and discovered the body of Jerry Fisher. He had been stabbed to death, a sharp letter opener still sticking out of his chest.

Lieutenant Miller's first unpleasant duty was to interview the

young lawyer's widow. Mona was distraught. "We were only married four months. I never met a man more romantic and honest. Why would anyone want to kill him?"

Jerry's law partner, Kyle Dyce, echoed her sentiments. "Jerry was a man I trusted completely, and a darn good lawyer. He was still working when I left. About 6 p.m. I walked across to the health club. I didn't work out, just used the tanning bed. I suppose I was jealous of Jerry's great Mexico tan."

The lieutenant spent the next hour going through Jerry's papers and discovered that the trusted Jerry Fisher had been skimming money from the law partnership. He also found the phone number of a woman—Gail Lowenski.

They located Ms. Lowenski just leaving the art gallery she managed. The attractive redhead was devastated by Jerry's death and even more devastated to hear that he'd been married. "We were together just this afternoon, at my apartment. The louse told me he was single. For two months he was stringing me on. I was so sure he was going to propose."

Lieutenant Miller and his partner showed up to witness Jerry Fisher's autopsy. "All three of them had motives," the partner whispered as they stared down at the cold, naked body. "The only trouble is, they didn't know they had motives."

"One of them knew," Miller said. "And I know which one."

Whom did the lieutenant suspect and why?

Answer on page 240

Would you believe that these stacks of square blocks are perfectly vertical?

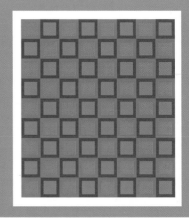

The pattern may be too much for your brain to handle. As your brain begins to organize the units into vertical columns, it assigns a "slant" to its processing. This produces the appearance of stacks that are slightly crooked.

TRIVIA

HISTORY & SCIENCE

148 Shiitake and enoki are what kind of food?

149 What element is abbreviated Pb?

150 What was the name of the B-29 bomber that dropped the atomic bomb on Hiroshima, Japan?

151 What sauce is usually used atop eggs Benedict?

152 What disease used to be called consumption?

Answers on pages 229 & 230

The Party's Over

Tony had promised to help clean up after the party, and Tony was a man of his word. Still nursing a hangover, Tony dragged himself over to Fernando's house. The two men had coffee, then walked into the fenced-in yard, scene of last night's birthday revels.

The lawn was strewn with blown-up balloons and bottles and streamers, but after an hour of work, they managed to get it cleaned up.

"Darn," Fernando said, pointing up to a tree by the edge of the eight-foot-high wooden fence. A balloon was stuck in a top branch. "I'd wait for a breeze to blow it off, but there hasn't been a breeze in days."

Fernando climbed the tree. He was just a few inches from

knocking free the balloon when he glanced into a window of Gil Dover's house next door. "Looks like a robbery," he yelled down. "Broken window. A big mess. Tony, my phone's not working. Go to the corner and call 911. I'll meet you by Gil's rear gate."

When the police arrived, Tony and Fernando were waiting outside the splintered gate to Gil Dover's backyard.

"That's how we found it," Fernando explained. "We didn't go in." Upon entering, the police found what Fernando had said: a broken window, a big mess in the den—plus ten missing rare coins worth $100,000.

Gil Dover wasn't too disturbed. "The coins were insured," he reported. "My uncle left me the collection, and frankly I'd rather have the money. I usually put the alarm on. But today's cleaning day. I don't put it on when the house cleaner comes."

But the cleaner had never come. Al, of Al's Domestic Service, was at his own house across town. He said he got a message from his answering service asking him to skip this week.

A sergeant checked his notes. "Dover says he left home at his usual time, 11 a.m. Fernando looked over the fence at 11:30. Anyone could have broken in during that half-hour period."

"Maybe," his captain replied. "But I have a good idea who's responsible."

Whodunit and how?

Answer on page 240

Which of these numbers appears more symmetrical? Make a choice, then spin this page upside down and look again.

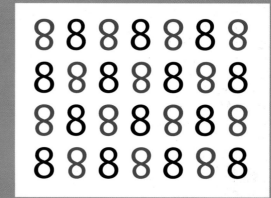

Again, we are familiar with the "bottom-heavy" appearance of the number 8. It's more easily accepted and so it doesn't seem imbalanced to us.

HISTORY & SCIENCE

153 What does a sphygmomanometer measure?

154 What general was known as "The Desert Fox"?

155 What language was invented by Ludwik Lejzer Zamenhof?

156 Who was the first president to be impeached?

Answers on page 230

The Smuggler and the Clever Wife

A Mexican border guard was talking to his wife over his cellular phone when he accidentally overheard a fragment of a static-filled conversation between a man and a woman. "I'll be waiting in Tecate at noon for your regular Monday shipment," said the man. "You don't think the border guards are getting wise?"

"No," the woman laughed. "We can keep this operation going forever." And then, just as suddenly as they'd come, the voices disappeared.

For a full month, customs officials kept track of the traffic at the relatively quiet border crossing. Only three women made a regular habit of crossing into Mexico each Monday morning.

The first woman, impeccably dressed, drove a black Mercedes. The second, a girl barely out of her teens, always crossed on an old red bicycle. The third drove a small van. "MexiCoast Spa" was marked on the side in fancy letters. Of the three, she was the only one declaring merchandise—a weekly supply of U.S.-made health foods and vitamins on which she paid a hefty tariff.

On the fifth Monday, they detained all three women. Methodically they searched, tearing every panel from the dark blue Mercedes, even checking inside the tire tubes. They did the same with the bicycle. Searching the van took the most time. Luckily, this week's shipment of health food was smaller than usual. The officers took samples from every box and bottle.

After finally allowing the women into Mexico, the guard who had intercepted the conversation got back on his cellular phone and reported every detail of the fiasco to his wife.

"From what you say, dear, I think I know who it is. When the woman I suspect crosses back into the U.S., ask passport control to detain her. If my theory is correct, it will be obvious what she is smuggling and how she's doing it." She explained her theory, leaving the guard to marvel at the brilliant woman he'd married.

Who's the smuggler? What is she smuggling? And how?

Answer on page 240

What color do you think this pattern of blue and yellow dots will appear when viewed from across the room?

The image takes on a green cast.

TRIVIA

HISTORY & SCIENCE

157 What was the name of the ship on which Charles Darwin sailed in the 1860s?

158 What is the Jewish New Year called?

159 Who invented dynamite?

160 What organization was George H.W. Bush the director of from 1976 to 1977?

161 Who are the four presidents depicted on Mount Rushmore?

Answers on page 230

The Suicidal House Guest

Doctor Paul Yancy tiptoed out of the sickroom, closing the door behind him. "Uncle Ben needs peace and quiet," he told his brother and sister-in-law. "The flu has left him weak and depressed. But the old man should make a full recovery."

"Thank goodness," replied Fritz with as much sincerity as he could muster. Uncle Ben had been staying with them ever since he got sick two weeks earlier. Every day Fritz had to remind himself of the 30 million good reasons why he and Caroline had to be hospitable to the cantankerous old man.

"Call me if he gets worse," Paul said as he left the house.

"Why can't Paul take Uncle Ben in?" Caroline whined, not for the first time.

"Very simple," Fritz explained again. "The nicer we are to the old buzzard, the more he'll leave us in his will."

A minute later, they heard the television go on in their uncle's ground-floor room. "At least when he's watching T.V., he's not making demands," Caroline sighed.

They listened as Uncle Ben channel-surfed for a few minutes, then switched off the set. An hour later, Caroline brought in his lunch on a tray. That's when they found Uncle Ben dead, a half-empty glass of water on his nightstand along with a completely empty bottle of liquid sleeping drops.

As the body was removed, Officer Warren inspected the room. It seemed to have every convenience for a bedridden man. He counted all the electronic or battery-operated devices: the T.V. set mounted in a ceiling corner, the radio/CD player within easy reach, the portable phone, the remote control for the blinds, an intercom, and, last but not least, the remote control to adjust the adjustable bed.

"According to the medical examiner, the overdose killed him in just a few minutes," a rookie officer informed his superior. "Since the bedroom window was locked from the inside and no one was seen entering the room, I think we can call this a definite suicide."

"Definite murder," Officer Warren countered.

What was it about the room that made Warren suspect murder? And whom did he suspect?

Answer on page 241

Can you believe that these two squares are the exact same size?

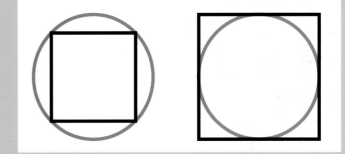

Only kidding. The square on the right is bigger. We thought we'd include this comparison to keep you guessing on line lengths and shape distortions.

TRIVIA

HISTORY & SCIENCE

162 What's the scientific name for the North Star?

163 What is the street address of the White House?

164 Who founded the Mormon Church?

165 What was the 48th state to enter the Union?

a) Montana

b) Alaska

c) Maine

d) Arizona

Answers on page 230

Long-Distance Murder

Nurse Abbott had just received her regular 10 p.m. call from Melba, the daughter-in-law of her patient, multimillionaire John Cord. As usual, Nurse Abbott put the irritating woman on the speakerphone as she tried to straighten up the kitchen. "Yes, I gave him his 9:30 medication," Nurse Abbott sighed. "Yes, he's in the study, having his tea. Is there anything else?" These conversations could go on for hours.

"Jimmy!" the nurse heard Melba shout to her husband. The annoying voice bellowed through the speakerphone. "Pick up the extension. Didn't you have a question for Nurse Abbott?"

The nurse sighed again. "Hello, Mr. Cord." She answered a few more useless questions from John Cord's son, then tactfully found a way to hang up.

Nurse Abbott finished her chore and then returned to the study. That's when she found the body of John Cord lying crumpled on the Oriental carpet. A breeze from the open French doors played through a scarf that was wrapped tightly around his neck.

The police combed the crime scene and found no clue to the killer's identity. Even the study's extension phone had been wiped clean of prints. "When did you last see the deceased?" asked the homicide captain.

"About 9:45," said Nurse Abbott. "I brought him his tea in the study. He was on the phone to his lawyer. Mr. Cord was always fiddling with his will. It got to the point where we no longer paid attention. I went to the kitchen to straighten up and wait for his daughter-in-law's call. It was just like any other evening."

"Not quite," said the captain. He was examining the phone records that had just arrived via fax. "Mrs. Cord telephoned from her home 30 miles away?"

"Yes. So it had to be an intruder," Nurse Abbott theorized. "Maybe a burglar or a hired assassin. Mr. Cord had his share of business enemies."

"No. I think it was someone a lot closer to home."

Whom did the captain suspect and why?

Answer on page 241

Are these lines parallel, or do alternate pairs come together and then spread apart?

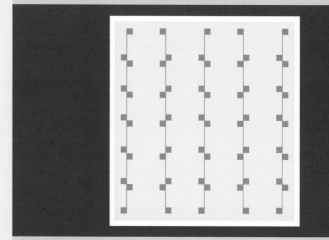

You may need a straightedge to check this out, but all of these lines are parallel. The offset squares trick your brain into creating imaginary tilts. These tilts produce the illusion of spreading and converging lines.

HISTORY & SCIENCE

166 What is the solid form of carbon dioxide commonly called?

167 On what date is Bastille Day celebrated in France?

168 What's the name of the political wing of the Irish Republican Army?

169 In what year did Abraham Lincoln make his Gettysburg Address?

170 Who led an expedition on a raft called Kon-Tiki?

Answers on page 230

The Queen Glendora Photos

"**Y**our regular two o'clock appointment is here," came the secretary's voice over the intercom.

Alicia Bonwit looked up from her cluttered desk. "What? Is it Wednesday already? I don't have time." Then she got a glimpse of her frazzled hair in the mirror. "Well, perhaps I'll make time. Send them in."

The team trooped into the editor's office—Fernando, a blond, clean-shaven hair stylist; Dodo, a tall, red-headed manicurist; and Mr. Mark, a distinguished, gray-bearded dress designer. Alicia pushed aside the stacks of work. "What a day!" she exclaimed with a sigh and delivered herself into their care.

"I've been so busy, I haven't even looked at the Queen Glendora photos." Alicia pointed to an unopened, padded envelope sitting among the editorial debris. "The paparazzi have been working overtime trying to catch a shot of the Albanian queen and her secret lover. Other magazines would pay a fortune for such pictures, but I got 'em. And I haven't had a free second to open the envelope. Oh, well, first things first. What are we going to do with my hair?"

For the next hour, the editor-in-chief of the fashionable tabloid Scoop Weekly allowed herself to be pampered. She gossiped, looked at fabric samples, and watched as her hair and nails were returned to their usual luster. It was only after the entourage had left that she noticed the missing envelope. "The Glendora photos," Alicia shrieked and immediately rang Security.

In the main lobby's trash can, right by the men's room door, a guard found the empty envelope, the reinforced paper neatly cut in a short, scalloped pattern. A week later, the pictures popped up in True Gossip Monthly.

"I had no idea they were stolen," the TGM publisher said with a shrug. "The photos were brought to us by a man wearing dark glasses, a fake beard, and a wig. Not unusual for us. We paid half a million in cash."

The police followed their one solid lead and quickly captured the thief.

What was the lead and who was the thief?

Answer on page 241

Count the number of times the letter "f" appears in the following paragraph:

> All forms of optical illusions seem to fascinate folks. In fact, my favorite friends find visual foolery fantastically fun, if not incredibly fascinating. But suppose such folks found illusions foolish and flat? If that were a fact, then books of this style might be defunct.

How many did you count? Was it twenty-one? Although you probably spotted the "f" in large words, you might have overlooked the "f" in shorter words, such as "of" and "if."

T R I V I A

HISTORY & SCIENCE

171 What is the familiar name of the scandal in which Albert Fall, former secretary of the interior, was convicted of accepting bribes in the leasing of the Elk Hills naval oil reserve?

172 What two presidents died on July 4, 1826?

173 Who is pictured on the $50 bill?

174 *The Watch Tower* is published by what religious group?

Answers on page 230

The Dirty Cop

For six months, a dirty cop had been leaking information to the mob, and Officer Bill Brady of Internal Affairs was going to catch him tonight. According to Brady's sources, Carmine Catrone, a mob boss, was scheduled to meet the dirty cop in Hannibal's, an out-of-the-way tavern.

Brady arrived at Hannibal's wearing a wig and false mustache. A familiar face was already on the premises—Marjorie Pepper, a desk sergeant from the Fourth Precinct. Brady watched as Marjorie ordered a drink, then lifted her left arm and checked her watch. Was she waiting for someone?

Seconds later, another familiar face entered, this time from the direction of the rest rooms. It was Adam Paprika of the Special Vice unit. As Adam used his right hand to zip up his trousers, Brady noticed the diamond pinkie ring. It reminded him of Carmine Catrone's pinkie ring.

Then came a third familiar face. Rookie patrolman Charlie Salt walked in and ambled over to an empty table. Charlie opened his briefcase and began writing down notes. When the young officer lifted his left hand to call over the waitress, Brady saw the glint of a gold fountain pen. Very expensive.

Brady had never counted on more than one officer showing up. What if they recognized each other? What if they recognized him?

As the bar grew crowded, Brady kept an eye on his subjects. All three were smoking. And all three occasionally got up to use the phone or buy cigarettes or use the rest rooms.

At the end of an hour, the suspects had all left, each one alone. Carmine Catrone had never shown up.

A frustrated Brady wandered past the pay phone. That's when he saw the matchbook in the wastebasket. On a hunch, Brady retrieved it, opening the flap. Four matches had been torn from the left side, and on the top flap was scrawled a phone number—Carmine Catrone's phone number.

Brady reasoned it out. One of his suspects had phoned Catrone, warning him not to come. And Brady knew just who it was.

Who was it? And how did Brady know?

Answer on page 241

Do the white letters appear "top heavy"?

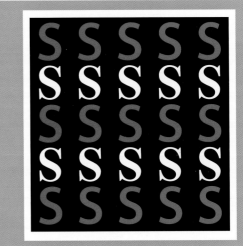

They're not. We get used to seeing an S with a slightly smaller top half. Therefore, when an S with two equal halves is presented, it appears asymmetrical.

TRIVIA

HISTORY & SCIENCE

175 What's the technical name for the thighbone?

176 What general was nicknamed "Old Blood and Guts"?

177 The three main classes of rocks are igneous, metamorphic, and what?

178 What mineral scores 10 on the Mohs' scale?

Answers on page 230

The Stolen Cleopatra

The silent alarm announced a break-in at the home of Jordan Marsh, the famous collector. When a patrolman arrived, he found two men waiting for him in the backyard of Marsh's suburban home, standing by a broken window.

"My name's Digby Dunne," the first man said. "Jordan's next-door neighbor. I caught this man red-handed, breaking in and stealing the Cleopatra coin."

"I caught him red-handed," the other man countered. "I'm Kenny Johnson, Jordan's other neighbor."

"One at a time," the patrolman said. "Mr. Dunne?"

"Jordan's been away for a month," Digby explained. "He gave me house keys and the alarm code. Every five days, I go in to water the plants. I was just about to do that this afternoon. I was in the process of unlocking Jordan's front door when I looked in. Kenny was in the living room, taking a small plastic frame from the display cabinet. It was Jordan's prized Cleopatra coin. Kenny saw me and rushed out into the kitchen. I raced around the house and caught up with him in the backyard."

"That's a lie," Kenny said. "I was in my second-floor office. When I heard the sound of breaking glass, I looked out. Digby was in Jordan's yard, by the kitchen door. He must have just broken a windowpane. In his hand I could see the plastic holder for the Cleopatra coin. I raced downstairs and surprised him before he could leave the yard. He must have gotten in with his key, stolen the coin, then faked the break-in to throw off suspicion."

The patrolman entered Jordan Marsh's house and found an empty spot in the display cabinet. By the doorway of the sun-lit kitchen, he examined a potted plant. The soil was dry and the lush, long leaves were bent toward the darkened living room. Re-emerging into the yard, he found the morning rain had left muddy patches. Rows of brown footprints trailed across the flagstones.

Both men insisted on being searched, but the patrolman refused. "I don't need to search anyone. I know which one of you is lying."

Whodunit? And where is the coin hidden?

Answer on page 241

Which arc appears bigger?

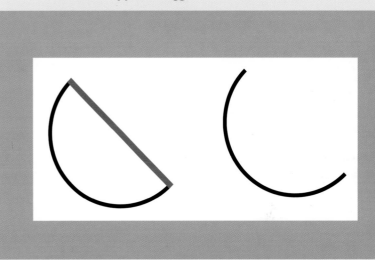

Most people think the open arc looks larger. This may be caused by one's tendency to shrink shapes that appear "closed in" while expanding shapes that appear surrounded by free space.

TRIVIA

HISTORY & SCIENCE

179 What was the name of the hill on which the Battle of Bunker Hill was fought?

180 What lowercase letter is used to represent the square root of negative one?

181 The Secret Service was formerly part of what Cabinet department?

182 What is the Tokyo Stock Exchange index called?

Answers on page 230

Archie's Christmas Surprise

"**M**r. Granger?" The secretary tried to speak calmly into the receiver. "This is Emily. Could you come down to the nineteenth floor? It's sort of an emergency."

Emily hung up. It was an emergency, alright. Archie Tatum, their chief financial officer, was in his office, hanging by a rope from an extremely strong light fixture. He had been like this when Hank, his assistant, came to work. Hank was used to seeing him in the office before anyone else, but not like this. Hank had waited for Emily to arrive. She'd know what to do.

Emily's reaction had been cool. "What a horrible thing—and on the last work day before Christmas! Call the police. I'll get Mr. Granger down here."

From the moment Gene Granger stepped out of the elevator, he was enmeshed in damage control. As president of Granger Productions, he had to break the news to the rest of the company and then deal with the press, the police, and Archie's family.

Granger didn't even think about returning to the twentieth floor until Emily reminded him at 5 p.m. "The Christmas party upstairs, Mr. Granger. People won't stay long, but I think everyone could use a little comfort."

Several employees were already gathered as Granger unlocked the door of his private conference room. A Christmas tree was in the corner, with a colorful jumble of presents under its branches. Emily crossed to the bar and immediately began serving. Despite the alcohol, the mood remained somber. Granger handed out a personally chosen gift to each worker, from the secretaries to the executive vice-president.

Hank was one of the last to leave. He took one final look at the empty floor under the tree, then turned to join his fiancée.

"What could have driven Archie to suicide?" his fiancée wondered. "Emily says he'd been very worried about company finances. You don't suppose that maybe he was embezzling . . .'"

"Archie didn't kill himself," Hank responded. He was murdered. And I know who did it."

Whodunit? And how did Hank know?

Answer on page 242

Describe this shape.

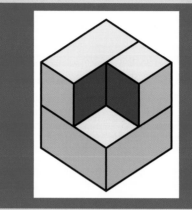

This is another image that can present two logical appearances. What it looks like depends on the direction you assign to the light source. If the light comes from above, the image looks like a simple cube that has its top corner missing. If, however, you assume that the light comes from below, it appears to be a small box that is positioned in the corner of a ceiling.

TRIVIA

HISTORY & SCIENCE

183 Who was the first vice president who didn't go on to become president?
a) Alexander Hamilton
b) Benjamin Franklin
c) Hannibal Hamlin
d) Aaron Burr

184 What last name was shared by three vice presidents?

185 What was Millard Fillmore's political party?

Answers on page 230

Postgraduate Murder

The time of death was firmly established. At 10:06 p.m. all three suspects said they heard a gunshot echo through the house. The house was shared by four graduate students; three, if you no longer counted Harry Harris, the victim who lay in his second-story bedroom, a bullet in his chest.

Harry, it seemed, had been a ladies' man. He had even bragged about seducing the girlfriend of one of his housemates. Unfortunately, the police didn't know which one. They separated the three remaining housemates and interviewed each one.

"I was working on my car," Bill Mayer insisted. "I plugged an extension cord into an outlet behind the house. Then I took a work light around to the side driveway, in front of the garage. When I heard the gunshot, it took me a second to realize it came from the house. Then I ran inside."

The second suspect entered the room with a noticeable limp. "I had just come home," explained Sonny Sorriso. "I parked in the alley behind the house. I was walking up to the back door when I tripped hard over some cord. I fell down, then just sat there, nursing my ankle. Maybe two minutes later came the gunshot. That got me moving."

The third suspect claimed that he had just come down to the kitchen. "I was starting to scoop out a bowl of ice cream," said Glen Gouly. "Then I heard a noise out back. I looked out, but it was dark. I went back to my ice cream. A couple minutes later I heard the shot."

The detectives circled the house. In the kitchen, they found a melted bowl of ice cream on the counter by the refrigerator. In the backyard, they saw an orange extension cord with a bent prong that had been ripped from an outdoor socket. Following the extension cord around, they found Bill Mayer's car in front of the garage, the work light suspended over the open hood.

"It's pretty clear who's lying," the chief detective mumbled. Whodunit?

Answer on page 242

Do you notice any problems with these columns?

These columns are perfectly straight, vertical, and parallel to each other. The slanted lines drawn in the columns create a false sense of 3-D. Your misguided visual processing goes to work and "repaints" the scene as a set of bent columns.

TRIVIA

HISTORY & SCIENCE

186 Who fought Athens in the Peloponnesian War?

187 How old do you have to be to become a U.S. senator?

188 What's the ninth month of the Muslim calendar?

189 Who was the first Secretary of State?

190 Who invented the helicopter?

Answers on page 230

The Last Poker Hand

A homicide sergeant stood in the hotel suite, gazing down at the body of Bugsy Ferret. "He was a card sharp," the sergeant told the hotel manager. "Bugsy preyed on tourists. He'd lure them to a hotel, start a friendly poker game, and take them to the cleaners. I guess someone came back this time and took Bugsy."

Bugsy lay sprawled amid a carpet of scattered playing cards and a bottle of Blush gin. He'd been stabbed in the chest.

"Looks like he didn't die right away," said the sergeant as he pointed to the five cards held in the victim's stiff grip. All diamonds. "Maybe he was trying to tell us something."

"We got our suspects," came a voice from the bedroom. The sergeant's partner emerged, holding a handwritten list. "Benny King, Jack Lawrence, Joe Blush, Alan Spade. He listed their hotels, too. Let's check 'em out."

The Reverend Benny King denied knowing Bugsy and vehemently denied ever playing poker. "My parishioners know I would never risk their money—or mine—in such a sinful pursuit. I don't know how my name got on that list."

Jack Lawrence told a different story. "Sure, King was there. And Al Spade and Joe Flush. The four of us first met yesterday at a hotel bar. We got to talking about cards and this Ferret character talked us into a game. Hey, you live and learn."

Alan Spade was a tad more sanguine. "He was a stinking cheat and he deserved to die. I was livid, but we all paid up and we left the rat in one piece. Someone must've come back, but it wasn't me."

Joseph Blush, an English professor, seemed an unlikely gambler. "At first we all won our share. But as the evening progressed, we lost more. I don't suppose you can give me my money back." The police assured him that no money had been found in Bugsy Ferret's suite.

"We should bring one of them in for questioning," the sergeant said after the final interview.

Which card player did he suspect?

Answer on page 242

$$
\begin{array}{r}
318 \\
303 \\
300 \\
104 \\
+\,215 \\
\hline
1240
\end{array}
$$

The above sum is correct. Nevertheless, it is possible to delete two of the figures above the line and still get the same correct answer.

Answer on page 245

Hidden Word–I

A three-letter word belongs in the rectangle below. Given the words below, figure out what it is.

0	1	2
HAS	CON	SON
	CAB	

Answer on page 252

Eye Spy

The American agent used his skeleton keys to work on the lock while his female partner acted as lookout. It was hard to see clearly in the dreary hall light in the dreary apartment building in the dreary winter weather of Beijing. But David Richman finally cracked the mechanism and opened the door. "Hurry," he whispered, motioning for Julia to join him. Inside it was just as chilly as the hall.

"We're looking for photographic negatives," he told Julia for perhaps the tenth time. "Thirty-five millimeter. Lu Ching hasn't had time to reduce them any further. Thank goodness it's a small apartment."

It was small, all right. The tiny studio contained a futon bed that doubled as a sofa. There were also a bookcase, a table, two chairs, and an old-fashioned desk fan that whirred noisily on top of a cluttered desk. A hot plate served as the apartment's kitchen. From a small adjoining bathroom came the sound of a leaky toilet.

"We have to find them," David whispered as he went directly for the bookcase. "The lives of a dozen Chinese contacts depend on our finding those eight negatives." He was already going through the books page by page, checking the covers for any telltale slits where the agent for the People's Republic might have stuffed them.

"Lu Ching didn't have a lot of time to hide them," David added. "And he needed to keep them in a pretty accessible place. It shouldn't be too hard."

But it was. They checked under everything, from the desk clutter to the chair seats. They checked the water flow in all the faucets and the toilet tank. David became so frustrated that he was almost ready to cut open the futon.

Julia stepped back and surveyed the room. "I see it now. I know where they probably are," she said softly.

What clue is Julia looking at?

Answer on page 242

Cut one of the pieces in two and then make the six pieces into a square.

Answer on page 245

Hidden Word–II

A five-letter word belongs in the rectangle below. Given the words below, figure out what it is.

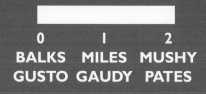

0	1	2
BALKS	MILES	MUSHY
GUSTO	GAUDY	PATES

Answer on page 252

The Piney Bluffers

"I was just pulling into the Piney Bluffs gas station," the shaken witness told the operator. "I heard a gunshot. And then I saw the men—two of them—running out of the station and hopping into a recreation vehicle. They'd killed the attendant." She gave a description of the R.V. and a general description of the men.

The R.V. was found, abandoned south of one of the road-blocks the highway patrol had set up. The vehicle was just feet away from Piney Bluffs State Park, which was enjoying its first rain in weeks. It was assumed that the men had hiked away into the hundreds of acres of parkland. Officers were sent in to interview the campers.

"Sorry we can't help you," Warren Hatchet told an officer. He and his brother were camping in a tent by a trout stream. They fit the general description. "We hiked in here last night. All day today we've been fishing. Got back just a little while ago."

"You fished in the rain?" the officer asked as he gazed at the two small trout frying in a pan. The brothers invited him to join them for dinner, but he refused.

A second pair of campers also fit the description. The officer joined them inside their tent, sitting on a knapsack in order to avoid the wet ground. "This morning we set up camp," Al Fishburn told him. "Then we went out hiking. When it started raining, we found a cave and holed up there for a few hours. We didn't see anyone—not until you came along."

A final pair of campers were discovered in an R.V. in a section of the park off-limits to vehicles. "I know we shouldn't be here," George Tingle said. "But we're not hurting anyone. A friend in Chicago lent me this R.V. That's why the registration's not in my name. If you want to call Chicago and check . . ."

"I don't need to call anyone," the officer replied. "I already know who's lying."

Whodunit? And how did the officer know?

Answer on page 243

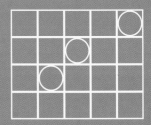

By using three lines, divide the page into seven sections, each containing only one egg.

Answer on page 245

Hound–I

A hound started on a square numbered 1, and moved from square to square numbering them in succession to the last one, numbered 20. The hound moved horizontally and vertically only, never entering any square twice. The numbers were then deleted. All we know is that the squares with circles had the numbers 5, 10, and 15, in some order. Figure out the path of the hound.

Answer on page 252

The Vandalizing Visitor

It was late at night at the Drakemore Hotel. A member of the cleaning staff was dusting the courtesy phones in the lobby when she heard the breaking of glass in the side lobby. And then the alarm went off.

The side lobby contained a display case holding memorabilia from the Drakemore's opening fifty years ago: the hotel's first menu, a laughably antiquated price list for rooms, a few rare coins and stamps from that year, photographs, and the dusty signatures of the first famous guests.

The night manager showed up a few seconds later. He and the staff member circled the lobby and discovered three guests who had been in the vicinity. Diplomatically but firmly, the manager suggested all three remain in the lobby until the police arrived.

"We've had them under constant observation," the manager told the responding officer. He pointed to a woman reading in an armchair. "Ms. Oakley said she had just returned from a business dinner. She was very cooperative. Just sat down and pulled a book out of her briefcase."

"Mr. Brier said he'd come down from his room to get some aspirin from the front desk. His wife had a headache. When we detained him, he called his wife on one of the pay phones. I listened in. He told her he would be delayed and not to worry."

The manager pointed to the last suspect, a sloppily dressed young man who looked like he'd had one too many. "Mr. Greenleaf had been in the hotel bar. The bartender refused to serve him any more alcohol, so he wandered in here. We found him by the elevator, jamming his finger into the 'up' button."

"Whoever did this wasn't counting on an alarm," the manager continued. "Perhaps he was scared off before he took anything. We may never know who tried to rob us."

"I have a good idea who it was," the officer said. "One of the suspects did something odd. Just let me have one thing checked."

Whom does the officer suspect and why?

Answer on page 243

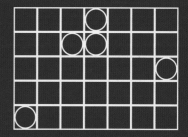

Copy the pieces onto a piece of paper and try to arrange them into a T. This puzzle first appeared in an advertisement for White Rose Ceylon Tea in 1903.

Answer on page 245

Hound–II

A hound started on a square numbered 1, and moved from square to square numbering them in succession to the last one, numbered 35. The hound moved horizontally and vertically only, never entering any square twice. The numbers were then deleted. All we know is that the squares with circles had the numbers 7, 14, 21, 28, and 35, in some order. Figure out the path of the hound.

Answer on page 252

An Attack of Gas

The island of Canary Rock had no police force and none was really needed—not until the fateful morning when Gerald Espy was found dead in his bed. The millionaire had been laid up with a broken leg, and although the local doctor was adept at setting bones, he was not well versed in murder. It wasn't until he saw the dead cat curled up in a corner that he even suspected foul play.

"Poison gas," the inspector guessed when he arrived. An empty glass container on the table was the primary evidence. "Pour one chemical on another." He pointed to the dead flies on the windowsill at the east end of the room. "In less than a minute everything in the room would be dead."

The body had been discovered by Espy's son, Melvin. "I was out with some friends on my boat. I dropped them off at about midnight, then motored back to Canary Rock. There were no lights on at the house, but every now and then the moon would peek through. I figured Dad was asleep. So I locked up the house and went straight to bed. This morning, I went to check up. He was dead."

The last person to admit seeing Gerald Espy alive was his business partner, Frank Townly, another island resident. "Frank came in here around midnight," the tavern owner testified. "He and Espy weren't getting along. Business was bad and they were both threatening lawsuits. Frank drank down a slew of scotches. He told me he had just been over to Espy's. When it came closing time, Frank was dead drunk and asleep. I just locked up and left him in there. He was still asleep at noontime when I opened up."

"When I left Gerald's house last night, he was alive," the hung-over Frank Townly said. "Check the time of death."

"I don't have to check the time of death," the inspector replied. "I have a pretty good idea when it was done and who did it."

Or, as we like to say: whodunit?

Answer on page 243

Trace or copy the picture above. Cut the card along the dotted lines into three pieces and exchange the two top parts. Suddenly there is an extra egg!

Hound–III

A hound started on a square numbered 1, and moved from square to square numbering them in succession to the last one, numbered 25. The hound never entered

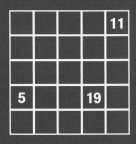

any square twice and moved horizontally and vertically only, except for one diagonal move to a neighboring square. All the numbers except those shown were then deleted. Figure out the path of the hound.

Answer on page 252

The Convent Mystery

"We have a little mystery at the Inner City Convent," the Mother Superior said as she poured a second cup of tea.

Inspector Griffith was immediately interested.

"It's the convent offices. We have three civilian employees there to handle the mail and the bills and the bookkeeping. Alice has been with us for years. Very reliable, even though she has a bit of a drinking problem and a husband who ... Let's just say he can use our prayers.

"Barbara is new. She worked at an Alaskan convent before coming here. She's seems wonderful, although we're still waiting for the sisters there to send us a character reference.

"Our third is Claudia. Ever since the city opened up riverboat gambling . . . Well, I'm not going to point fingers, but there have been some minor irregularities in our petty cash.

"As you know, the office is closed all weekend. On Monday morning I arrive first. I open up, check the mail, water the plants, turn off the alarm. We have this newfangled alarm system. It does all the usual. And it also automatically records whenever the alarm has been turned off. I never quite saw the sense of that. But four Mondays ago when I came in, I checked the log. The alarm had been turned off Saturday afternoon. For five minutes. Then it was switched back on. I didn't think anything of it. Someone probably came back to retrieve some forgotten item.

"The next Monday, I found the same thing. Turned off Saturday afternoon for five minutes. I asked the women—they all have alarm keys. All three denied having visited the office.

"This has been going on for four Saturdays now. Nothing is ever missing or changed. Even the petty cash is exactly the same as it was Friday evening. It's baffling—although I don't suppose there's any harm done."

"There could be harm," Inspector Griffith replied. "I can think of only one possible explanation. And I think we need to deal with this woman right away."

Whom does the inspector suspect and why?

Answer on page 243

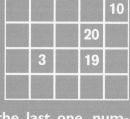

Just another dovetail? Seems impossible? It isn't. Can you see how to separate the two parts?

Answer on page 245

Hound–IV

A hound started on a square numbered 1, and moved from square to square numbering them in succession to the last one, numbered 25. The hound never entered any square twice and moved horizontally and vertically only, except for one jump move like a chess knight, shown at the left. All the numbers except those shown were then deleted. Figure out the path of the hound.

16				
				10
			20	
	3		19	

Answer on page 252

The Shortcut Robbery

It was 1 p.m. when the two officers heard the cry for help. They responded quickly, racing down an alley to find a woman sitting on the ground, massaging a nasty bump on the back of her head. It took them a minute to get her to speak coherently.

Her name was Mary Ramsey. She worked at a jewelry store and had been in the process of taking yesterday's receipts to the bank. "I do this every day. My boss warned me not to use the alley. Today I had a feeling I was being followed. Like an idiot, I took the alley anyway. I heard footsteps. Before I could even turn around, I was hit on the head.

"I fell down," Mary continued. "But it didn't quite knock me out. He was running away with my money bag. I only saw him from the rear. He was tall and had on blue jeans and a dark-colored cardigan."

The officers brought in two men for questioning: both tall and both dressed according to Mary's description.

"So, I was running," Stu Logan said angrily. He had been found two blocks from the site of the attack and ran as soon as he saw the patrol car. Stu had a string of priors, all misdemeanors. "Look, I was at the end of my lunch break. I can't be late getting back to work. I need this job." Stu, it turned out, worked at the deli right next to the jewelry store.

The second suspect was Ollie Oscar, a street person. "I wasn't even wearing this sweater," he protested as he unbuttoned his moth-eaten cardigan. "I picked it out of the garbage just before you pulled me in."

"And what about this money bag?" the officer asked, pointing to the other item found on him.

"I got that from a different garbage can. The ones behind the bank always have things like this. You didn't find any money on me. Right?"

The officers agreed that there was only one suspect worth considering.

Whodunit?

Answer on page 243

Do you see red spots in the intersections of the squares?

Broken M

We have formed six triangles by drawing three straight lines on the M. That's not enough. Starting with a new M, form nine triangles by drawing three straight lines.

Answer on page 252

The Locked Room

"I'm changing my will," Abigail Wallace announced. Her four children may have been adopted, but they were just as spoiled and ungrateful as any natural offspring. "Tomorrow I'm cutting you all off without a cent." And with that satisfying but reckless statement, Abigail rose from the dining room table and headed up to her bedroom.

No one was surprised when a gunshot rang out two hours later. The only surprise was that it had taken so long.

"I was downstairs reading," Manny later told the police. "As soon as I heard the shot, I ran upstairs and down the hall to Mother's room. It was locked from the inside."

Moe had also been downstairs, in the kitchen. "I ran up the back staircase. Manny was already at Mother's door, pounding and calling out her name."

"I was in my own room at the far end of the hall," said Jack, the third child to arrive at the scene. "I suggested looking through the keyhole. But Manny and Moe decided to put their shoulders to the door instead."

After a few tries, the door-jamb cracked open and the sons rushed in to find Abigail Wallace seated in her chair, her hand draped limply over the armrest with the gun on the rug right below.

The boys heard a gasp and turned around to see their sister, Sheila, behind them in the doorway.

"I'd been on the third floor," she later testified. "I heard the gunshot but didn't know what it was. When I heard everyone running, I came down to the second floor. They were gathered at Mother's door. Jack was looking through the keyhole. Manny and Moe shooed him away and started ramming the door. I just stood there. Only after they busted the door open did I come out of my daze and follow them in."

Faced with a locked room, the police were all prepared to call it suicide, until they heard about the will. Then they reviewed the evidence and arrested a suspect.

Whodunit? And how did the killer arrange the locked room?

Answer on page 244

Find the second car.

Answer on page 245

SHREWD CHALLENGE

Skin and Shoes

A white man is wearing a pair of white shoes, a black man is wearing a pair of black shoes, and a red-skinned man is wearing a pair of red shoes. In a gesture of friendship, they decide to exchange shoes. When they are done, each man has on one shoe from each of the other two men.

How many shoes will you have to look at to know which color of shoe each man is wearing on each foot, that is, which color shoe each man wears on his right foot and which color each man wears on his left foot? Note that when you look at a shoe, you can see that man's skin color.

Answer on page 252

A Chinese Lie Detector

When the emperor rose on that April morning, he immediately noticed the silence. "There's no cricket. Where's my cricket?" he demanded. The servants of the bed chamber checked all the usual places, but the cricket was gone—and so was its jeweled cricket box.

The entire royal court was thrown into turmoil until the chirping pet was finally found, housed in a lowly bamboo box and hidden in the corner of a public garden. The emperor was both relieved and outraged. "How dare someone steal from me!" He ordered the captain of the palace guard to find the still-missing box and the culprit.

Finding the box was easy. Lu Ping, a near-sighted gem dealer, bought it from a palace servant and only realized later what he had purchased. With the most abject apologies, he returned it to the emperor. "I don't know if I can recognize the man who sold it to me," he said with a squint. "I'll do my best."

From the gem dealer's description, the captain narrowed down the suspects to three. But the dealer couldn't make a positive identification, and none of the three would confess. "Hang them all," the emperor commanded.

That was when the court wizard intervened. "I can discover the guilty servant," he boasted. "Bring the three and come to the public garden."

The wizard led the way to the spot where the cricket had been found. He ordered each suspect to cut a stalk of bamboo. Then the wizard planted the stalks in the hard earth, making sure that each one stuck up the same height from the ground. "By dawn tomorrow," he announced in solemn tones, "the stalk of the guilty man will grow by the length of a finger joint."

By dawn the next morning, the wizard had kept his word. He had discovered the identity of the guilty servant.

How did the wizard do it?

Answer on page 244

Which of these two clowns is the larger one? Use a ruler to check. This is an optical illusion of German origin from the 1920s.

Fort Knox Jumping Frogs—I

Place 14 coins in the shape of a cross, as shown in the illustration. In seven moves, make seven piles of two coins each. Note: Only move the coins in a straight line; do not change directions.

Answer on page 252

The Brothers Ilirium

A church choir was picnicking in a rest area near Pine Gorge when they heard the distant squeal of tires. The choir members gazed out over the winding ribbon of road in time to see a red convertible slam through a guard rail and sail out into the steep gorge. The driver was thrown clear of the vehicle seconds before impact. Miraculously, there was no explosion.

The highway patrol found the bloodied body of Mike Ilirium smashed on the boulders. Inside the mangled car were several loose rocks, a tangle of broken branches, and more blood on the seat and the dashboard.

The Ilirium saga was well known to the area gossips. Mike had been engaged to a local beauty. They broke off the engagement when she confessed to having had an affair with one of Mike's brothers; no one knew which.

The authorities visited the Ilirium lodge a half mile up the road from the accident. Mike's two brothers seemed devastated by the news.

"Mike was in a funk," Dirk testified. "He'd been drinking all morning. Finally, he just grabbed his car keys and left. I yelled after him not to drive. I didn't hear any motor, so I thought he'd listened. Then a couple minutes later, I heard his car peel out. I would've gone after him, but there was this play-off game on T.V. I had no idea he'd kill himself."

Roger Ilirium confirmed his brother's story. "I was in the garage office, working on my computer when I heard the front door slam. I looked out the window and saw Mike stumbling around the driveway. I went back to work until I heard the ignition. I looked out again and saw Mike driving off in his convertible, weaving down the road. I wasn't too worried. Not until the highway patrol guys showed up."

The police concentrated their investigation on one of the brothers and soon had a confession.

Whodunit? What made the police suspicious?

Answer on page 244

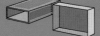
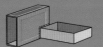

This puzzle is the brainchild of Oskar van Deventer. Glue the component parts of five empty matchboxes together as shown in the illustration. Now arrange them all in such a way that each box ends up in a casing.

Answer on page 245

Fort Knox Jumping Frogs—II

Place 12 coins on the three rings as shown in the illustration. In six moves, make six piles of two coins each. Note: Only move the coins around their own rings and always go clockwise in direction.

Answer on page 253

CRITICAL THINKING

****

Did you know that during periods of weight-lessness, astronauts lose bone mass? To prevent any serious loss, people in space must exercise. Stressing and stretching body parts help keep bone material from being reabsorbed into the body.

For a moment, let's imagine our weightless astronaut returning to Earth. She steps onto a scale and weighs herself. When the lab assistant asks her for her weight, she offers an obscure (but challenging) answer.

"According to this scale, I weigh 60 pounds plus half my weight."

Can you figure out how much this puzzling space traveler weighs?

****

Answer on page 238

TRICKY PUZZLE

Where is little Buttercup in this advertisement for Malt Bitter (1923)?

Answer on page 245

BRAINTEASER

89 My cousin Robert was pushed into a well measuring six feet in diameter and 10 feet deep, with smooth walls and its bottom covered with water. How did he emerge from the well?

90 What animal walks on all fours in the morning, on two legs at noon, and on three legs at dusk?

91 What is so fragile that when you say its name you break it?

Answers on page 210

CRITICAL THINKING

The total surface area of any cube is equal to the sum of the surface areas of each of the six sides. For example, the cheese cube below measures 2 inches on each side. Therefore, the surface area of each side equals 2 inches x 2 inches, or 4 square inches. Since there are six sides, the total surface area of this cube is 24 square inches.

Now, the challenge. Using as many cuts as needed, divide this cube into pieces whose surface area sum is twice the surface area of this 2 x 2 cube.

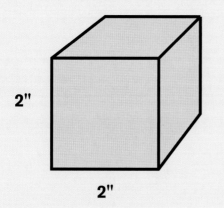

2"

2"

Answer on page 238

TRICKY PUZZLE

A hungry book-worm eats its way through 16 books. Each book is 2 inches thick and the cover is $1/4$ inch thick. The worm starts with page 1 of the bottom book and ends with the last page of the top book. How many inches of paper has he devored? (The principle of this puzzle goes back to 1800.)

Answer on page 245

BRAINTEASER

92 Among my siblings I am the thinnest. I am in Paris, but I am not in France. Who am I?

93 I can only live when there is light, although I die if the light shines on me. What am I?

94 A ship is anchored offshore. In order for the crew to reach the rafts, they must descend a 22-step ladder. Each step is 10 inches high. The tide rises at a rate of 5 inches per hour. How many steps will the tide have covered after 10 hours?

Answers on page 210

✳✳✳✳✳✳✳✳✳✳✳✳

Click, click, click, click. Like submarines, bats have a sonar system called echolocation. They use their echolocation to find objects. The clicking sounds made by bats move outward like the beam of a lighthouse. When the sounds strike an object (such as an insect meal), they are reflected back to the bat's large ears. With incredible speed, the bat's brain analyzes the echo return time and uses it to accurately locate the target's position.

Now, let's put that echolocation to work. Over a five-night period, a bat targets and captures a total of a hundred beetles. During each night, the bat captured six more beetles than on the previous night. How many beetles did the bat catch on each night?

✳✳✳✳✳✳✳✳✳✳✳✳

Proud as a peacock? So it seems, but is it true? Turn the picture upside down! The illustration was printed on a card from 1880 and was one in a series of cards known as the American Puzzle Cards.

Answer on page 245

BRAINTEASER

95 A 100-meter-long train moving 100 meters per minute must pass through a tunnel of 100 meters in length. How long will it take?

96 A cyclist takes 2 minutes and 13 seconds for every full lap of a circuit. Answer in 10 seconds: How long will he take to do 60 laps?

97 My bird can fly faster than any supersonic plane. How can this be?

Answers on page 210

Answer on page 238

CRITICAL THINKING

Two trains race against each other on parallel tracks. The Casey Jones Special is a coal-fed steam engine that travels at a respectable speed. The newer, oil-burning Metropolitan Diesel travels $1\frac{1}{2}$ times the speed of The Casey Jones Special. To make the race a closer competition, The Casey Jones Special begins the race $1\frac{1}{2}$ hours before its opponent. How long will it take the Metropolitan Diesel to catch up to the slower steam engine?

Answer on page 238

TRICKY PUZZLE

Help the animals find their way back to the woods. Henry Dudeney (1847–1930) found 600 ways to solve this puzzle without twice taking the same route or taking a wrong turn at a fork.

Answer on page 245

BRAINTEASER

98 Two trains travel on parallel tracks in opposite directions, at 70 and 50 miles per hour. When the trains are 60 miles apart, a bird flying at 80 miles per hour leaves the first train and flies off to the second. It keeps on flying back and forth until both trains cross. How many miles does the bird fly?

99 We drag a large stone over three logs measuring 50 inches in circumference each. What distance does the stone cover each time the logs make one rotation?

Answers on page 210

CRITICAL THINKING

Ed and his identical twin brother Ed build roller coaster tracks. They've just completed two hills that are both 40 feet high. As you can see, the slopes of the two hills are somewhat different. Ed (the older twin) rides a car that will travel along on a straight slope. Ed (the younger twin) rides a car that will travel along a curved slope.

If both cars are released at the exact same time, which Ed will arrive at the bottom of this slope first?

Answer on page 238

TRICKY PUZZLE

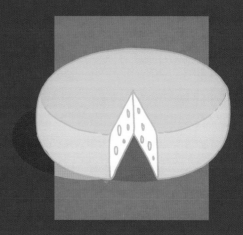

At first glance you would think that someone took a sizable piece out of this cheese. Look again and you will see that it is still there. But where?

Answer on page 245

BRAINTEASER

100 Two trains are moving on the same track in opposite directions. One goes 80 meters per minute and the other 120 meters per minute. After 12 hours, they are 1,700 meters apart. How far apart will they be one minute before they collide?

101 A snail is climbing up a one-meter-high wall. It advances three centimeters per minute and then stops for one minute to rest, during which it slides back down two centimeters. How long will the snail take to reach the top of the wall?

Answers on pages 210 & 211

CRITICAL THINKING

Unlike most liquids, water freezes into a solid that is less dense than its former liquid state. Since it is less dense, ice floats in water. At the surface, the ice acts as an insulator to help trap heat within the water below. This layer of frozen insulation actually insulates lakes, rivers, ponds, and oceans from freezing into a complete solid.

Now let's bring this information back to the kitchen. An ice cube floats freely in a glass filled to the brim with water. Will the water level rise or sink as the ice cube melts?

Answer on page 238

TRICKY PUZZLE

**Sam Loyd published this puzzle in the twentieth century. Turn the crescent moon into a cross.
Use pencil and paper.**

Answer on page 245

BRAINTEASER

102 A man is walking at night at a steady pace. As he passes by a street lamp, he notices that his shadow becomes longer. Does the top of the shadow move faster, slower, or at the same speed when the shadow is longer as when it is shorter?

103 A kid who is in the back seat of a car is holding the string of a helium balloon. The balloon is floating without touching the roof of the car, and the windows are closed. When the car accelerates, where does the balloon go? And when the car turns, where does it go?

Answers on page 211

CRITICAL THINKING

Ancient Egyptian pyramids were built as royal tombs. Within these massive stone structures were rooms, halls, and connecting passageways. Look at the figure below. Can you draw four paths that connect the matching symbols? The paths may not cross, nor may they go outside the large pyramid boundary.

Answer on page 238

TRICKY PUZZLE

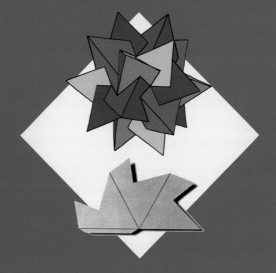

Twenty of the above pieces cut and folded together make a lovely star. Perhaps an early idea for Christmas?

BRAINTEASER

104 What was the biggest ocean in the world before Balboa discovered the Pacific Ocean?

105 How many cookies could you eat on an empty stomach?

106 Three mature and hefty women were walking in San Francisco under one regular-size umbrella. Why didn't they get wet?

107 What can a pitcher be filled with so it is lighter than when it is full of air?

Answers on page 211

CRITICAL THINKING

For this pyramid, can you place the numbers 1, 2, 3, 4, 5, and 6 in the circles shown below? Only one number may be placed in a circle and all numbers must be used. When the final arrangement is complete, the sum of each side's three numbers must all be the same number.

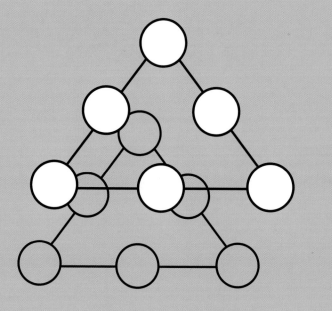

Answer on page 239

TRICKY PUZZLE

Happen to have a bill on you? Take two paper clips and fasten them onto the bill as shown above. Now with a short jerk pull both ends of the bill and see what happens.

Answer on page 245

BRAINTEASER

108 A dog is tied to a 15-foot long leash. How can the dog reach a bone that is 20 feet away?

109 I went into a store and found out that it cost $3 for 400, which meant that each part cost $1. What did I want to buy?

110 Last week, my uncle Peter was able to turn his bedroom light off and get into bed before the room was dark. The light switch and the bed are ten feet apart. How did he accomplish this?

Answers on page 211

CRITICAL THINKING

✱✱✱✱✱✱✱✱✱✱✱✱

The theater shows a double feature. The second movie is about Tarzan going into the moving business.

For his first job, Tarzan must raise a 35-pound crate into his neighbor's tree house. To do this, he first attaches a pulley to a tree branch. He then passes a rope through the pulley and ties it to the crate. Just as he is about to lift the crate, he is called away to help a nearby elephant.

A passing chimp observes the situation and decides to help. The chimp also weighs 35 pounds. As the chimp pulls down on the rope what happens to the crate?

✱✱✱✱✱✱✱✱✱✱✱✱

Answer on page 239

TRICKY PUZZLE

The above wall fell apart in five pieces. Can you rebuild it with these five pieces? There is a 3-D version of this puzzle called "Brick by Brick" which was marketed by Binary Arts Corporation. The inventor of this puzzle is the Dutchman, Ferdinand.

Answer on page 246

BRAINTEASER

111 How can you make 30 cents with only two coins if one of the coins is not a nickel?

112 Mary married John two years ago. She did not bring any money into the marriage and did not work during these two years, but she made her husband a millionaire. How did she do it?

113 My brother Mark says he is able to place a bottle in the middle of a room and by crawling on the floor, he can slide into it. How can this be?

Answers on page 211

CRITICAL THINKING

It's time to do some climbing. You have a choice of climbing one of three geometrically shaped mountains, which are all 10,000 feet high. One of the mountains is a perfect cylinder, another is in the shape of a cone, and the third looks like the top half of a sphere. Several out-of-work math teachers have constructed roads that go from the base to the summit of each mountain. All three roads are built so that you climb 1 vertical foot every 20 horizontal feet. If you wish to walk the shortest distance from base to summit, which mountain would you choose?

Answer on page 239

TRICKY PUZZLE

Is a man allowed to marry his widow's sister?

Answer on page 246

BRAINTEASER

114 Last Friday I flew to San Diego. It was a scary flight. About an hour after getting onto the plane, I saw a very thick fog and then the engines stopped due to lack of fuel. Why didn't we die?

115 While eating out, my brother-in-law Paul found a fly in his coffee. After taking the cup away, the waiter came back with a different cup of coffee. My brother-in-law got upset and returned it, saying that the coffee in the second cup was the same as in the first one. How did he know?

Answers on page 211

Now let's talk about something else that you might have, but not want, in your kitchen. While you are raiding the refrigerator, you look behind the stove and discover a slice of bread that you misplaced several weeks ago. Needless to say, it is covered with mold. Since the mold started growing, the area it has covered has doubled each day. By the end of the eighth day, the entire surface of the bread is covered. When was the bread half covered with mold?

Is this an elk? Or is there more to this? An American postcard from 1911, drawn by C. Levi.

Answer on page 246

Answer on page 239

BRAINTEASER

116 A mother has six children and five potatoes. How can she feed each an equal amount of potatoes? (Do not use fractions.)

117 The giraffe and its offspring are walking in a field. The little giraffe tells a friend, "I am the daughter of this giraffe, although this giraffe is not my mother."

118 A farmer has twenty sheep, ten pigs, and ten cows. If we call the pigs cows, how many cows will he have?

Answers on page 211

CRITICAL THINKING

A compass is a reliable tool that always points north—or does it? There are many reports of compass needles that unexpectedly turn away from north. The strangest natural cause for this disturbance may be a shooting star. As the meteor streaks across the sky, it upsets the electrical balance of the air and produces a magnetic force that some believe affects the compass reading.

We, however, will work with a compass that always gives a true reading. Suppose you start a hike by traveling directly south for 500 paces. Then, you turn and go due east for another 100 paces. You turn once more and go due north for 500 paces. You are now back where you started from, but in front of you is a bear. What color is it?

Answer on page 239

TRICKY PUZZLE

The never-ending story—on and on it goes!

BRAINTEASER

119 Where must a referee be to blow the whistle?

120 In the event of an emergency, can a Muslim baptize a Catholic?

121 It occurs once in a minute, twice in a week, and once in a year. What is it?

122 A man says, "I am going to drink water because I don't have water. If I had it, I would drink wine." What does he do for a living?

Answers on page 211

CRITICAL THINKING

✳✳✳✳✳✳✳✳✳✳✳✳✳

Did you know that 3 ounces plus 3 ounces doesn't always equal 6 ounces? As illogical as this may sound, it's true because of the behavior of the small particles (and spaces) that make up liquids. When different liquids are mixed, the particles tend to fill in some of the open spaces. As a result, the liquid becomes more compact and occupies less volume. It's only a small difference, but it is measurable.

Let's try mixing something whose volume does not change. Your challenge is to split some apple juice into three equal portions. The juice comes in a 24-ounce container. You have only three other containers, each holding 5, 11, and 13 ounces. How can you divide the juice into three equal portions?

HINT: At the very least, it will take four steps.

✳✳✳✳✳✳✳✳✳✳✳✳✳

Answer on page 239

TRICKY PUZZLE

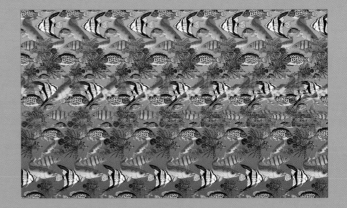

An aquarium full of fish:
Peaceful it seems, but danger lurks.
Look hard and see it come to the surface.

Answer on page 246

BRAINTEASER

123 My friend Albert the butcher wears a size 13 shoe, is six feet tall, and wears a 42-long suit. What does he weigh?

124 There are five apples in one basket and five people in a room. How can you distribute the apples so that each person receives one and there is one apple left in the basket?

125 A man is doing his work. He knows that if his suit tears, he will die. Can you guess his job?

Answers on page 211

CRITICAL THINKING

A wooden cube is painted grey. Suppose it is divided with four equal cuts into the smaller cubes as shown.

1. How many smaller cubes are there?
2. How many of these smaller cubes
   a. have only one side that is painted grey?
   b. have two sides that are painted grey?
   c. have three sides that are painted grey?
   d. have no sides that are grey?

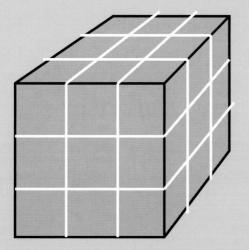

Answer on page 239

TRICKY PUZZLE

A fish's head is $2\frac{1}{2}$ inches long. His tail is as long as his head and half as long as his body. His body is half as long as his total length. How long is this fish?

Answer on page 246

BRAINTEASER

126 We have just invented two words: to sint and to sant. You cannot sint or sant in the street or in the office. You can do both things in the bathroom, the swimming pool, and the beach, but in the swimming pool and the beach you cannot sint completely. You cannot sint without clothes on and you need little or no clothing to sant. Can you guess what the words mean?

127 My cousin Henry can guess the score of a soccer game before the game begins. How can that be?

Answers on page 211

TRULY BAFFLING ILLUSION

The Dark Diamonds

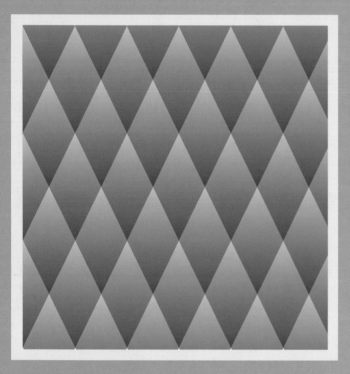

This illusion is made up of diamonds. The bottom part of each diamond is darker than the top. All the diamonds are exactly alike. Nevertheless, the diamonds in the top rows look darker than those in the bottom rows. Why? Nobody seems to know for sure.

SNEAKY THINKING

A foreign visitor to London wanted to ride up the escalator at the subway station, but did not do so. Why?

Clue on page 198/Answer on page 203

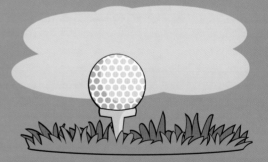

A golfer dreamed all his life of getting a hole in one. However, when he eventually did get a hole in one, he was very unhappy and, in fact, quit golf altogether. Why?

Clue on page 198/Answer on page 203

TRULY BAFFLING ILLUSION

A Luminous Illusion

Ask a friend which side of the box below is darker than the others. He or she will immediately point to the lid. Not so. Place paper strips covering the edges where the lid meets the walls of the box and you'll see they are all the same hue.

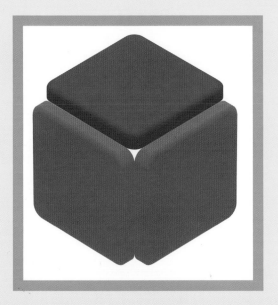

Why is this? It is probably because we compare the hues at the area where the sides meet. If the hues of two nearby areas with the same spatial orientation are identical, then we associate the areas to be alike. The edge of the lid has the same orientation as the walls, but it is slightly darker. Hence, we think the entire lid is darker than the walls.

SNEAKY THINKING

Why did a man write the same two letters over and over again on a piece of paper?

Clue on page 198/Answer on page 203

What major scientific blunder did Shakespeare include in his play *Twelfth Night*?

Clue on page 198/Answer on page 203

The Christmas Tree

If you look at the illustration above you will notice dark spots appearing and disappearing on the white circles. But if you try to fix your eyes on one of the dark spots, it will immediately disappear. This Christmas tree looks as if it has blinking lights.

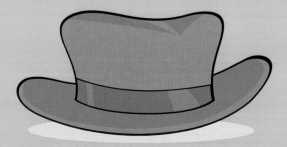

Why did the fashion for silk hats in the U.S. lead to an increase in the number of small lakes and bogs?

Clue on page 198/Answer on page 203

The ancient Greek playwright Aeschylus was killed by a tortoise. How?

Clue on page 198/Answer on page 203

TRULY BAFFLING ILLUSION

The Long Long Lizard

Suppose you see a car parked behind a tree. The front and the rear of the car are clearly visible but the middle is hidden by the tree trunk. Since you can't see behind the tree, for all you know, instead of one car, there could well be just two parts of a car with the tree hiding the gap. But, no matter how hard you try, you cannot imagine a car divided into two separate pieces. Why?

Some scientists think the completion of forms follows certain rules. One of them states that we perceive a continuous object when the extension of the surfaces of the parts at both sides of the covered object meet smoothly, and the volume enclosed by these surfaces can merge. The rule is so strong that, although we know lizards aren't this long, instead of imagining two animals, we cannot avoid seeing but one winding around the barber pole.

SNEAKY THINKING

A man stole a very expensive car owned by a very rich woman. Although he was a very good driver, within a few minutes he was involved in a serious accident. Why?

Clue on page 198/Answer on page 203

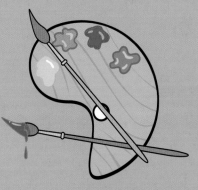

Leonardo da Vinci created some secret designs for his paintings that he did not want anyone to see. He hid them, but they were recently discovered. How?

Clue on page 198/Answer on page 203

TRULY BAFFLING ILLUSION

Floating Diamonds

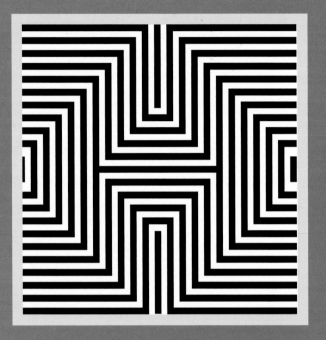

If you look at the illustration above for awhile you'll notice some strange things occurring. At first, it only looks like a group of lines. Suddenly, the lines seem to organize themselves into two diamond shapes, one inside the other. Sometimes the smaller diamond seems to float above the bigger, but an instant later, maybe after you blink, the smaller diamond seems to recede and the bigger advances toward you.

As an experiment, while looking at the figure, try to focus your eyes so that these two positions shift.

SNEAKY THINKING

Why did a woman send out 1,000 anonymous Valentine cards to different men?

Clue on page 198/Answer on page 203

A man was driving down the road into town with his family on a clear day. He saw a tree and immediately stopped the car and then reversed at high speed. Why?

Clue on page 198/Answer on page 203

TRULY BAFFLING ILLUSION

Visual Turbine

Hydroelectric dams produce energy by making a current of water flow through the slanted blades of a turbine. The water pushes the blades and the turbine spins. From a mechanical point of view, a water turbine transforms a straight motion into a rotational one. Here you'll do the same but, instead of water, you'll use your eyes.

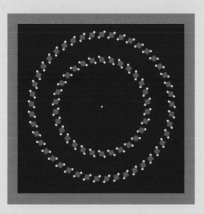

Place the book at reading distance, look directly at the central dot and slowly move your head forward and backward. The circles will spin in opposite directions—in one sense when you move forward and in the opposite sense when you move backward. If you can't make it work the first time, try placing the book at different distances. And don't forget to look at the dot.

SNEAKY THINKING

A mall café is pestered by teenagers who come in, buy a single cup of coffee, and stay for hours, and thus cut down on available space for other customers. How does the owner get rid of them, quite legally?

Clue on page 198/Answer on page 203

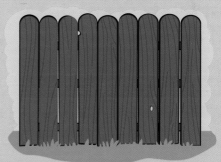

A man painted his garden fence green and then went on holiday. When he came back two weeks later, he was amazed to see that the fence was blue. Nobody had touched the fence. What had happened?

Clue on page 198/Answer on page 203

TRULY BAFFLING ILLUSION

Italics

Italic is a lettering style in which the words slant to the right. The curious thing about italics is that if, instead of tilting letters to the right, we tilt them to the left, they look much more slanted. Look at the illustration above. The number 7682 was written using the same font seen on many digital clocks and calculator screens and then slanted 15° to left and right. The result is that the number at the left looks more slanted than the right one.

Maybe this is because we are more used to seeing lettering slant to the right, since italics are found in everyday printed material. This can lead us to consider italic a "normal" font, paying no attention to its tilting. We only realize the letter is slanted when we see it tilted in the opposite direction. A simple observation seems to back up this theory: if we take figures other than letters, like the parallelogram and the arrow below, and apply the same tilt as above, the left and right slants look tilted by the same degree.

SNEAKY THINKING

A man, a woman, and a child are watching a train come into a station. "Here it comes," says the man. "Here she comes," says the woman. "Here he comes," says the child. Who was correct?

Clue on page 198/Answer on page 203

Why did the vicar only want a black dog?

Clue on page 198/Answer on page 203

TRULY BAFFLING ILLUSION

Perpetual Motion

The illusion above is based on a painting by French artist Isaiah Leviant. Look at the blue rings: some parts seem to be moving all by themselves. What makes them go round? Nobody is really sure. But if you erase the background rays, the movement will stop.

SNEAKY THINKING

A runner was awarded a prize for winning a marathon. But the judges disqualified him when they saw a picture of his wristwatch. Why?

Clue on page 198/Answer on page 203

Why are two little animals alone in a little boat in the middle of the ocean?

Clue on page 198/Answer on page 203

TRIPLE-WARPED TRIBAR

The figure above is a simple but profound elaboration of the Penrose Triangle. That tribar exhibited a single impossibility, while this figure has many. As your eye examines this figure—as with any impossible object—you must reappraise the drawing at every turn. The object has a convincing solidity, but if you tried to build such a thing it just wouldn't work out. This is the essence of impossible objects!

A famous dancer was found strangled. The police did not suspect murder. Why not?

Clue on page 198/Answer on page 203

A man standing in the middle of a solid concrete floor dropped a tomato six feet, but it did not break or bruise. How come?

Clue on page 198/Answer on page 203

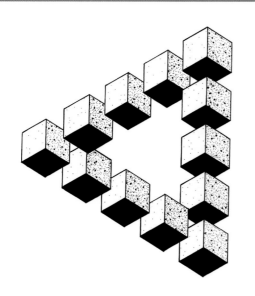

TWELVE-CUBE TRIANGLE

Geometric shapes are the best sources of inspiration for developing impossible objects. Take the simple cube, for instance. We see thousands of them in one form or another every day. As you can easily see in the figure above, we took one of the tribars from the previous page and broke it down into cubes. By doing that nothing was lost: this figure is just as profoundly impossible as its predecessor!

Constructed of a dozen cubes, this arrangement was laid out on a draftsman's board with a plastic 30°/60° triangle. The drafting triangle was useful in making sure that the individual cubes conformed to the overall perspective of the drawing. The impossibility, which takes advantage of this perspective, is accomplished by the false foreground-background placement of the rows of cubes, an effect similar to the one in the tribar. In other words, the drawing is held together through the incorrect connections of the normal rows of cubes.

A little shop in New York is called The Seven Bells, yet it has eight bells hanging outside. Why?

Clue on page 198/Answer on page 204

A man bought a pair of shoes that were in good condition and that fit him well. He liked the style and they looked good. However, after he had worn them for one day he took them back to the shop and asked for a refund. Why?

Clue on page 198/Answer on page 204

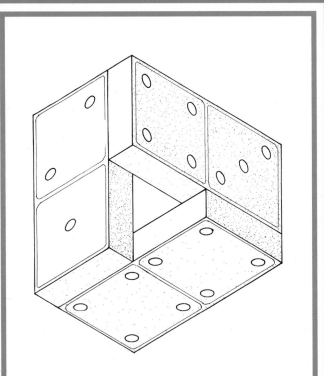

TRI-DOMINO

To accomplish what this three-piece suite appears to demonstrate would normally require four elements, not just three. Try it yourself the next time you play dominoes! To make a normal circle you need 360 degrees, but this object seems to close the 360-degree loop in just 270 degrees! Upon closer examination, it becomes apparent that this figure operates on a misplaced return in perspective—similar to that of the impossible tribar. This figure is really an impossible tribar in which the three perimeter elements have been replaced by the familiar game pieces.

A man who was paralyzed in his arms, legs, and mouth, and unable to speak a word, wrote a best-selling book. How?

Clue on page 198/Answer on page 204

A man is crowned king. Shortly afterwards, he is captured by enemy forces and chopped in two. Why?

Clue on page 198/Answer on page 204

IMPOSSIBLE OBJECT

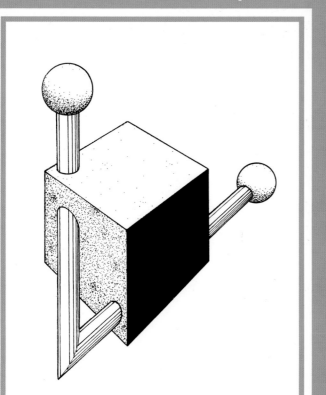

DOWEL BLOCK

The more sophisticated version of the tribar, shown on the facing page, was inspired by a child's building block and a Tinkertoy™. This object consists of a pair of complementary dowel-like components that penetrate the block and then intersect outside the block at an impossible juncture. It is the juncture alone that makes this impossible object possible, at least on paper! That this profound figure is a triangle is evident even in this simple two-element composition.

SNEAKY THINKING

A woman heard a tune which she recognized. She took a gun and shot a stranger. Why?

Clue on page 198/Answer on page 204

A police officer was sitting on his motorcycle at a red traffic light when two teenagers in a sports car drove by him at 50 miles per hour. He did not chase them or try to apprehend them. Why not?

Clue on page 198/Answer on page 204

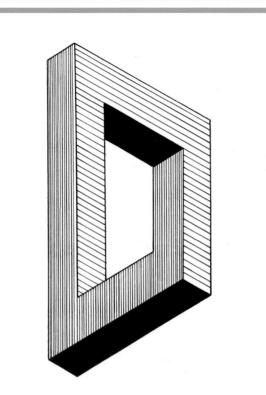

TRUNCATED TRIBAR

As we become more closely acquainted with the tribar and its seemingly limitless expressions, we now find a new and curious variation.

The Truncated Tribar is simply a tribar with one corner chopped off—truncated. As a result, the figure now has four sides. If this object were a window, what a job it would be to install the glass pane! (It would be a real pain!)

As with the impossible tribar, our eye accepts it as a solid object at first glance, but then sees it as a sort of window frame. It cannot really exist, of course, but then again it is a figure we cannot easily dismiss. The effectiveness of the Truncated Tribar illusion arises from a combination of misplaced perspective and false connections.

There is an orange in the middle of a circular table. Without touching or moving the orange or the table, how could you place a second orange under the first?

Clue on page 199/Answer on page 204

A young woman applied for a job as a secretary and typist. There were dozens of applicants. The woman could type only eleven words per minute, yet she got the job. Why?

Clue on page 199/Answer on page 204

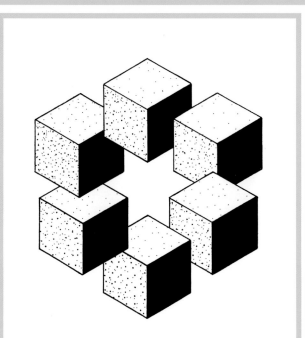

MENTAL BLOCKS

Children's blocks? Computer graphics? No, it's another version of the impossible tribar! The cube, as we have already seen, is a very useful element in constructing impossible objects. This is a simple but intriguing triangular arrangement of cubes. It functions with the same dynamics as its ancestor. The only real differences between this figure and the previous Twelve-Cube Triangle is that this figure consists of fewer cubes and provides a mentally challenging and subtle variation.

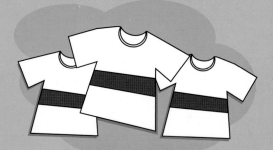

A change in the law in Italy resulted in large sales of white T-shirts with black bands on them. How come?

Clue on page 199/Answer on page 204

A man uses a stick to strike a part of an elephant and after a few seconds the part disappears. The man is then a lot richer. Why?

Clue on page 199/Answer on page 204

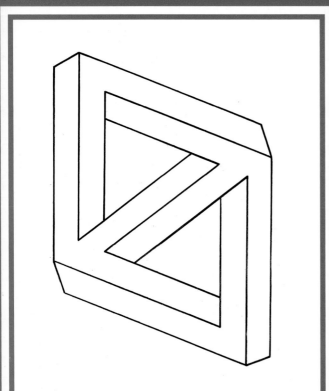

DIAMOND CROSSOVER

The enigmatic figure above derived from staring at a cross-truss that supported a stair landing at a two-level apartment complex. Again, the principle of the tribar is quite evident. The Diamond Crossover is essentially nothing more than two tribars glued together in the shape of a diamond. You could expand on this design by gluing together additional tribars here. Escher attached three tribars in his famous composition. There really is no limit. In fact, you could glue many such tribars together in a pattern that would be very effective in a pieced quilt or some other design. Otherwise, we leave it to you, the observer, to triangulate this squeamish, squashed, squarish thing!

A man was building a house when it collapsed all around him. He wasn't injured or upset, and he calmly started to rebuild it. What was going on?

Clue on page 199/Answer on page 204

Because it was raining, the firemen hosed down the road. Why?

Clue on page 199/Answer on page 204

THE SPACE FORK

With The Space Fork, we enter the very heart and essence of Impossibilia. It represents what is probably the largest distinct family of impossible objects. Almost everyone has seen it at one time or other. It was this object that appeared one day on Mr. Thomas's bulletin board in the author's high school woodshop class, labeled simply Space Fork. Even though I was unsuccessful in building such an object, I still got an "A" in Thomas's class, not to mention the fact that his pin-up triggered my interest in impossible objects, which led to a lifelong pursuit.

The notorious three-(or is it two-?) pronged impossible object began circulating among engineers and others in 1964. It first appeared in print as part of an advertisement by California Technical Industries in the March 23, 1964 issue of Aviation Week and Space Technology magazine. An article was published later that year by a psychology professor at Iowa State University in Ames, Iowa. It appeared in the December 1964 issue of the American Journal of Psychology. This was the first published writing about this ambiguous figure, which the author, Dr. Donald H. Schuster, called a "three-stick clevis." An actual shift in visual fixation is involved in perceiving and resolving (if that were possible) the incongruity in this new type of ambiguous figure. After much attention, scrutiny, and creative variations made by others over the years, Schuster's Space Fork has become a classic. A visually ambiguous trident or clevis-like device, of absolutely no practical use, it has also been called by some, simply, a "blivet." One rep from an aerospace manufacturer has suggested that its attributes be investigated for the design of an interdimensional cosmic tuning fork!

A keen ornithologist saw a rare bird that he had never seen before, except in illustrations. However, he was very upset. Then he was frightened. Why?

Clue on page 199/Answer on page 204

A horse walked all day. Two of its legs traveled 21 miles and two legs traveled 20 miles. How come?

Clue on page 199/Answer on page 204

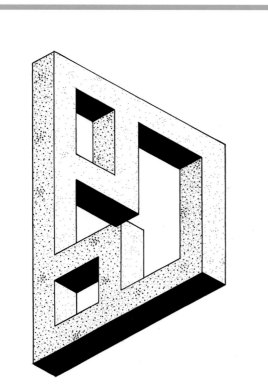

WARPED TRIBAR TRUNCATE

The Warped Tribar Truncate is, in essence, another chopped-off, or truncated, tribar with some internal variation. It looks as if it could be a surrealist design for a new style of furniture, but would certainly stop cold any carpenter who accepted an order for a dozen of these things. Then again, this piece of very expressive mini-art could open up a host of new ideas for everything from lawn chairs to plaza sculptures!

The visual arts cater to a wide variety of human needs. Impossible objects, like this one, present an amusing interplay of intrigue and entertainment. They could be called "recreational art"!

Four people were playing cards. One played a card and another player immediately jumped up and started to take her clothes off. Why?

Clue on page 199/Answer on page 204

A farmer has two pigs that are identical twins from the same litter. However, when he sells them he gets 100 times more for one than the other. Why?

Clue on page 199/Answer on page 204

IMPOSSIBLE OBJECT

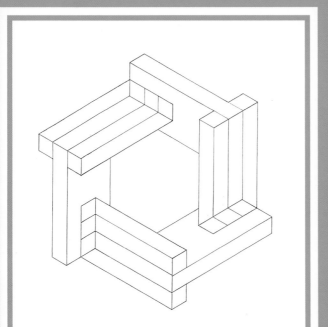

ETHEREAL HEXAGON

This rich new variation of the tribar, based on symmetry and repetition, is a design reminiscent of an image one might see in a kaleidoscope. You will notice that the grand underlying principle of the tribar is incorporated into this innovative design.

Like the other tribars, this one is relatively easy to create. It looks as though all you need is a potter's wheel to turn the drawing so that you can make all the extremities identical. It is easy to see that this figure, like all tribar figures, is based on a triangle.

SNEAKY THINKING

A man lies dead next to a feather that caused his death. What happened?

Clue on page 199/Answer on page 204

A man bought a beautiful and appropriate wedding gift for a friend's wedding. The gift was wrapped and sent. When the gift was opened at the wedding, the man was highly embarrassed. Why?

Clue on page 199/Answer on page 205

IMPOSSIBLE OBJECT

SNEAKY THINKING

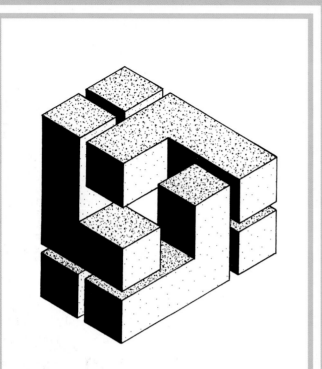

RECTANGULAR TRIHEDRON

In this concluding example of the tribar theme, we see yet another intriguing way to elaborate on the Penrose Triangle. In case you're wondering if the tribar model is now exhausted, rest assured that new ideas will always be coming up—that's guaranteed!

In principle, this figure functions very much like the other members of the tribar family. It is basically a three-dimensional equilateral triangle made up of rectangular solids that cause your gaze to search from one extremity to the other in an attempt to make sense out of the figure.

Adam was jealous of Brenda's use of a computer. He changed that by means of a hammer. After that, he could use the computer, but Brenda could not.
What did he do?

Clue on page 199/Answer on page 205

There is a reason why men's clothes have buttons on the right while women's have buttons on the left. What is it?

Clue on page 199/Answer on page 205

IMPOSSIBLE OBJECT

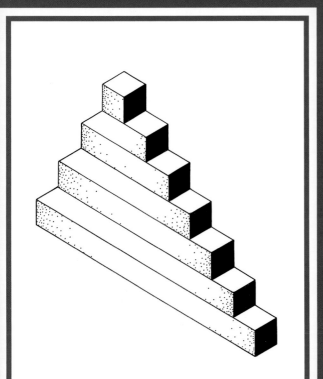

FOUR-SEVEN STICK STACK

This profusely stepped specimen could have been inspired by a stack of railroad ties. As a climber anticipating your negotiation of the steps, you have the option of taking it in four steps or seven. It looks as if your ascent to the top would be easier in an approach from the left. However, until you actually try it, you cannot know for sure. The laws of energy conservation and expenditure may not apply in this uncanny world of the impossible!

The illusion has been accomplished by taking advantage of its equally spaced parallel lines in treating the end detail of the sticks, some of which seem to twist in order to comply with the illusion.

SNEAKY THINKING

Two frogs fell into a large cylindrical tank of liquid and both fell to the bottom. The walls were sheer and slippery. One frog died but one survived. How?

Clue on page 199/Answer on page 205

A butterfly fell down and a man was seriously injured. Why?

Clue on page 199/Answer on page 205

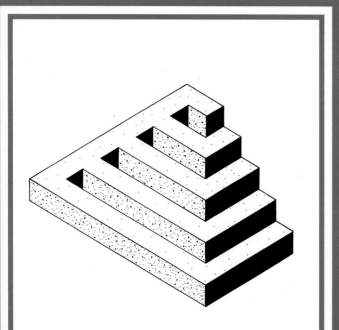

AMBIGUOUS
STEPPED PYRAMID

In the figure above, you have a choice: you may take the route on the right side and climb five full steps to get to the top, or, simply take one step onto the platform at the left, which will lead you ethereally to the top!

In the Ambiguous Stepped Pyramid each of the horizontal shafts between the voids at the left of the figure leads to a step on the right end, each at a different level. Also noteworthy is the fact that the opposite ends of the figure are not the same length, yet the number and size of tread elements are equal at both ends. The nagging question is, are there five steps or just one?

Why did a man who knew the time and had two accurate watches phone a clock that speaks the time?

Clue on page 199/Answer on page 205

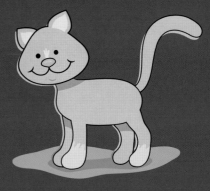

A man who did not like cats bought some fresh salmon and cream for a cat. Why?

Clue on page 199/Answer on page 205

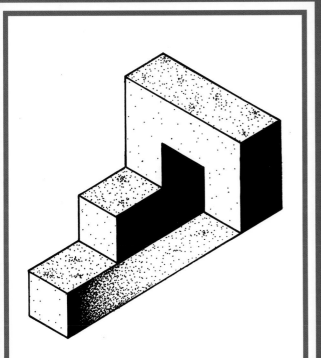

INCONGRUOUS
STEPPED WALL

With this intriguing new figure, another impossible object is making its debut in this book. It combines subtle elements from the Space Fork and other impossible objects. These influences become evident, one way or another, when you examine the figure closely.

You will see that the figure is tied together by a single profound discontinuity: the front surface of the lower step "twists" toward the right and becomes a "floor" at the base of the wall. At the same time this effect causes us to confuse the opening in the wall with the shaded face of the second step.

A man undressed to go to bed and hundreds of people lost their jobs. Why?

Clue on page 199/Answer on page 205

A New York City hairdresser recently said that he would rather cut the hair of three Canadians than one New Yorker. Why?

Clue on page 199/Answer on page 205

TRICKY PUZZLE

Can you bring this lady's pooch back?
An English postcard from 1906,
part of a series called the Valentine Series.

Answer on page 246

EYE-POPPER

You don't need curved lines to distort an appearance. Notice how this pattern of triangles tricks your brain into seeing slightly slanted walls.

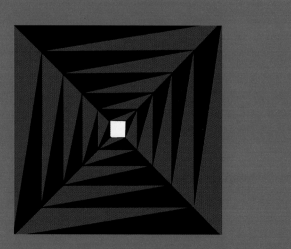

MIND-BENDER

75 Three dollar bills were exchanged for a certain number of nickels and the same number of dimes. How many nickels were there? Read this puzzle to a group of friends and see how long it takes to come up with the answer. You may be surprised!

76 In this multiplication problem, x, y, and z represent different digits. What is the sum of x, y, and z?

$$\begin{array}{r} yx \\ \times\ 7 \\ \hline zxx \end{array}$$

77 Alex, Ryan, and Steven are sports fans. Each has a different favorite sport among football, baseball, and basketball. Alex does not like basketball; Steven does not like basketball or baseball. Name each person's favorite sport.

78 Let's say 26 zips weigh as much as 4 crids and 2 wobs. Also, 8 zips and 2 crids have the same weight as 2 wobs. How many zips have the weight of 1 wob?

79 Find the hidden phrase or title.

Look U Leap

Answers on pages 220 & 221

TRICKY PUZZLE

Can you remove six heads of lettuce and still have horizontal, vertical, and diagonal rows of four crops?

Answer on page 246

EYE-POPPER

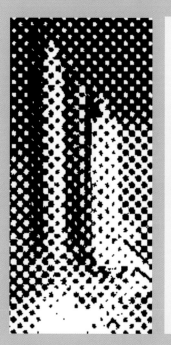

Even the photographic images in newspapers are illusions. Use a magnifying lens and you'll see that regions that appear as shades of gray are actually made up of varying sizes of black ink dots.

MIND-BENDER

80 There is a certain logic shared by the following four circles. Can you determine the missing number in the last circle?

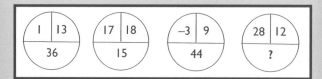

81 What is $\frac{1}{2}$ of $\frac{2}{3}$ of $\frac{3}{5}$ of 240 divided by $\frac{1}{2}$?

82 Find the hidden phrase or title.

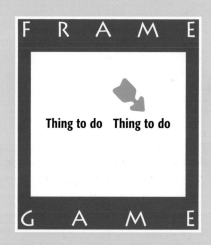

F R A M E

Thing to do   Thing to do

G A M E

83 Can you determine the next letter in the following series?

A   C   F   H   K   M   ?

84 The three words below can be rearranged into two words that are also three words! Can you decipher this curious puzzle?

the red rows

Answers on page 221

TRICKY PUZZLE

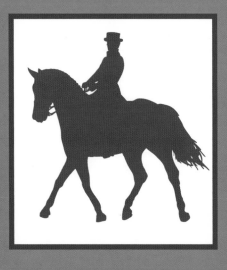

In which direction are horse and rider riding?
Toward you or away from you?

EYE-POPPER

Back in the 1960s, Op Art was very popular. This illustration style used highly contrasting shapes and patterns to produce a sensation of movement called visual vibration. Look into this figure and you'll see that many of the edges appear to have an "electric" or glowing quality.

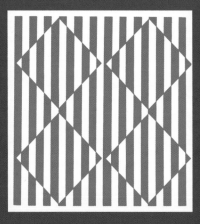

MIND-BENDER

85 One of the figures below lacks a common characteristic that the other five figures have. Which one is it and why?

Hint: This does not have to do with right angles or symmetry.

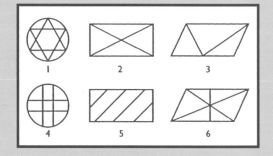

86 Find the hidden phrase or title.

F R A M E

evil EVIL

G A M E

87 If the length of a rectangle is increased by 25 percent and its width is decreased by 25 percent, what is the percentage of change in its area?

Answers on page 221

TRICKY PUZZLE

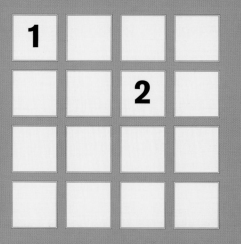

Fill in the remaining squares so
that a magic square is formed and you
can move from number 1 to 7 with
two Knight's chess moves.

Answer on page 246

EYE-POPPER

The pattern of angles in this illustration gives the
illusion of depth.

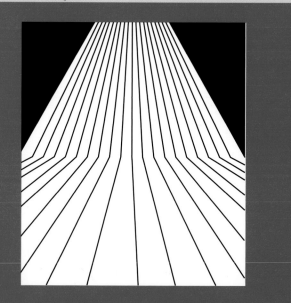

MIND-BENDER

88 Try your luck at this "trickle-down" puzzle.
Starting at the top, change one letter of
each succeeding word to arrive at the
word at the bottom.

TOOK

———

———

———

BURN

89 A car travels from point A to point B (a distance of one mile) at 30 miles per hour. How
fast would the car have to travel from point
B to point C (also a distance of one mile) to
average 60 miles per hour for the entire trip?

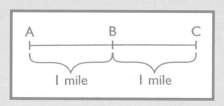

90 The design on the left is made up of three
paper squares of different sizes, one on top
of the other. What is the minimum number
of squares needed to create the design on
the right?

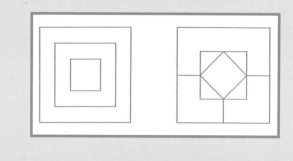

Answers on page 221

Entertain Your Brain 175

TRICKY PUZZLE

Are both the inner squares an equal shade of gray?

Answer on page 246

EYE-POPPER

This "sliced" circle has a 3-D appearance created by the checkerboard pattern. Notice how the shape seems to bend in regions that have compressed checkerboard squares.

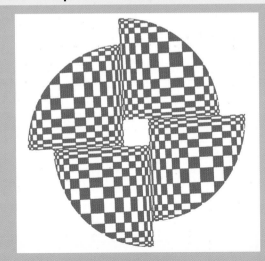

MIND-BENDER

91 A friend has a bag containing two cherry gumdrops and one orange gumdrop. She offers to give you all the gumdrops you want if you can tell her the chances of drawing a cherry gumdrop on the first draw and the orange gumdrop on the second draw. Can you meet your friend's challenge?

92 Here's a variation on an old classic. On what side of the line does the "R" go?

A B D   O P Q
        C E F G H I J K L M N

93 Find the hidden phrase or title.

94 Given the initial letters of the missing words, complete this sentence.

There are 100 Y in a C.

Answers on page 221

TRICKY PUZZLE

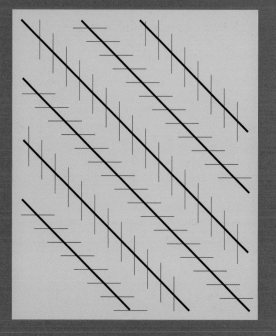

Are the bold lines all running parallel?

EYE-POPPER

Take a look at this thick line with two bumps. By itself, it creates a slight feeling of depth. But once it is repeated in a pattern, its 3-D effect intensifies.

MIND-BENDER

95 If I tripled one-quarter of a fraction and multiplied it by that fraction, I would get one-twelfth. What is the original fraction?

96 Two toy rockets are heading directly for each other. One is traveling at 50 miles per hour and the other is traveling at 70 miles per hour. How far apart will these two rockets be one minute before they collide?

97 Find the hidden phrase or title.

98 Think of five squares that are the same size. In how many ways can these five squares be combined, edge to edge? (No mirror images allowed.)

99 What number is four times one-third the number that is one-sixteenth less than three-thirty-seconds?

Answers on page 222

TRICKY PUZZLE

Trace the diagram on a piece of paper, but do it in one continuous line, i.e., without taking your pencil off the paper or going over the same line more than once. Now to make it even more difficult, the lines cannot cross each other anywhere.

Answer on page 246

EYE-POPPER

The red or the blue box can seem to be on top of the stack. Can you switch their positions in your mind?

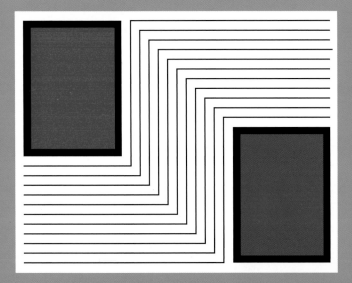

MIND-BENDER

100 Below are five words. By adding the same three letters at the beginning of each word, you can come up with five new words. What three letters will do the trick?

her

ion

or

if

to

101 If x^2 is larger than 9, which of the following is true?

    a. x is greater than 0.

    b. 0 is greater than x.

    c. x is equal to 0.

    d. x^3 is greater than 0.

    e. There is insufficient information to determine a solution.

102 Based on the following information, how many pleezorns does Ahmad Adziz have?

    Molly O'Brien has 22 pleezorns.

    Debbie Reynolds has 28 pleezorns.

    Roberto Montgomery has 34 pleezorns.

103 What is 10 percent of 90 percent of 80 percent?

104 A mixture of chemicals costs $40 per ton. It is composed of one type of chemical that costs $48 per ton and another type of chemical that costs $36 per ton. In what ratio were these chemicals mixed?

Answers on page 222

TRICKY PUZZLE

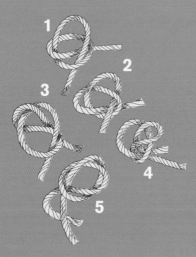

Above you see five knots. Although they appear to be, they're not all genuine knots. Can you detect the real ones?

Answer on page 246

EYE-POPPER

Look closely into this image and you'll see that the shapes are not painted with brush strokes. Instead, they are created solely by dots. This style, known as Pointillism, uses points of paint on a surface so that, from a distance, they blend together. It was made famous in the 1800s by the French artist Georges Seurat.

MIND-BENDER

105 Find the hidden phrase or title.

106 Find the hidden phrase or title.

107 If the ratio of 5x to 4y is 7 to 8, what is the ratio of 10x to 14y?

Answers on page 222

TRICKY PUZZLE

Many scientists have pored over this diagram in the pyramid of King Tut and wondered how many triangles there were.

Answer on page 246

EYE-POPPER

Copy this pattern onto a sheet of paper. Use a pair of scissors to cut it out. Poke a hole through the center circle and place the disk on a lazy Susan. Spin the rotating plate moderately and steadily.

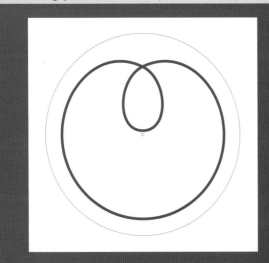

MIND-BENDER

108 How many triangles of any size are in the figure below?

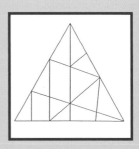

109 Decipher the following cryptogram:

WLA'P XLJAP RLJO XGMXBSAE NSQLOS PGSR GCPXG.

110 Find the hidden phrase or title.

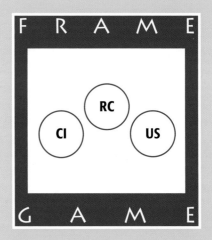

111 How many four-letter words can you find in the word "twinkle"? (Try for at least 15.)

112 Do this quickly: Write down twelve thousand twelve hundred twenty-two.

Answers on pages 222 & 223

TRICKY PUZZLE

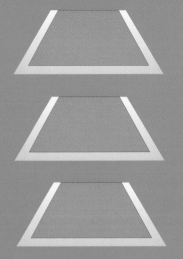

Copy the above figures, cut them out, and arrange them in such a way as to form a pyramid. Just looking at them, would you say they're all the same size?

Answer on page 246

EYE-POPPER

Here's another weird spinner that creates the illusion of lines that twist and bend. To see this effect, all you have to do is rotate the book. For its strongest effect, photocopy this shape onto a sheet of paper. Cut it out and punch a hole in its center. Place this on a lazy Susan. Spin and watch the never-ending twists.

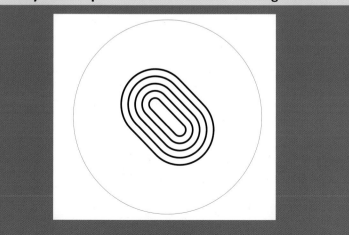

MIND-BENDER

113 Below are four sets of letters that are related in a way known to virtually everyone. Can you find the missing two letters? (*Hint:* Some people have been known to take months to solve this!)

ON
DJ
FM
AM
? ?

114 Find the hidden phrase or title.

115 In the strange land of Doubledown the alphabet appears to be hieroglyphics, but it isn't really much different from ours. Below is one of the Doubledown months spelled out. Which month of ours is comparable?

Answers on page 223

TRICKY PUZZLE

Two ships sail on the horizon. Look at the ship on the left with your right eye, while closing your left eye. Slowly bring the book closer to your eye and suddenly the ship on the right will disappear.

TRICKY PUZZLE

Copy this disc and stick a skewer through the center. Spin the top and see various colors appear. The principle of the Mason disc phenomenon has never been proved.

MINDTRAP

◆ "I wouldn't want this musty old dump if you gave it to me," snapped Ida Gamble. "Look," replied Sam Sham, "Clem may have been a whacked-out hermit, but I have a feeling he hid a fortune on this property. This house has been boarded up for 7 years. All you need to do is pay the back taxes and, er, my modest fee, and this little gem is all yours!" "I'm outta here!" cried Ida. "Wait, just let me show you the secret staircase I found." Sam pulled back the oakpress paper paneling to reveal the hidden staircase. "Look, that step is loose, and there's something shiny behind it!" Sam pulled back the loose step to discover a small collection of shiny sterling silver cutlery. "I knew it!" exclaimed Sam, "This house contains a fortune! I think I'll buy it myself." "Not so fast," replied Ida, "you offered me the house and I just bought it." How do you know that Ida has just been scammed?

Answer on page 248

116 Find the hidden phrase or title.

117 Quickly now, which is larger, 2^{67} or the sum of $2^{66} + 2^{65}$? How about 2^{67} or the sum of $2^{66} + 2^{66}$?

118 Unscramble this word:

GORNSIMMAROCI

119 Given the initial letters of the missing words, complete this sentence.

There is one W on a U.

120 Below are six rays. Choosing two of the rays, how many angles of less than 90 degrees can you form? (Angle ACB is less than 90 degrees.)

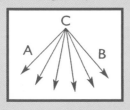

Answers on page 223

121 By arranging all nine integers in a certain order, it is possible to come up with fractions equal to $\frac{1}{2}$, $\frac{1}{3}$, $\frac{1}{4}$, $\frac{1}{5}$, $\frac{1}{6}$, $\frac{1}{7}$, $\frac{1}{8}$ and $\frac{1}{9}$. See if you can come up with one of these.

Example: $\dfrac{1}{8} = \dfrac{3{,}187}{25{,}496}$

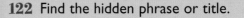

122 Find the hidden phrase or title.

123 What are the two missing numbers in the series below?

8, 15, 10, 13, 12, 11, 14, 9, 16, 7, ?, ?

124 What is the value of **z** in the following problem? (Each number is a positive integer between 0 and 9.)

$$\begin{array}{r} x \\ y \\ +z \\ \hline xy \end{array}$$

Answers on pages 223 & 224

MIND-BENDER

125 Joe takes three-fifths of a bag of candy. Bob has three-fourths of Pete's share of the remaining candy. What fraction of the total number of pieces of candy does Pete have?

126 What is the value of F in the following system of equations?

$$
\begin{aligned}
A + B &= Z & (1) \\
Z + P &= T & (2) \\
T + A &= F & (3) \\
B + P + F &= 30 & (4) \\
A &= 8 & (5)
\end{aligned}
$$

Answers on page 224

Irregular Circuit

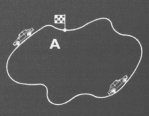

Two cars start from point A at the same time and drive around a circuit more than one mile in length. While they are driving laps around the circuit, each car must maintain a steady speed. Since one car is faster than the other, one car will pass the other at certain points. The first pass occurs 150 yards from point A.

At what distance from A will one car pass the other again?

Answer on page 253

MINDTRAP

◆ Sid Shady was waving frantically as Shadow pulled up to Sid's oceanfront home. "Hurry!" shouted Shady. "My wife's been murdered!" Shadow opened the bedroom door and surveyed the gruesome scene. Mrs. Shady lay dead on the floor, a knife planted in her back. The smell of a recently extinguished candle permeated the air. A puddle of water and a broken jug lay near her head. As always at this time of night, a light breeze blew off the ocean through the open window. Shadow crossed the room, pulled the window shut and turned to face Shady. "I was downstairs when I heard a loud crash and a scream," began Shady. "I raced upstairs to find my wife lying on the floor. Rather than touch anything, I immediately called the police." "That's a lie!" replied Shadow. Why would he say that?

Answer on page 248

MIND-BENDER

127 The following words can all be transformed into new words by prefixing the same three letters, in the same order, at the beginning of the words. What are the three letters?

___ ___ ___ **PENT**
___ ___ ___ **RATE**
___ ___ ___ **VICE**
___ ___ ___ **VILE**

128 Can you quickly write down the numbers 1 through 5 so that no two consecutive numbers are next to one another? The first number is not 1, and the second, third, and fourth numbers must increase in value.

Answers on page 224

SHREWD CHALLENGE

Place Your Cards

You have three cards: an ace, a queen, and a six. One is a diamond, one is a heart, and one is a spade, although not necessarily in that order.

The diamond sits between the queen and the heart.

The six is immediately to the right of the spade.

Write in the picture below where each card is located.

Answer on page 253

TRICKY PUZZLE

Determine in which sequence these 22 square pieces of paper were laid on top of each other. All papers are the same size.

Answer on page 246

TRICKY PUZZLE

You can cover all 64 squares of a chessboard with 32 dominoes. But if you try to cover the chessboard with 31 dominoes, it will never work. Which color do the leftover squares always end up being?

Answer on page 246

129 Arrange the four squares below to create five squares of the same size. You cannot interlock or overlap the squares.

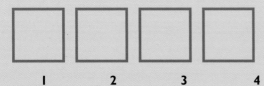

    1   2   3   4

130 Determine the relationships between the pictures and the letters to find the solutions:

Answers on page 224

Nice Discounts

A bookstore has a nice discount policy. If you buy a $20 book today, you get a 2% discount on your next purchase. If you buy a $15 book, you get a 1.5% discount on your next purchase. If you have to buy three books that cost $10, $20, and $30, you could buy the $30 book today, the $10 tomorrow (on which you'll get a 3% discount), and the $20 book the following day (on which you'll get a 1% discount). Or you could buy the $30 book and the $20 book today, and the $10 book tomorrow (with a 5% discount).

What is the cheapest way to buy five books priced at $10, $20, $30, $40, and $50?

Answer on page 253

MINDTRAP

◆ Mike Peters was surprised to see his window slide open and was positively shocked when he saw two strangers climb inside. What transpired next could only be described as a despicable act of thievery. Mike watched with rapt fascination as the two thieves systematically began to remove the priceless Persian carpets, artwork, and jewelry. Having stripped the room, the thieves climbed back out the window. Incredibly, Mike went back to what he had been doing before the thieves arrived and soon he'd forgotten about the entire incident. Why wouldn't Mike, who was in perfect health, have tried to stop the thieves, or at the very least, called the police after they had left?

Answer on page 248

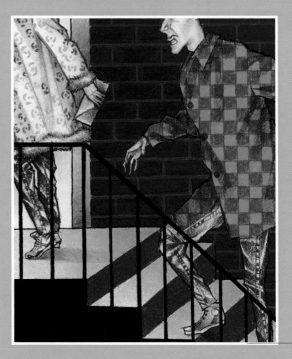

131 Find the hidden phrase or title.

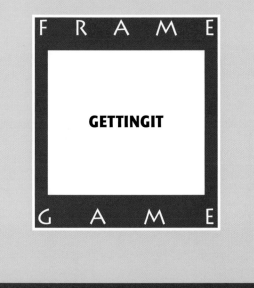

Answer on page 224

Enigmatic Fares

Professor Zizoloziz always adds the five digits on a bus transfer. Yesterday, he rode route 62 with a friend. As soon as he got the tickets, which were consecutively numbered, he added the numbers on them and then told his friend that the sum of all ten digits was exactly 62. His logical friend asked him if the sum of the numbers on either of the tickets was by any chance 35. Professor Zizoloziz answered and his friend then knew the numbers on the bus tickets.

What were the numbers on the two bus tickets?

Answer on page 253

Are these all perfect squares?

Answer on page 246

The slip of paper with the four numbers was accidentally ripped in two. When you add 30 to 25 and square the sum, the outcome is the same as the total figure on the note! So 30 + 25 = 55, and 55 x 55 = 3025. Amazing, isn't it? Now the question is: Can you find a different four-digit figure that has the same magic properties?

Answer on page 246

132 What comes next in this number sequence?
Hint: Get primed for this puzzle.

5   8   26   48   122   ?

133 The words *assign* and *stalactite* form a relationship that produces the word *ignite* in parentheses. Can you find a similar relationship between the words *double* and *stationary* that will form a new word in the blank?

assign   (ignite)   stalactite
double   (_____)   stationary

Answers on page 225

134 What is 1,449 in Roman numerals?

135 Here's a balance puzzle. Where does the 25-lb. weight on this teeter-totter go (how many feet from the fulcrum)?

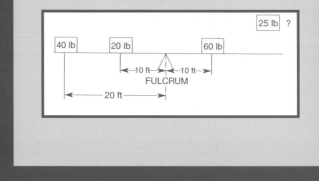

Answers on page 225

MINDTRAP

◆ "I have the only key to the room containing the jewelry of my late Aunt Maggy," said Sid Shady. "Since her death a week ago, neither I nor anybody else has entered this room. I was quite pleased to hear that all her jewelry was to be sold and the proceeds to go to charity," continued Shady as he stepped around a large plant on his way to the safe. While Shady was spinning the combination lock, Shadow crossed the room to sit on the ledge of the large bay window. Shady opened the safe and removed the bag of jewels. "I'm sure these jewels of Aunt Maggy's will fetch a fortune for charity," said a smiling Sid Shady. "I'll bet these jewels are either fake or there are a few missing," replied Shadow. What made him suspicious?

Answer on page 248

Eve's Enigma

After heaven, the earth, the grass, and all the animals were created, the snake, who was very smart, decided to make its own contribution.

It decided to lie every Tuesday, Thursday and Saturday. For the other days of the week, it told the truth.

"Eve, dear Eve, why don't you try an apple?" the snake suggested.

"But I am not allowed to!" said Eve.

"Oh, no!" said the snake. "You can eat it today since it is Saturday and God is resting."

"No, not today," said Eve, "Maybe tomorrow."

"Tomorrow is Wednesday and it will be too late," insisted the snake.

This is how the snake tricked Eve.

On what day of the week did this conversation take place?

John Cash

John Cash saw his face on a poster nailed to a tree. As he approached, he saw "WANTED, DEAD OR ALIVE." Under his picture, it read "REWARD: ___ DOLLARS."

There was a three-digit figure on the poster. John drew his Colt and shot at the first number (in the hundreds column).

He had just reduced the price on his head by five times.

"Good Lord!" said the doctor's daughter, who was sitting on the other side of the tree doing her math homework.

John blushed, and shot again at another number (in the tens column).

He had just reduced the price on his head by another five times.

"Nice shooting!" said the young girl.

"Thank you, miss," said John. He spurred his horse and never returned.

What was the initial reward offered on John's head?

Answer on page 253   Answer on page 253

MIND-BENDER

136 Find the hidden phrase or title.

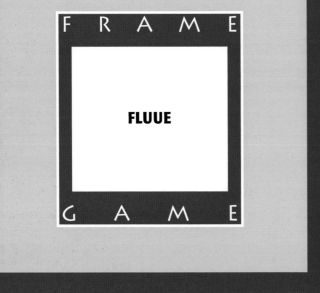

```
F R A M E

     FLUUE

G A M E
```

Answer on page 225

MIND-BENDER

137 What is $1/3$ divided by $1/5$ divided by $2/3$ times $3/5$?

138 A group of students at a major university was polled to see which courses they were taking. Sixty-four percent were taking English, 22% were taking a foreign language, and 7% were taking both. What percentage of the students polled were taking neither subject?

Answers on page 225

MINDTRAP

◆ Art Bragg caught Charles Pompuss in the lobby of the Soul-Ace Hotel and recounted his latest adventure. "While cutting through the heavy Amazon growth, I suddenly looked up into the business end of a 6-foot long blowgun with a painted savage on the other end. Soon after, I'm bound hand and foot to a stake. Having studied the famous Harry Houdini, I managed to free myself and make a run for it. One of the savages saw me and gave chase. I hid behind a tree and ambushed him. I knocked him silly, took his blowgun, and headed for the river. Hearing the rest of the tribe coming, I jumped into the river and hid underwater. I must have stayed underwater for close to an hour, breathing through the blowgun. When I felt it was safe, I followed the river back to civilization." "I hope you don't expect anyone to believe that yarn," retorted Charles Pompuss. Why isn't Art's story believable?

Answer on page 248

Russian Roulette

Russian roulette was created by Count Ugo Lombardo Fiumiccino, who successfully died during his first presentation of it.

He placed six jars on a shelf, as in the drawing below. After staring at them, he closed his eyes and told his friend to fill them up with the ingredients, making sure that each jar contained an ingredient other than the one shown on its label.

When she was finished, the count asked:

"Dear Petrushka, would you be so kind as to tell me where the salt is?"

"Under the jar containing snuff," answered Petrushka.

"My dear friend, would you tell me where the sugar is?" he asked.

"Immediately to the right of the jar containing coffee," she answered.

Ugo Lombardo Fiumiccino, confirming his desire to commit suicide, reached immediately for the jar containing arsenic.

Where is the arsenic?

The Calculator Keys

Several times Professor Zizoloziz mentioned that he feels uncomfortable looking at his pocket calculator. Yesterday, he was elated because he had found the reason why. The layout of the keys from 1 to 9 and the "minus" and "equal" signs look like they are doing subtraction. It's an incorrect equation however, because 789 minus 456 does not equal 123. Zizoloziz thought of changing the numbers to achieve a correct equation. He exchanged 7 with 3, then 3 with 4, and 9 with 6, resulting in 486 − 359 = 127. He made only three changes to achieve this.

Using the keypad below as a reference, can you obtain a correctly subtracted number with only two changes?

Answer on page 253   Answer on page 254

139 You need to match three items, A, B, and C, with three numbers, 1, 2, and 3. But you are given some peculiar information by which to determine how to match them up. From the following rules, can you find a solution?

(a)   If A is not 1, then C is not 3.

(b)   If B is either 2 or 1, then A is 3.

(c) If C is not 2, then A cannot be 3.

(d)   If C is not 1, then A is not 3.

(e)   If C is 3, then B is not 1 or 2.

(f) If B is 3, then A is not 2.

Answer on page 225

140 Find the hidden phrase or title.

Answer on page 226

MINDTRAP

◆ It seemed just yesterday he had taught his wife gymnastics in high school, Sid Shady thought. Today, however, it was free climbing. Suddenly Sid couldn't believe his good luck. His wife had inexplicably succumbed to an animal-like fear of heights and stood frozen against the rock. Seizing his chance and aware of spectators below, Shady began coaxing his wife to obey his commands. Gradually she turned around and put her back against the rock. Shady knew she would do what he said out of blind obedience and sheer terror. Sid drove a piton into the rock and secured the line. He knotted a safety clip to the other end and threw it to his wife's feet. Sid then instructed her to bend over and pick up the clip while being careful not to move her feet or bend her knees. As soon as she began to do so, she suddenly plunged to her death. When Shadow heard the details, he had Shady arrested. Why?

Answer on page 248

Strangers in the Night

The midnight train is coming down the Strujen-Bajen mountains. Art Farnanski seems to be dozing off in his seat.

Someone knows that this is not true.

At the station, all the passengers get off the train, except one. The conductor comes and taps him on the shoulder to let him know they have arrived. Art Farnanski does not answer. He is dead.

"His heart?" asks commander Abrojos, looking at the dead body.

"Strychnine," answers the forensic doctor.

Hours later, the four people that had shared the train compartment with the dead man are at the police station.

The man in the dark suit:

"I'm innocent. The blonde woman was talking to Farnanski."

The blonde woman:

"I'm innocent. I did not speak to Farnanski."

The man in the light suit:

"I'm innocent. The brunette woman killed him."

The brunette woman:

"I'm innocent. One of the men killed him."

That same morning, while he is serving him coffee, the waiter at the Petit Piccolo asks commander Abrojos:

"This is an easy case for you, isn't it?"

"Yes," answers the commander. "Four true statements and four false ones. Easy as pie."

Who killed Farnanski? (Only one person is guilty.)

The Foreigners and the Menu

A particular inn always offers the same nine dishes on its dinner menu labeled A, B, C, D, E, F, G, H, and I.

Five foreigners arrive. Nobody tells them which dish corresponds to each letter and so they each select one letter without knowing what they will eat.

The innkeeper arrives with the five dishes ordered and puts them in the center of the table so that they can decide who eats what.

This goes on for two more nights.

The foreigners, who are professors of logic, were able to deduce by the dishes they ordered which letter represents what dish.

What could have been the dishes ordered each of the three nights?

Answer on page 254　　Answer on page 254

141 Here is a five-letter "trickle-down" puzzle. Change one letter at a time to reach the final word.

TIMER
——————
——————
——————
DUNKS

142 Given the initial letters of the missing words, complete this sentence:

There are 6 O in an I.

Answers on page 226

143 Quickly now, solve this puzzle! You are taking a long drink of water. Which happens first?

The glass is $^5/_{16}$ empty.
The glass is $^5/_8$ full.

144 Quickly now, finish this mathematical analogy:

$^1/_5$ is to 5 as 5 is to ___?___ .

Answers on page 226

MINDTRAP

◆ Professor Quantum had purchased an old Scottish castle that was in desperate need of repair. One of his first priorities was to have the tunnel leading to the antiques storage room in the cellar wired. Luigi, the electrician, had just finished the basement wiring but had failed to label which of the three switches belonged to the storage room. Quantum had a small flashlight that would enable him to find the storage room; however, he didn't like the thought of returning for a small item armed with only a small light. Knowing he would be back, Quantum wanted to be certain he could correctly label which switch belonged to the storage room with only one trip. How did he do it?

Answer on page 248

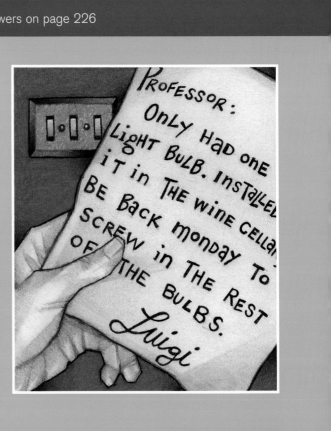

Bertha's Travels

Bertha is a woman who normally travels with other people. She doesn't travel by walking or running, nor by plane or boat. She provides a service to passengers.

The Tracks of My Tires

The police didn't ask any questions but merely used their powers of observation. When the police arrived, none of the three suspects was carrying a weapon or wearing blood-stained clothing. The police correctly deduced that the woman was the murderer.

Sick Leave

Walter was human and physically normal. The hospital was a normal hospital. He wasn't able to walk into the hospital or out of it.

The Upset Woman

He was an unwelcome intruder. He had visited before, so she left some food for him. She wanted him to die.

Top at Last

William didn't cheat. He didn't revise or work any harder than usual. He wasn't particularly happy to be top of the list.

In the Middle of the Night

He didn't hear or smell anything that might have helped him. The watch wasn't luminous. None of the objects could be seen in the pitch dark.

Criminal Assistance

The police notices were to warn people about certain types of thieves. The thieves observed people's reactions to the signs.

Material Witness

They are perfectly normal curtains and not special.

Shell Shock

The game is rigged. The dealer is fast, but it isn't speed alone that deceives the player.

Plain and Simple

The tree was normal and the boy was normal. Trees grow differently from boys.

Wonderful Weather

The accident happened at night. No other craft was involved. The accident happened in winter.

Rush Job

He exploited a different need of the miners. He turned the tents to some other use—not accommodation. The tents were made of heavy denim material.

Denise and Harry

Denise and Harry harmed people. They weren't humans but they weren't animals either.

The Office Job

The man's age, appearance, gender, and dress didn't matter. Everyone had completed the form correctly and in a similar fashion. The man showed that he had a skill required for the job.

Mechanical Advantage

The problem wasn't with the engine of his car. It was raining. He bought something sweet and used that to solve the problem.

Co-lateral Damage

Some damage is fatal to a plane and some is not. The returning planes are not a true sample of all the planes and all the damage. U.S. bomber command used the information about damage on returning planes to strengthen planes and so reduce losses.

Lifesaver

Any speech of the same length would have had the same effect. Someone made an attempt on his life.

The Single Word

Other people also heard what she had to say. There is no sexual connotation to this story. The narrator could be male or female. The word I said summarized a decision that would significantly affect the woman. None of my companions was allowed to speak in the woman's presence.

Unfinished Business

The work isn't necessarily big. Many people undertake this work. None of them can ever truly complete it.

Inheritance

Both sons reached the shore. The younger was judged to have touched the shore first. The younger son took drastic action.

The Deadly Dresser

If he had not dressed, he would not have died. He died by accident. He was poisoned.

Golf Bag

Paul removed the bag without touching it. He did not deliberately set fire to the bag since that would have incurred a penalty. He indulged in a bad habit.

Landlubber

He circumnavigated the world and crossed every line of longitude. There was nothing special about his boat or on his boat. He sailed his boat around the world but always stayed within a few miles of shore. He did it from November to February.

Flipping Pages

I did this deliberately in order to produce a specific result. I could do this only in certain places. I should have gotten permission from the publisher first.

Another Landlubber

He went around quite quickly. He saw Africa, Asia, Europe, North America, and South America. He didn't sail the ship.

The Test

Each boy deserved the grade he was given. There was something unusual about the test. Jerry was not as diligent as he should have been.

Not Eating?

The hungry man wanted to eat and there was no medical, religious, or financial reason for him not to eat. He was physically fit, healthy, and normal. He was in the same room as his plate and the plate had food on it. But he wasn't able to eat it.

Chimney Problem

He came down very slowly. The chimney was not the same after he finished his descent.

Superior Knowledge

Nobody said anything, but there was visible evidence of the man's presence. It had nothing to do with shaving.

Alex Ferguson

Soccer is played in Singapore. Alex Ferguson's style of coaching would be appropriate. One of his personal habits would not be acceptable in Singapore.

The Engraving

What she received wasn't what she expected. A fine artist had created the picture she received. The engraving had already been put to use.

One Mile

The one-mile kink is not associated with any physical or geographical feature of the landscape. The land there is the same as elsewhere along the border. There was no mistake in the original map and none in the current map. Actions were taken to speed up the survey of the border.

Half for Me and Half for You

Lucrezia Borgia's companion died of poisoning. The apple was taken at random from a bowl of perfectly good apples. Lucrezia deliberately killed her companion.

Dali's Brother

Salvador Dali is recognized as a brilliant surrealist painter. Salvador Dali's younger brother was actually a brilliant surrealist painter but his older brother never knew this. The two brothers had something important and unusual in common.

Who Did It?

The teacher didn't threaten or bribe any child. No child admitted the misdemeanor or tattled on anyone else. The teacher gave the class an exercise to do.

Window Pain

Both the windows are perfect squares. Their areas are different. They look different.

Lethal Relief

They didn't die of hunger, disease, or food poisoning. The relief was delivered to remote areas. The people died before they opened the packages of food.

Nonconventional

They are not prohibited from speaking altogether. They do not use signs, gestures, or codes. They are extremely courteous and concerned for the well-being of their companions.

Page 150 There was no one else around. The foreign visitor saw a sign. He was very obedient.

Page 150 It was not a good shot that got him the hole in one. He should have been more careful. The golfer's ball rebounded into the hole. Another person was involved.

Page 151 He is not trying to form words or to communicate or send a message. The man is working on a cross-word puzzle. The letters he writes are S and E.

Page 151 The blunder did not involve physics, chemistry, mathematics, or astronomy. The blunder concerned the twins, Viola and Sebastian.

Page 152 The same environmental change would have occurred if felt hats or woolen hats had become very popular. More silk hats were sold and fewer other hats were sold. Fur hats were out of fashion.

Page 152 Aeschylus did not trip over the tortoise or slip on it. He did not eat it or attempt to eat it. He was not poisoned or bitten by the tortoise. No other human was involved in his death.

Page 153 Driving conditions were excellent, but the thief found the woman's car very difficult to drive. She had had the car modified. The rich woman suffered from some of the same frailties as other old people. There was nothing unusual about the car's engine, gears, wheels, steering, or bodywork.

Page 153 Leonardo hid the designs in a place where he thought nobody would ever find them, but they were not buried or locked away. People carefully stored the hidden designs for years without real-izing they had them.

Page 154 She didn't know the men and didn't like any of them. She had selfish intentions. There was poten-tial financial gain for her.

Page 154 There were many trees along the side of the road. The man had never seen or noticed this tree before. There was something different about this tree. His primary concern was safety. The tree itself was not a threat to him.

Page 155 The café owner did not change the menu or prices or music in the café. He changed the interior of the café in a way that embarrassed the teenagers.

Page 155 No other person or animal was involved. The change in color was not caused by the sun or wind. The change in color was caused by the rain, but every other house and fence in the area remained unchanged in color.

Page 156 Do not take this puzzle too seriously—it involves a bad pun. The child was correct. But why?

Page 156 The fact that he is religious is not relevant. The vicar is particular about his appearance.

Page 157 The wristwatch was perfectly legal and did not give the runner an unfair advantage. The man had cheated. The clue to his cheating was that his wristwatch had changed hands.

Page 157 They were deliberately cast adrift from a famous boat. These animals can sometimes offend the senses.

Page 158 She was strangled to death with a scarf. No dancing was involved. She should not have been in such a hurry.

Page 158 The tomato fell six feet. It was a regular tomato. The man was fast.

Page 159 The shopkeeper can easily change the sign, but chooses not to do so. No superstition about num-bers is involved. Many people notice the discrepancy.

Page 159 The shoes fit him comfortably, but there was something uncomfortable about them. They were made of different material from his other shoes. They were fine when worn outside, but not when worn inside.

Page 160 It was a long process. Somebody helped him. He used a part of his body that was not paralyzed.

Page 160 Twelve candidates had started out in the attempt to become king. The one that succeeded was one of the few to survive.

Page 161 She was in her home when this happened. She had heard the tune many times before. Normally she was happy when she heard this tune. The stranger was trying to rob her.

Page 161 The police officer was perfectly capable of chasing the teenagers and he was not engaged in any other task at the time. The officer was conscientious and always chased and apprehended those he saw breaking the law.

Page 162 The second orange goes under the first orange but the first orange remains on the table.

Page 162 She was chosen on merit. She was a good typist.

Page 163 The T-shirts were designed to circumvent the law. The law was a traffic regulation. The black band was a diagonal stripe.

Page 163 The man is very skillful in his use of the stick. The man strikes something made of ivory.

Page 164 Although he constructed it with great care, the man thought that the house might fall down. He didn't intend that he or anyone else live in the house.

Page 164 They used regular water. The road was not contaminated in any way. It was for a special event. They did not hose down the entire road.

Page 165 The bird was just as beautiful and rare as he had imagined. He wasn't disappointed with its appearance. What happened to the bird placed him at risk. He saw the bird through a small window.

Page 165 The horse was alive throughout and was not exceptional. The horse was a working horse. The two legs that traveled farthest were the front left and back left.

Page 166 They weren't playing strip poker, and stripping wasn't a forfeit or penalty involved in the game. The actual card game isn't relevant. She took off her clothes to avoid harm.

Page 166 They were sold on the same day at the same market. Each was sold for a fair price. The two pigs looked the same, but when they were sold one was worth much more than the other. One was sold for food—the other was not.

Page 167 The man was physically fit and healthy. The feather had touched him. He was a circus performer.

Page 167 He was embarrassed and ashamed when his gift was opened. His gift wasn't offensive to the bride and groom in any religious, political, or moral way. He had bought an expensive gift but then made a mistake and tried to save money.

Page 168 Adam did not use the hammer on the computer. The computer was undamaged. Brenda had a disability.

Page 168 This is not a fashion issue. It has to do with right- and left-handedness. When buttons first came into use, it was the better-off who used them.

Page 169 The frogs were physically identical. One managed to survive the ordeal because of the result of its actions. The nature of the liquid is important.

Page 169 The butterfly was not a live butterfly. The man walked into trouble. The model butterfly served as a warning.

Page 170 He was not interested in the time. He wanted to make an innocuous telephone call. He was cheating.

Page 170 He wanted the cat to do something for him.

Page 171 The man was a movie star. The people who lost their jobs worked in the garment industry.

Page 171 The New York hairdresser has nothing against New Yorkers and no particular love of Canadians. He charges everyone the same price for one haircut.

Page 10 You will see a lightbulb with a glowing yellow center. Yellow is the reverse color of blue. These opposite colors are known as complementary colors.

Page 11 The choice is yours. Did you notice that the caption says, "How many can can you see?"

Page 12 A part of Hearn's act is shown close-up. From a distance, it resembles the performer.

Page 13 They are both the same height. The lines of perspective help to create the illusion of one being taller than the other.

Page 14 Turn the page 90° clockwise to reveal the circus.

Page 15 The message, made up from the pale background shapes, says, "Can you find the words."

Page 16 Turn the page upside down and he looks exactly the same.

Page 17 It's a dog curled up on a rug. Turn the page so that the arrow points upwards to reveal the dog.

Page 18 The fourth one down reads "something."

Page 19 Your guess is as good as mine. It's impossible to tell.

Page 20 From a distance, it's a skull. Close up, it's a man and woman sitting at a table.

Page 21 Turn the page 90° upside down.

Page 22 Napoleon's silhouette is found between the two trees on the right.

Page 23 The face can belong to either the man or the woman.

Page 24 It is a magic square. Each horizontal, vertical, and diagonal line of four numbers adds up to 264. It also works if you turn it upside down.

Page 25 Each circle will seem to revolve on its axis. The inner cog wheel will appear to rotate in the opposite direction.

Page 26 It is supposed to be the longest sentence that still reads the same when you turn it upside down.

Page 27 Turn the page upside down.

Page 28 Look at the lion's mane. You will see some of the old British colonies: Canada, India, Australia, New Zealand, and African colonies.

Page 40 It says, "We see but we we don't observe."

Page 41 The zebra is descended from a solid black animal. The white stripes are superficial tufts on the black background color of the animal's skin.

Page 42 The old lady's face shows her life. You can see her as a baby, a young girl, courting, in marriage, and finally in death. This type of art is based on the work of Archimboldo, a painter in Italy who lived from 1517 to 1593.

Page 43 Turn the page upside down to see them smiling. Now they are married.

Page 44 The young woman's chin becomes the nose of the old lady.

Page 45 The shapes spell the word "eye." The shelf is an impossible object

Page 46 The drum appears to spin. The word "rotator" is a palindrome; it reads the same backwards and forwards.

Page 47 Mona Lisa.

Page 48 Look closely and you'll find the profiles of Adam and Eve. The phrase "Madam I'm Adam" is a palindrome; it reads the same backwards and forwards.

Page 49 Turn the page 90° counterclockwise. His face will appear.

Page 50 The circle appears to be in two different shades of color.

Page 51 Bring the page close to your face. The bee and flower will come together.

Page 52 Pile B. Were you surprised? Measure each of them to check.

Page 53 A black cat down a coal mine eating a stick of licorice at midnight.

Page 54 The secret word is "hello." Look at the page in the direction of the arrow at eye level.

Page 55 It changes direction!

Page 56 Look at the reflection of this page in the mirror.

Page 57 At first glance, you see a bearded man. On closer inspection, you'll find a phoenix.

Page 58 Turn the page upside down and you will see the mother's head. The baby's diaper becomes the mother's head scarf.

Page 59 It appears to follow you, but it's just an illusion. This design was used as a recruiting poster for the British Army.

Page 60 Turn the page upside down and you will see a slice of cake. The name "Otto" has both horizontal and vertical symmetry. And it's also a palindrome!

Page 61 The choice is yours!

Page 62 Bring the page closer to your face. The figures will come together.

Page 63 Take your pick!

Page 64 No. The set of stairs is impossible.

Page 65 They are both the same size. Trace one of them and measure it against the other. Their curve tricks us and creates the illusion.

Page 66 It depends on what direction you see the bird flying. Either answer is correct.

Page 67 The letter E. Try looking at the page from a distance.

Page 68 The right eye and bridge of the nose form the heads of Romeo and Juliet. This form of art was popular in the 19th century in Europe.

Page 69 The choice is yours. It all depends on what you saw first. Horizontally, it reads A, B, C. Vertically, it reads 12, 13, 14.

Page 70 A person riding a horse. See the illustration.

Page 90 The previous one was 1881. The next one will occur in the year 6009.

Page 91 It's a crate. Look at the illustration to the right. It's easier to see the crate with the added lines.

Page 92 "I've got a a big head."

Page 93 There are six F's in the sentence.

Page 94 You might see a medal or two people having an argument.

Page 95 "X" marks their spots. See illustration.

Page 96 The middle leg is impossible.

Page 97 Look at the markings on the cow's back. You will see a sideways map of the United Kingdom.

Page 98 It says, "Optical illusions are magic."

Page 99 To tie mules to.

Page 100 Slowly bring the page closer to your face. At a certain point, the matches will join together.

Page 101 Look at the sequence of the words. It says, "the with." It should be "with the."

Page 150 The foreign visitor saw a sign saying, "Dogs must be carried." He did not have a dog!

Page 150 The golfer's ball rebounded off the head of another golfer who was crossing the green. The ball bounced into the hole. However, the man who was hit died.

Page 151 The man is given the world's most difficult cross-word and offered a prize of $100 for every letter he gets right. He puts "S" for each initial letter and "E" in every other space. S is the commonest initial letter and E the commonest letter in the English language.

Page 151 The identical twins Viola and Sebastian are different sexes. This is impossible.

Page 152 Because silk hats came into fashion, the demand for beaver hats decreased. More beavers meant more small lakes and bogs.

Page 152 Aeschylus was killed when the tortoise was dropped on him from a height by an eagle who may have mistaken the bald head of Aeschylus for a rock on which to break the tortoise.

Page 153 The rich woman was very nearsighted, but did not like wearing glasses or contact lenses. So she had her windshield ground to her prescription. The thief could not see clearly through it.

Page 153 Leonardo hid the secret designs by painting over them with beautiful oil paintings. He knew that no one would remove such masterpieces. But he did not know that modern X-ray techniques would allow art historians to see through the oil paintings and reveal his designs.

Page 154 She was a divorce lawyer drumming up business!

Page 154 The man saw a tree lying across the road. He was in Africa and he knew that blocking the road with a tree was a favorite trick of armed bandits, who then waited for a car to stop at the tree so that they could ambush and rob the passengers. He guessed correctly that this was the case here, so he reversed quickly to avoid danger.

Page 155 The café owner installs pink lighting that highlights all the teenagers' acne!

Page 155 The man had made green paint by mixing yellow paint and blue paint. The blue paint was oil-based, but the yellow paint was water-based. Heavy rain had dissolved the yellow paint, leaving the fence decidedly blue.

Page 156 The child was correct. It was a mail train!

Page 156 The vicar wears black suits and knows that light-colored dog hairs will show up on his suits, but that black ones will not be noticed.

Page 157 A picture of the runner early in the race showed him wearing his watch on his right wrist. When he crossed the finishing line, it was on his left wrist. The judges investigated further and found that one man had run the first half of the race and his identical twin brother had run the second half. They had switched at a toilet on the route.

Page 157 The two animals were skunks that had been ejected from Noah's Ark because of the stench they were causing.

Page 158 The famous dancer was Isadora Duncan, who was strangled when the long scarf she was wearing caught in the wheel of her sports car.

Page 158 He caught it just above the ground.

Page 159 It was originally a mistake, but the shopkeeper found that so many people came into his shop to point out the error that it increased his business.

Page 159 The man found that the synthetic shoes generated a buildup of static electricity when he wore them around his carpeted office. He constantly got electric shocks, so he rejected them and went back to his old leather shoes.

Page 160 He winked one eye and thereby indicated to a very dedicated assistant each letter, word, and sentence of the book. He was Jean-Dominique Bauby, the French writer. The book he wrote by blinking, *The Diving Bell and the Butterfly*, was published just before his death in 1996 and became a best-seller.

Page 160 This is normal in a game of checkers (or draughts).

Page 161 The woman was alone and asleep in her house in the middle of the night when she was awakened by the sound of her musical jewel box. She knew that a burglar was in her bedroom. She reached under her pillow, pulled out a gun, and shot him.

Page 161 The teenagers were traveling on the road that crossed the road the police officer was on. They drove through a green light.

Page 162 Put it under the table.

Page 162 Typing eleven words per minute is going quite fast, if the language is Chinese!

Page 163 A law was introduced making the wearing of seat belts compulsory for car drivers and passengers. Many Italians tried to circumvent the law. They wore the T-shirts in order to give the false impression that they were wearing seat belts.

Page 163 The man is playing billiards (or snooker or pool) with balls made of ivory. By pocketing a ball with his cue, he wins the match.

Page 164 The man was building a house of cards.

Page 164 This incident occurred just before the start of the Monaco Grand Prix race, which is held in the streets of Monte Carlo. Part of the course runs through a tunnel. When it rains outside, the firemen hose down the road in the tunnel in order to make the surface wet. This improves consistency and safety.

Page 165 The ornithologist was sitting on a plane coming in to land when he saw the rare bird, which was sucked into the jet engine, causing the engine to fail and the plane to crash-land.

Page 165 The horse worked in a mill. It walked around in a circle all day to drive the millstone. In the course of the day, its outer legs walked a mile farther than its inner legs.

Page 166 When one player went to play a card, she knocked over a mug. The hot drink poured over the other player, who immediately jumped up and started to take her clothes off.

Page 166 This happened in France. One pig was sold for bacon. The other had been painstakingly trained to sniff out truffles and was, therefore, much more valuable.

Page 167 The man was a circus sword swallower. In the middle of his act someone tickled him with the feather and he gagged.

Page 167   The man selected a beautiful crystal vase in a gift shop, but he knocked it over and broke it. He had to pay for it, so he instructed the shop to wrap it and send it anyway. He assumed that people would think that it had been broken in transit. Unfortunately for him, the shop assistant carefully wrapped every broken piece before sending the package.

Page 168   Brenda was blind and she depended on her Braille manual when using the computer. Alan flattened the pages with a hammer.

Page 168   Most people are right-handed and find it easier to fasten a button which is on the right through a hole which is on the left. This is why men's buttons are on the right. When buttons were first used, it was the better-off who could afford clothes with buttons. Among this class the ladies were often dressed by maidservants. The servant would face the lady, and so it was easier for right-handed servants to fasten buttons that were on the lady's left.

Page 169   The frogs fell into a large tank of cream. One swam around for a while but then gave up and drowned. The other kept swimming until his movements turned the cream into knobs of butter, on which he safely floated.

Page 169   The butterfly was made of plastic and was put on a large plate-glass window to indicate the presence of the glass. After it fell off, a man walked into the window and was seriously injured.

Page 170   The man is having an affair. Once he has phoned his mistress, he calls for the time so that if his wife should later press the redial button she will not find out anything he does not want her to know.

Page 170   The man was a television cable engineer who needed to thread a cable from the back of a house, under the floor, to the front. He released the cat with a string attached to it into a hole at the back of the house. The cat was lured by the smell of the cream and salmon to find its way under the floor to the front of the house. The string was used to pull the cable through.

Page 171   The man was Clark Gable, the screen idol, who took off his shirt in a movie in which he was about to go to bed. He was not wearing an undershirt. So great was his influence that men stopped wearing undershirts, and factories making them had to close down. In a later movie, he wore an undershirt and restored it to fashion.

Page 171   He gets three times as much money!

1 Only once, because the second time you will be subtracting from 24 instead of 30.

2 The number 8. (It is made up of two zeroes, one on top of the other.)

3 By using Roman numerals. The upper half of XII is VII.

4 1 and 9.

5 Any number and 1.

6 2 and 2.

7 It is easy to eliminate possibilities. For example, it has to be an even number; none of the digits can be zero (or else the product would be zero); and the product of the digits must be less than or equal to 48 (otherwise two times the product would have three digits). If you think of the remaining possibilities, you will find the answer, $36 = 2 \times 3 \times 6$.

8 1, 2, and 3, because $1 \times 2 \times 3 = 1 + 2 + 3 = 6$.

9 $25 = 5^2$ and $36 = 6^2$.

10 $9^{9^9} = 9^{387420489}$, which is a number with more than 369 million digits.

11 The father is 41 and the son is 14.

12 10 cents.

13 $1.10 for the outlet and $0.10 for the light bulb.

14 $3 \times 75 = 225$ qualities distributed among 100 persons, so at least 25% of them have all three.

15 The number of passing grades is a whole number less than 32, and 5% of it is also a whole number. It can only be 20. If 20 is the number of passing grades, the number of students from New York that took the test is one.

16 If half of the 83% tip the usher 10 cents and the other half leaves no tip, it is the same as if all 83% had tipped him 5 cents, which is the same amount as what the remaining 17% tipped. The usher received 4,800 cents, or more simply, 48 dollars.

17 Turn the page upside down. It will read $108 = 6 \times 18$.

18 He will need twenty "9's," one for the numbers 9, 19, 29, 39, 49, 59, 69, 79, 89, 90, 91, 92, 93, 94, 95, 96, 97, and 98, and two for 99.

19 At each stop, passengers can buy a ticket for any of the 24 remaining stops. Therefore, the number of tickets will be $25 \times 24 = 600$.

20 Let's imagine that the inhabitants are as different as possible (one will be bald, another will have only one hair, another two, another three, and so on, until we get to someone having 100,000 hairs). Inhabitant number 100,002 will have the same number of hairs as someone among the first 100,001 inhabitants. The total population is more than 200,000 people, which means that there will be more than 100,000 inhabitants with the same number of hairs as other people in town.

21 Three: one red, one blue, and one brown.

22 There are 6 chestnut trees per side, making a total of 12.

23 Two birds and one olive tree.

24 There is only one winner, so the remaining 110 players were defeated in 110 matches. Therefore, they used 110 balls.

25 Twelve muffins. When John ate half the remaining muffins plus three more to leave none, he must have eaten six muffins. So Peter ate half the muffins and left six, meaning that there were twelve to start.

26 The shepherd that is talking had 5 sheep and the other one had 7.

27 Three cages and four canaries.

28 Each sardine costs 1 dollar. Therefore, 7½ sardines would cost 7½ dollars.

29 Since ½ brick weighs 3 pounds, 1½ bricks weigh 9 pounds.

30 Since 18 sardines are the same as 1½ dozen, they cost 9½ dollars.

31 Since 1 man eats 1 pie in 1½ minutes, 1 man eats 20 pies in 30 minutes, which means 3 men eat 60 pies in 30 minutes.

32 11 times (one fewer than the number of times he went in).

33 Three ducks.

34 The person who won three games must have also lost six games, since his opponent won $3. In total, they played 9 games.

35 1.25¢

36 We measure the inside diameter and the height of the liquid, obtaining the volume of the liquid. Then, we turn the bottle upside down and measure the volume of the empty part. If we add both, we obtain the total capacity of the bottle and can calculate the percentage of the liquid. An easier way is to measure only both heights, because both have the same size base.

37 At 8 P.M. Each hour the volume triples, so it is one-third full one hour before it is full.

38 By leaving a task half done (for example, peeling potatoes) so that the next soldier can finish it, they can do all the tasks in 1 hour and 30 minutes.

39 If the length of the rope + 2 yards = 3 times the length of the rope, then the rope is 1 yard long.

40 29 days. One spider would have covered half of the space on the 29th day, and on the 30th day would repeat what had been done, covering the space completely. Two spiders would each have covered half of the space in 29 days, therefore covering the entire area.

41 If the length is 6 yards + half the length, then half the length is 6 yards. Therefore, it is 12 yards long.

42 No mud at all, because a hole can only contain air.

43 There are only three people, a daughter, her mother, and her grandmother. The mother received 25 books from the grandmother and then gave eight to her daughter.

44 Dolores is taller than Emily, who is taller than Ann.

45 Joan is 6 years older than Rose.

46 Emily speaks in a softer voice than Dolores (Emily < Ann < Dolores).

47 Peter is sitting between Philip (on his right) and James (on his left).

48 A pound of $10 gold coins has twice the amount of gold than half a pound of $20 coins. Therefore, it is worth more.

49 He made each candidate ride another candidate's horse. Each one would, of course, try to come in first, because in that way the owner of the horse that a particular candidate was riding would lose the race.

50 The store lost $40 given as change plus the value of the umbrella, or $10. The transaction was only between the sales person and the customer. The bank teller did not take part in the transaction.

51 If it is a traditional scale with two dishes, you can place the apples in one dish and dirt in the other until they balance. Then, replace the apples with weights and you will know the weight of the apples. If it is a spring scale, you weigh the apples first, then write down the mark on the scale and replace the apples with weights until you reach the previous mark. The weights will show the real weight of the apples.

52 The pitcher with water contains exactly the same amount of wine as water in the pitcher of wine. Both pitchers have the same volume of liquid before and after mixing water and wine, so mixing them makes no difference.

53 Put one marble in one box, three in another and five in a third one. Then place the three boxes inside the fourth box.

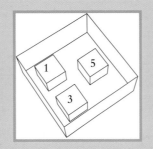

54 The weight of the fish bowl increases by the same amount as the weight of the liquid displaced by the fish.

55 The reaction of the air that the little bird is pushing down in order to fly will partially affect both the dish of the scale and the floor of the room. The scale will show one pound minus some portion of the 5 ounces that the bird weighs.

If the cage were sealed, the air would affect only the dish of the scale and the scale would continue to read one pound.

56 One weighing. Take one ball from the first sack, two from the second, three from the third, and so on until you reach the last sack, from which you take ten balls. Since 1 + 2 + 3 + ... + 9 + 10 = 55, if all of the balls weighed 10 ounces each, the total weight would be 550 ounces. In this case, the weight will be 550 − N, where N is the number of the sack containing nine-ounce balls.

57 The minimum number of parts that could have been left is 3 (the link that is cut and the two disconnected parts of the chain). The maximum number will be 6, as shown in the figure below.

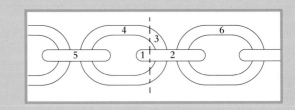

58 We identify each sack by the number of balls taken from it. We must find a way to obtain different results from all possible sums of the digits that identify the sacks. The easiest way would be powers of 2: 1, 2, 4, 8, 16, ... (20, 21, 22, 23, 24, ...). Therefore, we will take one ball from one sack, two from another, four from another, etc.

The resulting weight will be 1023 − N, where N can only be obtained by adding certain sack numbers. If N is 27 ounces, the sacks containing 9-ounce balls will be those from which we took 1, 2, 8, and 16 balls, because, using just the powers of 2, 27 can only be obtained by adding 1 + 2 + 8 + 16.

Let's call "1" the sack from which we took 1 ball, "2" the one from which we took 2 balls, "3" the one from which we took 4 balls, etc. The number 27, in binary, is 11011. The position of the 1's in this binary sequence reveals the solution. The 1's are in first, second, fourth, and fifth position, which means that the sacks containing the 9-ounce balls are 1, 2, 4, and 5.

59 Put five marbles in one cup, four in another, and one in another. Put the cup with one marble inside the one containing four. There are other solutions, all based on the same trick. Another solution, for example, involves putting three marbles in one cup, three marbles in the second cup, and four marbles in the third cup, and then putting the second cup inside the third one. This leaves three marbles in the first cup, three marbles in the second cup, and seven marbles in the third cup.

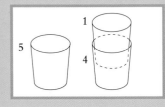

60 The best solution is to open four links from one of the pieces and use them to join the remaining five parts in one chain. The total cost will be 4 × 60 = 240 cents, or $2.40.

61 The worst case scenerio is to take two white, two black, and one red marble. The sixth marble has to be either white or black.

62 By cutting the third link, we obtain three pieces of one, two, and four links each. The first day, she pays with the one-link part. The second day, she pays with the two-link part and gets the one-link piece back as change. The third day, she pays with the loose link. The fourth day, she pays with the four-link part and receives back the three links, and so on.

63 The clock that doesn't work will show the precise time twice a day, but the fast one will take 2 × 60 × 12 = 1,440 days to show the precise time. Therefore, the broken clock shows the correct time more often.

64 His statement must be "I will be hanged." If they want to hang him, the sentence is true, and therefore, they will not be able to hang him. For the same reason, he cannot be drowned because his statement would be false and they could not drown him if his statement is false. (Based on *Don Quixote*, by Cervantes.)

65 Two glasses. Pick up the second glass, pour its contents into the ninth glass, and put it back. Then pick up the fourth glass, pour its contents into the seventh glass, and put it back. Note that the seventh and ninth glasses are not moved.

66 100% probability, because if four marbles are in their corresponding cups, the fifth one must be in its corresponding cup, too.

67 It happened to Gioacchino Rossini, who was born on February 29, 1792, and who died on November 13, 1868. Remember that 1800 was not a leap year. All years that are divisible by four are leap years, except those that end in "00." They are only leap years if they are divisible by 400.

68 Three. The first two can be of different colors, white and black, but the third sock will be one of these two colors, and thus complete one pair.

69 Four hours, the time between 8 and 12.

70 Four. There are three different colors, so the first three socks may not match, but the fourth one will match one of the previous three socks.

71 Neither. The yolk of an egg is yellow.

72 The first 12 gloves can be six white left gloves and six black left gloves. Therefore, the 13th glove will make a pair with one of the previous 12 gloves. No matter what the first 12 gloves are, if no two have made a pair yet, the 13th will.

73 He would have drunk the same number of cups of coffee. The difference is that the conversation would have taken place on March 14.

74 Take one marble from the box marked BW. If it is white, the other marble must also be white. This means that the box marked BB must have black and white marbles and the box marked WW must have only black marbles. You can apply the same principle if the first marble you take is black.

75 Time to have the clock fixed.

76 After being inverted twice, the hourglass continued working in its initial position. Therefore, the extra hour that it measured was a consequence of these two inversions, half an hour each time. If it was inverted for the second time at 11:30, the first time had to be a half-hour earlier, at 11:00.

77 Ten times (you can verify it yourself).

78 Four seconds (it takes two seconds between 2 consecutive strikes).

79 There is 1 second between 2 strikes. Therefore, it will take 11 seconds for the clock to strike 12 times.

80 He lived 59 years, because there is no "0" year.

81 It is not "I am going in" or "I am not going in." The opposite is "I am leaving."

82 Friday.

83 Three days and two nights. She left yesterday and will return tomorrow.

84 The man's birthday is December 31 and he was talking on January 1. He's 36 now, the day before yesterday he was 35, this calendar year he will turn 37, and next calendar year he will turn 38.

85 INVENT.

86 The word "incorrectly."

87 Lounger.

88 It's a matter of language. Consider "four twenty" as $4.20. Then it is true.

89 Wet.

90 Humans. When we are little, we crawl on all fours. When we are adults, we stand on two feet. When we are old, we use a cane.

91 Silence.

92 The letter "i."

93 A shadow.

94 None. The ship floats and it always weighs the same in the water. It will rise with the tide, so its flotation line will always be the same. So the ladder will still be 22 steps underwater.

95 Two minutes. During the first minute, the front of the train will pass through the tunnel, and during the second minute, the rest of the train will pass through the tunnel.

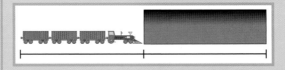

96 Two hours and thirteen minutes. (If you multiply by 60, the minutes become hours and the seconds become minutes.)

97 If you put my bird inside any supersonic plane and make it fly in the same direction as the plane, it will be going faster than the plane.

98 The combined speed of the trains is 50 + 70 = 120 miles per hour. It will take them half an hour to travel the 60 miles between them. During this time, the bird will travel 40 miles.

99 100 inches. The stone moves relative to the log and the log to the terrain.

100 The combined speed of the trains is 80 + 120 = 200 meters per minute. One minute before crashing, they will be 200 meters apart.

101 You might think that the snail would take 200 minutes in traveling 100 centimeters, but you have to realize that at the end of the 194th minute it will be three centimeters away from the end. This means that in the 195th minute, the snail will reach it and will not slide down again. The answer is 195 minutes.

102 This point maintains a constant speed, independent of the length of the shadow.

103 When the car speeds up, the inertia pushes the air back inside the car, compressing the air behind the balloon and thus pushing the balloon forward. When the car turns, the balloon will move toward the inside of the turn.

104 The Pacific Ocean. Even though it had not been discovered or named by Balboa, it was still the biggest ocean.

105 One cookie, because after eating one you would no longer have an empty stomach.

106 Because it wasn't raining.

107 Holes.

108 By walking and dragging the rope with it. The text does not say that the leash is tied to something.

109 The number 400, to hang on a house. This number is formed by three digits, costing $1 each.

110 It was daytime, so the room was light.

111 With one quarter and one nickel. The puzzle says that one of the coins is not a nickel, and it is true since a quarter is not a nickel.

112 When he got married, he was a billionaire. Because of his wife's spending habits, he became a millionaire.

113 He goes to the next room and by crawling toward the bottle, he slides into the room.

114 The plane had not yet taken off.

115 He had already put sugar in his coffee.

116 By serving mashed potatoes.

117 It is a male giraffe, so it is the father and not the mother of the offspring.

118 Ten cows. We can call the pigs cows, but it doesn't make them cows.

119 He must always be behind the whistle.

120 There is no reason to baptize him. If he is Catholic, he is already baptized.

121 The letter "e."

122 He is a farmer. He needs plenty of water, so if he lacks water he has no income and he won't be able to buy or even make wine.

123 Since he's a butcher, he weighs meat.

124 The first four people pick one apple each, and the fifth one takes the basket with the apple in it.

125 Either a deep-sea diver or an astronaut.

126 "To sint" means to take off your clothes, and "to sant" is to go into the water to bathe.

127 Because before the game begins, the score is always 0-0.

Bertha's Travels

She was "Madame Guillotine," the deadly invention of Joseph Guillotin that was used in France to execute people.

The Tracks of My Tires

The woman was the only person in a wheelchair.

Sick Leave

Walter was a newborn baby.

The Upset Woman

He was a mouse caught in a mousetrap.

Top at Last

William's name was William Abbott, and the results were given in alphabetical order.

In the Middle of the Night

He turns on the light.

Criminal Assistance

The police put up notices that read, "Beware of Pickpockets." The pickpockets stood near a sign and noticed that when people saw it they immediately checked that their purses and wallets were safe. The pickpockets then knew where their victims carried their purses and wallets—which made them easier to steal.

Material Witness

They are on the window!

Shell Shock

The pea isn't under any of the shells. It's slipped under a shell by the operator as he lifts it. Sometimes the operator places the pea under a player's choice to encourage dupes.

Plain and Simple

The boy will be six inches taller than the nail. The tree grows from the top, so the nail won't rise.

Wonderful Weather

The ship was the Titanic, which hit an iceberg on a fine night when the sea was very calm. If the weather had been worse, then the lookouts would have seen waves hitting the iceberg or heard the iceberg. (Icebergs make groaning noises when they move.) Unfortunately, the iceberg wasn't seen, and the rest is history.

Rush Job

He used the tough tent cloth to make trousers for the miners. His name was Levi Strauss.

Denise and Harry

Denise and Harry were hurricanes.

The Office Job

This happened in the 1800s. The man had applied for a job as a telegraph operator. Among the background noise was a Morse code message saying, "If you understand this, walk into the office." It was a test of the candidates' skill and alertness. He was the only candidate who passed.

Mechanical Advantage

It was raining heavily and the man discovered a leak in the roof of his car. He bought several packs of chewing gum, chewed them, and then used the gum as a waterproof filler until he could reach a garage.

Co-lateral Damage

They strengthened the parts of the aircraft that had not been hit. Antiaircraft fire is random in nature. The returning planes showed damage that had not been fatal. But this sample excluded information from the planes that had not returned and had sustained fatal damage. It was deduced that they had sustained damage on the parts not hit on the returning planes. By adding armor to the planes, overall losses were reduced.

Lifesaver

The politician was Teddy Roosevelt, the American president. In 1912, in Milwaukee, he was shot in the chest. He was saved because the bullet was slowed as it passed through the folded manuscript of the speech in his breast pocket. He went on to make the speech later on the same day that he was shot!

The Single Word

The word was "Guilty." I was foreman of the jury at the woman's trial.

Unfinished Business

His autobiography.

Inheritance

The younger son took his sword and cut off his hand before hurling it ashore. Since he had touched the shore before his brother, he was able to claim his father's kingdom. (This story is told of the kingdom of Ulster, and to this day a bloody red hand is used as the symbol of the province.)

The Deadly Dresser

The last thing he put on was his shoe and it contained a deadly spider that bit him, and he died soon after.

Golf Bag

To deliberately ignite the paper bag would be to interfere with the lie of his ball and incur a penalty. So while he pondered the problem he smoked a cigarette. He discarded the cigarette onto the bag and it burned. No penalty was incurred.

Landlubber

He sailed around the coast of Antarctica.

Flipping Pages

I was photocopying the book.

Another Landlubber

He was an astronaut in a spaceship.

The Test

The final instruction in the test was to ignore all the previous questions. The teacher had repeatedly told the students to read over the entire exam before beginning. The test was given to see how well the pupils could follow instructions.

Not Eating?

His plate is his dental plate.

Chimney Problem

The man on the tall chimney had a penknife in his pocket. With this he pried loose a brick from the top layer. He used the brick as a hammer. In this way, he gradually demolished the chimney by knocking out all the bricks and lowered himself to the ground.

Superior Knowledge

One of the toilet seats had been left up.

Alex Ferguson

Alex Ferguson chews gum incessantly during soccer games. The sale and use of non-therapeutic chewing gum are illegal in Singapore.

The Engraving

She received a used British postage stamp.

One Mile

When it was originally surveyed, two teams were sent out down the west side of South Dakota. One started from the north and one from the south. They missed! It was easier to put the kink in the border than to redo the survey.

Half for Me and Half for You

Lucrezia Borgia put a deadly poison on one side of the blade of a knife. When she cut the apple, only one half was poisoned.

Dali's Brother

Salvador Dali died at age 7. Nine months later his brother was born and was also named Salvador. It was the younger Salvador Dali who became the famous surrealist painter.

Who Did It?

One of the words that was not rude was spelled incorrectly (for example, "The headmaster is a horribul %$@*&@!"). The teacher gave a spelling test that included the word and the guilty child spelled it wrong again.

Window Pain

Initially the square window has sides of about 1.4 feet and an area of 2 square feet. The second window has sides of 2 feet and an area of 4 square feet.

Lethal Relief

The food was dropped by parachute in remote areas. Several people were killed when the packages fell on them.

Nonconventional

If a nun wants the salt, she asks the nun nearest the salt if she would like the mustard, which is near the first nun. The second nun would reply, "No, but do you want the salt?"

1 **16.** The numbers increase by 3.

2 **b.** Feminine.

3 **14, 5.** There are 2 alternate patterns: one increasing by 2, one decreasing by 2.

4 **5.** The lines diminish counterclockwise.

5 **juniper.** The other words are: tulip, orchid, carnation, and gardenia.

6 **row.**

7 **81.** The square of the diagonally opposing number.

8 **6.** The figures become smaller from left to right.

9 **12.** Multiply the three numbers in the outside squares and divide the sum by 3.

10 **New York.** It's the only city that is not a capital.

11 **12.** Alternately multiply each number by 2.

12 **x.** The letters progressively skip 1, 2, 3, 4 places.

13 **Montreal.** The other cities are: Bangor, Phoenix, Detroit, Galveston, and Portland.

14 **2.** Multiply the first two numbers and then divide the sum by 3.

15 **5.** In this figure, the cross is with the black box and the x is with the white circle.

16 **53.** Every number is multiplied by 2 and then alternately changed +1, −1.

17 **cardinal.** It is the only choice that is not a chess piece.

18 **1.** Multiply the order values of the first two letters.

19 **89, 153, 121.** Every number is multiplied by 2 and then added to: +1, +2, +3, +4, +5.

20 **b and c.** They both have a circular form.

21 **2.** The three series alternate ears, hair, and eye shapes.

22 **Denise.**

23 **2.** Multiply the letters in the circles, subtract the number in the square, and divide the sum by 2.

24 **a.**

25 **4.** Each figure reverses, loses a line, and alternates circle colors.

26 **4.**

27 **whale.** It's the only mammal. The other words are anchovy, trout, herring, sardine, and shark.

28 **49, 3, 53.** Each row numbers adds +2, −4, +8, −16, +32 or −2, +4, −8, +16, −32, in alternation.

29 **(c) bassoon.** They are all woodwinds.

30 **j, n, r.** The letters skip 3 in the rows and 2 in the vertical columns.

31 **love.** Uses numerical order of letters.

32 **2.** Each row comprises has three basic types: circle, square, diamond; and 1, 2, and 3 base lines.

33 **364.** Add the two outer numbers and then divide by 2.
13. Add all the numerals in the outer numbers together.
15. Subtract the second outer number from the first and divide the result by 5.

34 **i, d.** Skip a letter going up the alphabet in the diamond boxes and down a letter in the square boxes.
o, c. The letters go up the alphabet in a 1, 2, 3, 4 series in the diamond boxes and down the alphabet in the square boxes.

35 **2,241.** There are two alternate series. Multiply the first number by itself and subtract the next number from the result.

36 **1.** The outer figure progressively moves toward the shaded figure. The dotted lines alternate.

SELF-SCORING

Less than 14 = Poor — —
From 15 to 19 = Adequate — ☆
From 20 to 24 = Fair — ☆☆
From 25 to 29 = Good — ☆☆☆
From 30 to 36 = Excellent — ☆☆☆☆

1. **bedspread.** The other words are: closet, couch, nightstand, bureau, and chair.

2. **17, 8.** The first set of numbers increases by +1, +2, +3, +4, +5. The second set of numbers decreases by 5, 4, 3, 2, 1.

3. **pen, dam.**

4. **i, r, g.** Each series skips a letter.

5. **6120 (fat).** Numerical value of letters.

6. **15.** Add all the single numerals.
   11. Multiply the numbers outside the parentheses and divide the product by 6.
   7. Subtract the numbers outside the parentheses and divide the difference by 5.

7. **4.** The sum of each column is 10.

8. **64.** There are two patterns. The first pattern increases by +1 from the number 2. The second pattern cubes each number in the first pattern.

9. **5.** The figures are added together.

10. **c, c, c.**

11. **12.** To solve for the triangle, add the numerical values of the letters in the circle and subtract the value of the letter in the square.

12. **b.**

13. **2.** Two lines are progressively eliminated while also alternating between solid and dotted lines.

14. **1.**

15. **6.** In every figure series, there are 4, 3, 2 circles; 2, 1, 0 windows; and 3, 2, 1 vertical lines.

16. **14.** The pattern alternates between adding 5 and subtracting 2.

17. **Beijing.** It's the only non-European city.

18. **c.** All are names of mountains in North America.

19. **24, 6, 32.** The pattern runs horizontally: +1, −2, +4, −8, +16 and −1, +2, −4, +8, −16, in alternation.

20. **horseshoe.** All other choices are pointed objects.

21. **cribbage.** It's a card game. The other words are: curling, lacrosse, wrestling, rugby, archery.

22. **own.**

23. **75.** Add the first number and the second number, the second with the third, etc., and add 1 to each sum.

24. **6.** Subtract the second figure from the first figure.

25. **4.** Add the numbers in the outside squares, subtract the diamond from the sum, and divide by 2.

26. **elbow.** It is the only word with two syllables.

27. **8.** The pattern alternates between adding 3 and subtracting 5.

28. **z.** The pattern alternately skips 3 and 2 letters.

29. **forearm.** The others are names of bones: tibia, femur, patella, and humerus.

30. **16.** Multiply the first two numbers in each row and double the product.

31. **4.** It's the only figure that combines two of the same shape.

32. **730.** Cube the preceding number and add 1.

33. **b.**

34. **87.** Multiply the first two numbers and subtract 3 from the product.

35. **6.** It is the only figure that has two squares on one side.

36. **3.** The figure progressively advances direction. The orange and yellow shapes alternate.

SELF-SCORING

Less than 14 = Poor	—
From 15 to 19 = Adequate	☆
From 20 to 24 = Fair	☆☆
From 25 to 29 = Good	☆☆☆
From 30 to 36 = Excellent	☆☆☆☆

1 $4^4 + 44 = 300$

2 It would appear in column B. Divide by 7 whatever number you wish to place, and see what the remainder is. If the remainder is 1, the number goes in column A; if the remainder is 2, the number goes in column B; and so on. (If the remainder is zero, however, the number goes in column G.)

3 Audrey will reach the destination first. Suppose they cover 12 miles, both walking at a rate of 2 miles per hour and running at a rate of 6 miles per hour. Use the formula $rt = d$ (rate × time = distance) to find each person's time.

Nancy (walks half the distance and runs half the distance):

$2t = 6$ mi., so $t = 3$ hrs. walking
$6t = 6$ mi., so $t = 1$ hr. running
$t = 4$ hours total time

Audrey (walks half the time and runs half the time):

$$2(\tfrac{1}{2}t) + 6(\tfrac{1}{2}t) = 12 \text{ mi.}$$

$$t + 3t = 12$$
$$4t = 12$$
$$t = 3 \text{ hours total time}$$

4 Each reads the same when held upside down.

5 Lead by example.

6 15. Simply add the sum of the two digits in any number to the sum of the two digits in the adjacent number to get the corresponding number in the row below. For example:

8 + 9 (89) and 5 + 3 (53) = 25
5 + 3 (53) and 1 + 7 (17) = 16

To find the missing number, add:

1 + 6 (16) and 1 + 7 (17) = 15

7 His younger daughter received more—$4,000 more—than the older daughter. One way to solve this is to set up an equation that represents who received what:

$$x = \frac{1}{3}x + \frac{1}{5}x + \frac{1}{6}x + 9{,}000$$

$$x = \frac{10}{30}x + \frac{6}{30}x + \frac{5}{30}x + 9{,}000$$

$$x = \frac{21}{30}x + 9{,}000$$

Multiplying both sides of the equation by $\frac{30}{9}$, we get

$$\frac{30}{9}x = \frac{21}{9}x + \frac{270{,}000}{9}$$

$$\frac{30}{9}x - \frac{21}{9}x = 30{,}000$$

Then

$$\frac{1}{3}x = \$10{,}000 \text{ (wife)}$$

$$\frac{1}{5}x = \$6{,}000 \text{ (son)}$$

$$\frac{1}{6}x = \$5{,}000 \text{ (older daughter)}$$

8 The missing number is 4. Simply add the first and second rows together to get the third row, like this:

65,927
14,354
80,281

9 If you know that 2:17 is the correct time, find the difference, positive or negative, of the other clocks:

clock 1	2:15	−2
clock 2	2:35	+18
clock 3	2:00	−17
clock 4	2:23	+6
clock 5	2:17	0
5 clocks		5 minutes

As a group, the clocks average 1 minute fast.

10   The answer is $\frac{1}{12}$. If we convert each fraction to twelvths, the series looks like this:

$$\frac{8}{12}, \frac{7}{12}, \frac{6}{12}, \frac{5}{12}, \frac{4}{12}, \frac{3}{12}, \frac{2}{12}, \mathbf{\frac{1}{12}}$$

11   Cheaper by the dozen.

12   Pages 6, 19, and 20 are also missing. Newspapers are printed double sided, two pages to a sheet. The first and second pages are attached to the second-to-last and last pages—in this case, pages 23 and 24. The rest of the pages are attached as follows:

1–2 with 23–24
3–4 with 21–22
5–6 with 19–20
7–8 with 17–18
9–10 with 15–16
11–12 with 13–14

13   The value of c is 14. To solve the problem, set up the following equations:

(1) $a + b = 13$
(2) $b + c = 22$
(3) $a + c = 19$

Solve for b in equation (1):
$$b = 13 - a$$

Substitute this into equation (2):
$$13 - a + c = 22$$
$$-a + c = 9$$

Then combine equations (2) and (3) and solve for c:
$$-a + c = 9$$
$$\underline{a + c = 19}$$
$$2c = 28$$
$$c = 14$$

14   Rotate the first square 90 degrees to the right to obtain the second square.

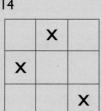

15   MOVE
MORE
MARE
BARE
BARK

16   Sarah is the second oldest; Liz is the oldest.

17   The missing number is 14. The first and last numbers added together make 19, as do the second number and the next-to-last number. Moving toward the middle in this fashion, each successive pair of numbers adds up to 19.

18   Broken promise.

19   There are 23 triangles.

20   2^{73} is larger by a long way.

21   You are out of touch.

22   e. $\dfrac{1}{10\sqrt{10}}$

23   The chances are 1 in 5. The possibilities are:

Blue$_1$, Blue$_2$
Blue$_1$, Green
Blue$_1$, Yellow
Blue$_2$, Green
Blue$_2$, Yellow

24   Carrot juice (The symbol before "juice" is called a "caret.")

25   Yardstick

26   $16^2/_3$ lbs. Calculate the answer as follows:
$$(1)\ A + B = 50 \text{ lbs.}$$
$$\text{and } (2)\ \$8A + \$5B = 50 \times \$6$$

Then, multiply the first equation by −5, so:
$$-5A - 5B = -250$$

Next, combine with equation 2:
$$\$8A + \$5B = \$300$$
$$\underline{-5A - 5B = -250}$$
$$3A = 50$$
$$A = 16^2/_3 \text{ lbs.}$$

27 Your cup runneth over.

28 The correct answer is 20. Don't forget that the number 33 has two threes.

29 Place "end" at the beginning of each word:

endear

endless

endanger

30 The answer is 3.

$$\frac{3}{4} \times \frac{1}{2} \times 16 = \frac{48}{8} \quad = 6$$
$$\frac{1}{2} \times 6 = 3; 6 - 3 \quad = 3$$

31 It will take 63 moves. For any number of discs n, the number of moves can be found by using the formula $2^n - 1$.

32 Here's a list of 15 words. Are they anywhere near the words you came up with?

serve	vice	rice
ice	see	seer
veer	sieve	eve
rise	ever	sever
cerise	rive	verse

33 The last number is 625. Subtract each individual digit in the numbers from 10 to crack the code.

34 A single discount of 12 percent is greater.

$$12\% \times 100 = 12.00$$
then
$$6\% \times 100 = 6.00$$
$$100 - 6 = 94$$
$$6\% \times 94 = 5.64$$
$$6.00 + 5.64 = 11.64$$

12.00 is greater than 11.64

35 Traffic congestion.

36 The answer is zero!

37 YOU ARE A GENIUS. Move each of the letters in the puzzle back by three letters in the alphabet.

38 Draw a line from point 3 to point 12 and cut along the line to divide the figure. Turn the smaller figure upside down, then connect points 1 and 12 on the smaller figure with points 17 and 13, respectively, on the larger figure.

39 The next perfect number is 28 ($14 + 7 + 4 + 2 + 1 = 28$).

40 An upward turn in the economy.

41 False. Some pibs may be rews, but it is not definite.

42 Milepost 900. To solve this problem, recall that rate $\times$ time = distance. Let x be the time it takes the *Seneca Streamer* to reach the milepost. Then:

$$60 \text{ mph} \times (x + 3) = 75 \text{ mph} \times x$$
$$60x + 180 = 75x$$
$$15x = 180$$
$$x = 12 \text{ hrs.}$$
$$75 \times 12 = 900 \text{ mi.}$$

43 The first calculation is $\frac{1}{3} \times \frac{1}{3}$ of 12×12, or $\frac{1}{9}$ of 144, which equals 16. The second calculation is $(12 \div 3 \div 2)^3$, or $(\frac{4}{2})^3$, or 2 cubed, which is 8. The correct answer is the first calculation.

44 The cyclist can take 96 ($4 \times 8 \times 3$) different routes.

45 The correct answer is (d). To solve this, we need to find

$$\frac{\frac{3}{7}}{\frac{4}{9}}$$

Invert the denominator and multiply:

$$\frac{3}{7} \times \frac{9}{4} = \frac{27}{28}$$

46 Making up for lost time.

47 Because there are two sides to the coin, the chances are always one in two.

48 Place a decimal point between the two numbers to get 4.5.

49 The weight should be placed five feet from the fulcrum. First, calculate foot-pounds on the left side:

$$(5 \times 10) + (6 \times 5) = 80 \text{ ft.-lbs.}$$

The right side must equal the left side:

$$16x = 80$$
$$x = 5$$

50 The probability is 1 in 132,600.

$$\tfrac{1}{52} \times \tfrac{1}{51} \times \tfrac{1}{50} = \tfrac{1}{132,600}$$

51 It weighs approximately 1,700 pounds! One cubic foot of water weights 62.4 pounds; one cubic yard (27 cubic feet) of water weighs 1,684.8 pounds.

52 It must win 90 percent of the games. This is probably best expressed as follows: If a team wins 60 percent of one-third of the games, it is the same as winning 20 percent of all the games. Therefore,

$$20x + \tfrac{2}{3}x = 80x$$
$$\tfrac{2}{3}x = 60x$$
$$2x = 180$$
$$x = 90$$

53 There are 50 stars on the United States flag.

54 It would be 4. The best way to solve this is by setting up proportions:

$$\frac{\tfrac{1}{2} \times 24}{8} = \frac{\tfrac{1}{3} \times 18}{x}$$
$$\tfrac{12}{8} = \tfrac{6}{x}$$
$$12x = 48$$
$$x = 4$$

55 Here's one way to solve the puzzle:

PART
WART
WANT
WANE
WINE

56 Upper crust.

57 The answer is 1,234,321.

58 Six.

$$6m = b$$
$$8b = f$$
$$3f = y$$

We can find the number of bops in a yump by multiplying 8×3, or 24, and the number of murks in a yump by multiplying 24 times 6, or 144. So,

$$\frac{144 \text{ murks in a yump}}{24 \text{ bops in a yump}} = 6$$

59 Growing concern.

60 The missing number is 448. In each triangle, multiply A times B and subtract 2 to get C.

61 It is 27 cubic yards—divide the number of cubic feet by 27 to get cubic yards.

62 A pear costs $.05. Here's one way to solve the problem. Letting p = pears and r = oranges, we have

$$(1) \quad 3p + 4r = 0.39$$
$$(2) \quad 4p + 3r = 0.38$$

Multiply equation (1) by 3 and equation (2) by –4:

$$9p + 12r = 1.17$$
$$-16p - 12r = -1.52$$
$$-7p = -0.35$$

Now we can solve for p:

$$-7p = -.35$$
$$p = .05$$

63 227. In each column, divide the top number by 3 to get the bottom number. Then, add 3 to the sum of the top and bottom numbers to get the middle number.

64 $\frac{1}{2}$ or $-\frac{1}{2}$

$$\frac{1}{5} \times x \times 4 \times x = \frac{1}{5}$$
$$\frac{4x^2}{5} = \frac{1}{5}$$
$$4x^2 = 1$$
$$x^2 = \frac{1}{4}$$
$$x = \frac{1}{2} \text{ or } -\frac{1}{2}$$

65 Think of it this way: If the leader receives twice as much as each of the others, that's the same as having seven members all earning the same amount, which would be $175 each. If the leader earns twice as much, he or she would therefore receive $350 per gig.

66 The missing number is 3. The numbers correspond to letters on the telephone keypad or dial.

67 Double play.

68 Close encounters of the third kind.

69 You would say *birta farn*. Notice that the adjectives follow the nouns.

klar = red
fol = shine
birta = apples
pirt = bicycles
farn = big
obirts = often

70 The numbers are 61, 62, and 63. To solve this, let x be the first number; then $x + 1$ is the second number and $x + 2$ is the third number. An equation can be set up as follows:

$$x + (x + 2) = 124$$
$$2x + 2 = 124$$
$$2x = 122$$
$$x = 61$$

71 It equals 26. The midpoint between 20 and 32 is 26, and the midpoint between 16_a and 36_a is 26.

$$16_a = 20$$
Midpoint: $26_a + 26$
$$36_a = 32$$

72 Over and over again.

73 The word is "geometric."

74 Knock on wood.

75 There were 20 nickels and 20 dimes. To solve this, set up the following equations, where n = nickels and d = dimes:

$$n = d$$
$$.05n + .10d = 3.00$$
$$.05n + .10n = 3.00$$
$$.15n = 3.00$$
$$n = 20$$

76 $x = 5$, $y = 6$, and $z = 4$, so the sum is 15. The variable x can be either 0 or 5. It must be 5 because there is no number that ends in 0 when multiplied by 7 ($x \times 7$, resulting in x). Therefore, a 3 is carried over to the y. Since x is 5, y must be 6 because $7 \times 6 = 42$. Add the 3 that was carried over and you get 45. Therefore, z is 4.

77 It might be helpful to set up a grid as follows:

	BASKETBALL	FOOTBALL	BASEBALL
Alex	x		o
Ryan	o		
Steven	x	o	x

We can see that Ryan must like basketball since neither Alex nor Steven does. Steven does not like basketball or baseball, so he must like football, leaving Alex liking baseball.

78　Seven zips have the weight of 1 wob. The problem can be set up as follows:

$$26z = 4c + 2w$$
$$8z + 2c = 2w$$

Rearranging, we get

(1) $26z = 4c + 2w$

(2) $8z = -2c + 2w$

Multiply equation (2) by 2 so that the c factor drops out, and combine the two equations:

$$
\begin{aligned}
26z &= 4c + 2w \\
16z &= -4c + 4w \\
\hline
42z &= 6w \\
7z &= w
\end{aligned}
$$

79　Look before you leap.

80　The missing number is 10. The numbers in each circle add up to 50.

81　The answer is 96. Set up the following equations:

$$\tfrac{1}{2} \times \tfrac{2}{3} \times \tfrac{3}{5} = \tfrac{6}{30} = \tfrac{1}{5}$$
$$\tfrac{1}{5} \times 240 = 48$$
$$48 \div \tfrac{1}{2} = 96$$

82　It's the right thing to do.

83　The next letter is P. The differences between letters form the pattern 1, 2, 1, 2, 1, 2…

84　The answer is "three words."

85　Figure 4 is the only one that doesn't contain a triangle.

86　The lesser of two evils.

87　6.25 percent. Remember, length × width = area. Let l = length and w = width. Then

$$l + .25l = 1.25l$$
$$w - .25w = .75w$$
$$1.25l \times .75w = 93.75\%$$

Finally,

$$100\% - 93.75\% = 6.25\%$$

88　Here's one way to solve the puzzle:

TOOK
BOOK
BOON
BORN
BURN

89　It is impossible to average 60 miles per hour for this trip. At 30 miles per hour, the car would travel one mile in two minutes; at 60 miles per hour, the car would travel two miles in two minutes. So, in order to average 60 mph, the entire trip of two miles would have to be completed in two minutes. But the driver has already used two minutes going from point A to point B; there's not time left to get from point B to point C.

90　Five.

91　The chances are 1 in 3. Here are all the possible draws (C1 = first cherry gumdrop, C2 = second cherry gumdrop, O = orange gumdrop):

First draw	Second draw
C1	C2
C1	O
C2	C1
C2	O
O	C1
O	C2

Among the six possible draws, O appears twice in the second-draw column; thus, the chances are 2 in 6, or 1 in 3.

92　The "R" goes above the line. The letters above the line are closed with a space inside them.

93　Time slips into the future.

94　There are 100 years in a century.

95 Let x = the fraction. Then:

$$(3 \times {}^1\!/_4 x) \times x = {}^1\!/_{12}$$

$$^3\!/_4 x^2 = {}^1\!/_{12}$$

$$x^2 = {}^1\!/_9$$

$$x = {}^1\!/_3$$

96 Two miles. They are actually eating up the distance at 120 miles per hour (50 + 70 mph):

$$\frac{120 \text{ miles}}{60 \text{ minutes}} = \text{two miles in one minute}$$

97 Pocket full of money.

98 They can be combined in 12 different ways.

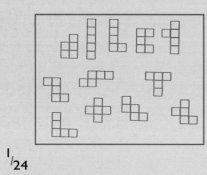

99 $^1\!/_{24}$

$$\frac{3}{32} - \frac{1}{16} = \frac{1}{32}$$

$$4 \times \left(\frac{1}{3} \times \frac{1}{32}\right) = \frac{4}{96} \text{ or } \frac{1}{24}$$

100 The letters "mot" will create the words "mother," "motion," "motor," "motif," and "motto."

101 The answer is (e). Remember, x may be a negative number.

102 He would have 20 pleezorns. Count the letters in each name and multiply by 2.

103 $.1 \times .9 \times .8 = .072$, or 7.2%.

104 The ratio is 1 to 2. One way to solve this problem is to set up an equation in which x equals the amount of $48 chemical used and y equals the amount of $36 chemical used:

$$48x + 36y = 40(x + y)$$
$$48x + 36y = 40x + 40y$$
$$8x = 4y$$
$$\frac{x}{y} = \frac{1}{2}$$

105 Line dance.

106 Traffic jam.

107 The ratio is 1 to 2. It might help to set up the problem as follows:

$$\frac{5x}{4y} = \frac{7}{8}$$

$$40x = 28y$$
$$10x = 7y$$

Thus, $10x$ to $7y$ is a 1-to-1 relationship. We are asked for the ratio of $10x$ to $14y$; since $14 = 7 \times 2$, we can see that it is a 1-to-2 relationship.

108 There are 31 triangles.

109 Don't count your chickens before they hatch.

110 Three-ring circus.

111 Here are 20 four-letter words:

twin	wine	lint	kiln
kilt	lent	wink	wilt
like	link	welt	kine
tine	tile	lien	newt
kite	line	went	wile

112 The answer is 13,222.

$$
\begin{array}{r}
12,000 \\
+1,222 \\
\hline
13,222
\end{array}
$$

113 JJ. The letters are the initial letters of pairs of month names, starting with October-November.

114 Forward thinking.

115 Draw a line as follows and you'll see the answer June:

116 Double-decker sandwich.

117 In the first case, 2^{67} is larger. In the second case, they are equal.

118 Microorganism.

119 There is one wheel on a unicycle.

120 Fifteen angles of less than 90 degrees can be formed.

121 Here they are:

$$\frac{1}{2} = \frac{6,729}{13,458}$$

$$\frac{1}{3} = \frac{5,832}{17,496}$$

$$\frac{1}{4} = \frac{4,392}{17,568}$$

$$\frac{1}{5} = \frac{2,769}{13,845}$$

$$\frac{1}{6} = \frac{2,943}{17,658}$$

$$\frac{1}{7} = \frac{2,394}{16,758}$$

$$\frac{1}{8} = \frac{3,187}{25,496}$$

$$\frac{1}{9} = \frac{6,381}{57,429}$$

122 *i* before *e* except after *c*.

123 The missing numbers are 18 and 5, respectively. There are actually two alternating series of numbers in this puzzle. Look at every other number, beginning first with 8 and then with 15.

124 The value of z must be 9 in all cases.

125 Pete has $^8/_{35}$ of the candy. After Joe takes $^3/_5$ of the candy, $^2/_5$ of the bag is left. If we let Pete's share be x and Bob's share be $^3/_{4}x$, we have:

$$x + {}^3/_4 x = {}^2/_5$$
$$^7/_4 x = {}^2/_5$$
$$x = {}^2/_5 \times {}^4/_7$$
$$x = {}^8/_{35}$$

126 F = 23. Substituting Eq. (1) in Eq. (2), gives us

$$A + B + P = T$$

And substituting Eq. (5) in this last equation gives us

$$8 + B + P = T \qquad (6)$$

If we then substitute Eq. (3) in Eq. (4), we get

$$B + P + T + A = 30$$

Substituting Eq. (5) in this last equation gives us

$$22 - B - P = T \qquad (7)$$

Adding Eqs. (6) and (7) gives us the following:

$$8 + B + P = T$$
$$\underline{22 - B - P = T}$$
$$30 = 2T$$
$$\text{So, } T = 15 \qquad (8)$$

Substituting Eqs. (5) and (8) in Eq. (3) gives us

$$F = 15 + 8 = 23$$

127 SER.

128 The order should be 4, 1, 3, 5, 2.

129 One possible answer:

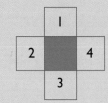

130 1) CAGI
2)

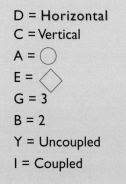

The breakdown of the relationships:

D = Horizontal
C = Vertical
A = ◯
E = ◇
G = 3
B = 2
Y = Uncoupled
I = Coupled

131 Getting it all together.

132 168. The pattern behind this sequence can be revealed by factoring the individual terms:

$$5 = 2^2 + 1$$
$$8 = 3^2 - 1$$
$$26 = 5^2 + 1$$
$$48 = 7^2 - 1$$
$$122 = 11^2 + 1$$

This shows that the squares of the prime numbers are involved. So the next term in the sequence must be 168:

$$13^2 = 169$$
$$169 - 1 = 168$$

133 Bleary. Take the last three letters of each pair of words to form the new words.

134 MCDXLIX.

135 It should be placed 16 ft. to the right of the fulcrum.

Left side: Currently there are a total of 20 ft × 40 lb + 10 ft × 20 lb = 800 + 200 = 1,000 ft-lb.

Right side: Currently there are 10 ft × 60 lb. = 600 ft-lb. Since this is less than what's on the left side, the 25-lb weight must go somewhere on the right side. Let's call the exact distance from the fulcrum y:

$$10 \times 60 + 25y = 1,000$$
$$25y = 400$$
$$y = 400/25 = 16 \text{ ft}$$

136 A bad spell of flu.

137 $1\frac{1}{2}$

138 21%. If you were to pick a student at random, the probability that he or she was taking at least one of the courses is 64% + 22% − 7% = 79%, which means there is a 21% chance that the student was taking neither course.

139 A = 1, B = 3, C = 2. We can arrive at the answer via a plan of attack that examines the rules one at a time to chart the possibilities:

Rule (a): This tells us too little at this point.

Rule (b): This raises two clear possibilities:

(1) B = 2, A = 3, C = 1
or
(2) B = 1, A = 3, C = 2

Let's assume one of these is correct and look at the next two rules.

Rule (c): This eliminates possibility (1).

Rule (d): This eliminates possibility (2). But what if C = 3 while B = 1 or 2? That raises the following two possibilities:

(3) B = 2, A = 1, C = 3
or
(4) B = 1, A = 2, C = 3

Rule (e): This eliminates possibilities (3) and (4). Thus, B is not 1 or 2 and so it must be 3.

Rule (f): If B = 3, then A, not being 2, must be 1. And C, therefore, must be 2.

140 "All Things Great and Small."

141 Here's one way:

TIMER
TIMES
DIMES
DINES
DUNES
DUNKS

142 There are six outs in an inning.

143 The glass is $5/16$ empty. $5/8$ is equal to $10/16$, which means that if the glass were $10/16$ full, you would have emptied $6/16$ of it. You empty $5/16$ of the glass first.

144 125. 5 is 25 times $1/5$; likewise, 125 is 25 times 5.

MOVIES & TELEVISION

1 Huey, Dewey, and Louie. [100%]

2 *The Daily Planet.* [97.5%]

3 Captain Kangaroo. [95%]

4 Green. [87.5%]

5 The Teletubbies. [85%]

6 *Home Improvement.* [80%]

7 c) Ed Bradley. [80%]

8 *Love Story.* [77.5%]

9 Jack Benny. [75%]

10 Suzanne Pleshette. [75%]

11 Clint Eastwood. [75%]

12 Jean-Claude Van Damme. [72.5%]

13 Cosmo. [72.5%]

14 *M*A*S*H.* [72.5%]

15 *Happy Days.* [72.5%]

16 Shirley MacLaine. [72.5%]

17 Jerry Springer. [70%]

18 Susan Sarandon. [70%]

19 Florida. [70%]

20 Richard Kimble. [67.5%]

21 Geraldine Jones. [67.5%]

22 Helen Hunt. [67.5%]

23 *Heidi.* [67.5%]

24 *Steamboat Willie.* [65%]

25 Grape Nehi. [65%]

26 Sean Connery. [65%]

27 Cary Grant. [65%]

28 Greg, Marcia, Peter, Jan, Bobby, Cindy. [62.5%]

29 Woody Allen. [60%]

30 Carlton. [60%]

31 Blythe Danner. [57.5%]

32 *The Godfather Part II.* [57.5%]

33 Vera. [55%]

34 MacGillicuddy. [55%]

35 Sensurround. [55%]

36 b) Annette Bening. [55%]

37 General Lee. [52.5%]

38 Marcel Marceau. [52.5%]

39 *Lou Grant*, *Phyllis*, and *Rhoda*. [52.5%]

40 Ken Burns. [52.5%]

41 Robert Redford. [52.5%]

42 *Bull Durham.* [52.5%]

43 Fred Grandy. [50%]

44 Jake and Elwood. [50%]

45 Garry Trudeau. [47.5%]

46 Michael Jackson. [47.5%]

47 Kim Basinger. [47.5%]

MUSIC, ARTS & LETTERS

48 Capulet and Montague. [92.5%]

49 Nevermore. [90%]

50 88. [90%]

51 Chattanooga Choo-Choo. [87.5%]

52 *The Merchant of Venice.* [80%]

53 Quasimodo. [75%]

54 Plié. [75%]

55 "All the News That's Fit to Print." [70%]

56 Bob Dylan. [67.5%]

57 London and Paris. [67.5%]

58 Michael Crichton. [67.5%]

59 Buddy Holly, Ritchie Valens, and the Big Bopper (J.P. Richardson). [65%]

60 Leviticus. [65%]

61 Baroque. [65%]

62 Maya Angelou. [62.5%]

63 Elton John. [62.5%]

64 The Spanish Civil War. [62.5%]

65 a) *The Catcher in the Rye* by J.D. Salinger. [62.5%]

66 *Uncle Tom's Cabin.* [60%]

67 Stephen King. [60%]

68 *Cabaret.* [60%]

69 *The Mousetrap* by Agatha Christie. [57.5%]

70 *Cats.* [52.5%]

71 17. [52.5%]

72 Eagle and lion. [52.5%]

73 Frank Zappa. [52.5%]

74 Alaska, Hawaii, and Texas. [50%]

75 Claude Monet. [50%]

76 Jim Morrison. [50%]

77 Grant Wood. [50%]

78 Princess Diana. [47.5%]

79 Polly. [47.5%]

80 Milli Vanilli. [47.5%]

81 Sisyphus. [47.5%]

82 Pointillism. [47.5%]

83 Coventry, England. [42.5%]

84 *Mad.* [42.5%]

85 R.L. Stine. [42.5%]

86 *The Time Machine* by H.G. Wells. [42.5%]

87 Dashiell Hammett. [42.5%]

88 Florence, Italy. [42.5%]

89 William Faulkner. [40%]

90 Baby, Posh, Scary, and Sporty. [40%]

91 José Carreras. [40%]

92 *La Bohème.* [37.5%]

93 Emma. [35%]

94 *The Firm* by John Grisham. [35%]

95 Ian Fleming. [35%]

96 *The Unfinished Symphony.* [35%]

97 *Frankenstein.* [35%]

98 Napoleon. [32.5%]

99 Bob Woodward. [32.5%]

100 Leo Tolstoy. [32.5%]

101 Isadora Duncan. [32.5%]

102 Lincoln Center. [32.5%]

103 *La Gioconda.* [30%]

104 Grover's Corners. [30%]

105 Kurt Vonnegut Jr. [30%]

106 Modest Mussorgsky. [30%]

107 221B Baker Street. [27.5%]

108 John. [27.5%]

109 *Damn Yankees*. [27.5%]

110 Goneril, Regan, and Cordelia. [27.5%]

TRAVEL & GEOGRAPHY

111 Annapolis, Maryland. [90%]

112 Australia. [90%]

113 Nova Scotia. [90%]

114 Punxsutawney. [85%]

115 Instanbul, Turkey. [85%]

116 Denver. [85%]

117 Minnesota. [82.5%]

118 Deutschland. [82.5%]

119 Oahu. [77.5%]

120 Oxford. [77.5%]

121 Mount Kilimanjaro. [75%]

122 Gibraltar. [75%]

123 Gobi. [72.5%]

124 Colorado. [72.5%]

125 Mecca, Saudi Arabia. [72.5%]

126 Tropic of Capricorn. [72.5%]

127 Israel. [70%]

128 Utah. [67.5%]

129 K2. [67.5%]

130 Colorado. [67.5%]

131 Paris. [67.5%]

132 Arizona, Colorado, New Mexico, and Utah. [65%]

133 Topeka. [65%]

134 New Hampshire. [62.5%]

135 Wyoming. [62.5%]

136 Dominican Republic and Haiti. [62.5%]

137 Switzerland. [62.5%]

138 Montana. [60%]

HISTORY & SCIENCE

139 Laughing gas. [100%]

140 Stonehenge. [92.5%]

141 24. [87.5%]

142 Ash Wednesday. [87.5%]

143 Self-contained underwater breathing apparatus. [85%]

144 Pegasus. [85%]

145 Vitamin C. [85%]

146 Dwight D. Eisenhower. [85%]

147 Socks. [85%]

148 Mushrooms. [85%]

149 Lead. [82.5%]

150 *Enola Gay*. [82.5%]

151 Hollandaise sauce. [80%]

152 Tuberculosis. [80%]

153 Blood pressure. [75%]

154 Erwin Rommel. [75%]

155 Esperanto. [75%]

156 Andrew Johnson. [75%]

157 *Beagle*. [75%]

158 Rosh Hashanah. [72.5%]

159 Alfred Nobel. [72.5%]

160 The CIA. [72.5%]

161 George Washington, Thomas Jefferson, Abraham Lincoln, and Theodore Roosevelt. [70%]

162 Polaris. [70%]

163 1600 Pennsylvania Avenue. [67.5%]

164 Joseph Smith. [67.5%]

165 d) Arizona. [67.5%]

166 Dry ice. [67.5%]

167 July 14. [65%]

168 Sinn Fein. [65%]

169 1863. [62.5%]

170 Thor Heyerdahl. [62.5%]

171 Teapot Dome. [62.5%]

172 John Adams and Thomas Jefferson. [62.5%]

173 Ulysses S. Grant. [60%]

174 Jehovah's Witnesses. [60%]

175 Femur. [60%]

176 George S. Patton. [60%]

177 Sedimentary. [60%]

178 Diamond. [57.5%]

179 Breed's Hill. [57.5%]

180 i [55%]

181 Treasury Department. [55%]

182 Nikkei. [55%]

183 d) Aaron Burr. [55%]

184 Johnson (Richard, Andrew, and Lyndon). [52.5%]

185 Whig. [52.5%]

186 Sparta. [50%]

187 30. [50%]

188 Ramadan. [47.5%]

189 Thomas Jefferson. [47.5%]

190 Igor Sikorsky. [47.5%]

LAZY DAYS OF SUMMER

The 24 four-digit numbers that can be formed using the digits 1, 2, 3, and 4 sum to 66,660.

To obtain this sum without adding up the 24 numbers, note that each column of the sum involves six 1's, six 2's, six 3's, and six 4's. The sum of these 24 digits in each column is 6 × (1 + 2 + 3 + 4) = 6 × 10 = 60. Therefore, to obtain the sum in question, you line up the 60's in each of the four columns and add:

```
      60
      60
      60
      60
  _____
  66,660
```

PIECES OF EIGHT

The length of a side of a smaller cube is four units, or one-half the side of the big cube.

SOMETHING IS MISSING

3	11	21	41	91
6	14	15	23	53
3	5	6	8	12

The third row is obtained by adding together the numbers in the first two rows and then taking the square root. (3 is the square root of 3 + 6 = 9; similarly, 5 is the square root of 11 + 14 = 25, etc.) The missing number is therefore 12, because 91 + 53 = 144, and 12 is the square root of 144.

SEEING SPOTS

Three spots are in the center—one each for the 1, 3, and 5 faces. Sixteen spots are in the corners—for the 2 (two), 3 (two), 4 (four), 5 (four), and 6 (four) faces. That leaves two spots for the sides, and both of these are found on the 6 face.

FILL IN THE BLANKS

12 ÷ 2 + 7 − 4 = 9

HOW FAR?

To prove that a given number is prime, you only need to check as far as the largest prime number less than the number's square root. Why? Because in any pair of factors for the number, one factor will be greater than the square root and the other factor will be less. (If the number is a perfect square, then it will have two factors that equal one another, but we're not going to waste our time showing that a perfect square isn't prime!) The point is that if you haven't come across a factor by the time you reach the square root, you never will. In the case of 907, the largest whole number less than the square root of 907 is 30, and so the largest prime you need to consider is 29.

ON ALL FOURS

148. To arrive at this answer, simply start dividing a string of 4's by 3 until you get no remainder.

When you start dividing, you see that 3 goes into 4 once, with a remainder of 1. Bring down a 4, making 14. Then 3 goes into 14 four times, with a remainder of 2. Bring down another 4, making 24. 3 goes into 24 precisely 8 times, so 444 divided by 3 equals 148.

DON'T LEAVE ME OUT

If Jerry was not on the starting team, he would be one of two players who were left out. There are six others overall, and each of these six could be paired with Jerry to sit out, so there are six teams that do *not* include Jerry as a starter. Because there are 21 possible teams in all, Jerry must be a starter on 21 − 6 = 15 of those teams.

Where does the 21 come from? It comes up because $21 = \frac{7!}{(5!)(2!)}$, where $n!$ equals the product of all whole numbers from 1 to n inclusive. The idea is that when choosing a team, you have 7 choices for the first player, 6 choices for the second player, and so on, down to 3 choices for the fifth player. But because the order in which you selected the team doesn't matter, you have to divide by the total number of ways of arranging the five players, which is 5!. (In other words, the team you got by choosing Alex, Brian, Clifford, Dave, and Elmer is the same as the team you would have gotten by choosing Dave, Brian, Elmer, Alex, and Clifford.)

SO FAR, YET SO CLOSE

The plus sign has been changed to a 4!

5 + 5 4 5 = 550

WAGERING ABOVEBOARD

If the second man has a net gain of three dollars but lost three games in the process, then overall he must have won six games and lost three. Since there were no draws, a total of nine games were played.

ALL IN THE NEIGHBORHOOD

Sarah will be four times as old in just five days. Sarah is always 24 days older than Melanie. To be four times as old as Melanie, this difference of 24 days must be three times Melanie's age. Since

$^{24}/_3 = 8$, when Melanie is 8 days old, Sarah will be four times older at 32 days. Since Melanie will be 8 days old in five days, the answer is five days from today.

THROUGH THE LOOKING GLASS

There are many, many palindrome years you could use for this problem. Here are a few examples:

A) 110 years apart — 1771 and 1881

B) 11 years apart — 1991 and 2002

C) 10 years apart — 575 and 585

D) 2 years apart — 99 and 101

HEAD START

Let P equal the probability that Chris will win the game. To compute P, we start by noting that obviously the game is over if Chris flips "heads" on the first try, and that will happen with probability $^1/_2$.

If Chris flips "tails" (probability $^1/_2$) there is also a probability of $^1/_2$ that Jean will flip "tails," in which case the game would return to how it was at the beginning. The combined probability of Chris and Jean flipping "tails" equals $^1/_4$. The equation that expresses all of the above is that P = $^1/_2$ + $^1/_4$(P).

Solving the equation yields $(^3/_4)$P = $^1/_2$, so P = $^2/_3$.

For another method, note that the probability is $^1/_2$ that Chris will win immediately. But if that doesn't happen, Jean is in the same position that Chris was in originally, so her chance of winning is precisely $^1/_2$ of his chance. Since the two probabilities must add to 1, the only possible solution is that Chris's probability of winning is $^2/_3$ and Jean's chance is $^1/_3$.

PLAYING THE TRIANGLE

The third side must have length 17. The only other choice is that the length of the third side is 8 (remember, the triangle is isosceles, so two sides have the same length). However, a length of 8 is impossible, because if two sides of a triangle were both 8, they could never reach the third side (length 17), even if laid end to end! (In general, the sum of any two sides of a triangle must be greater than the third side. This principle is called the "triangle inequality.")

FULL OF HOT AIR

The red balloon was the highest. Using algebra, our equations are as follows:

$$R + B = 140$$
$$B + Y = 135$$
$$R + Y = 155$$

A neat way to solve symmetrical equations like this is to add all three together. Here, we get:

$$2R + 2Y + 2B = 430, \text{ so}$$
$$R + Y + B = 215.$$

Now that we have the sum of the three heights, we can simply subtract each of the three original equations from it in turn to find the individual values. We get $R = 80$, $Y = 75$, and $B = 60$.

MY THREE SONS

The equation is $x + (x + 3) + (x + 6) = 57$, where x is the age of the youngest son. This simplifies to $3x = 48$, so $x = 16$. The sons are therefore 16, 19, and 22 years old.

Alternatively, the man's age must be three times the age of the middle son, because the other sons are spaced equally to either side. The middle son is therefore $^{57}/_3 = 19$ years of age.

THE A&P

If L and W are the length and width of the rectangle, then we can solve as follows, using a neat factoring trick:

$$LW = 2L + 2W$$
$$LW - 2L - 2W = 0$$
$$LW - 2L - 2W + 4 = 4$$
$$(L - 2)(W - 2) = 4$$

Since L and W are whole numbers, we can match $(L - 2)$ and $(W - 2)$ with factors of 4. Since 4 factors as both 4×1 and 2×2, we get two solutions:

$L - 2 = 4$ and $W - 2 = 1$ (so $L = 6$ and $W = 3$) or
$L - 2 = 2$ and $W - 2 = 2$ (so $L = 4$ and $W = 4$)

There are two solutions: a 4×4 square or a 6×3 rectangle.

MISSED ONE!

The only decade of the 20th century that lacks a multiple of 11 is the 1970s. The key step is to notice that the only way a decade could lack a multiple of 11 is for the first year of the following decade to be a multiple of 11, which reduces to examining the numbers from 191 through 200 (the final zero doesn't contribute to a number's divisibility by 11). The only multiple of 11 among this group is 198—note that the outer two digits add up to the middle digit, which is characteristic of certain multiples of 11. Therefore the decade prior to 1980 is the one we want.

SIX-SHOOTER

The only way that a number can be divisible by 6 is if it is divisible by both 2 and 3. Note that $n(n + 1)(2n + 1)$ is always divisible by 2, because either n or $n + 1$ must be even. As for divisibility by 3, if n leaves a remainder of 2 upon division by 3, then $n + 1$ must be divisible by 3. And if n leaves a remainder of 1 upon division by 3 (the only other possibility), then $2n + 1$ must be divisible by 3. Any way you slice it, $n(n + 1)(2n + 1)$ is divisible by 2 and 3, and therefore by 6.

By the way, $\frac{n(n+1)(2n+1)}{6}$ equals the sum of the *squares* of the first n whole numbers, so it's always a whole number!

LOOK BEFORE YOU LEAP

The area of the rectangle is increased by 300 percent. Note that an increase of 100 percent for a side of the rectangle is the same as doubling it. Doubling both sides multiplies the area by four. And multiplying a number by four is the same as increasing it by 300 percent—not 400 percent!

STRANGE SEQUENCE

The last number in the sequence is 5. The rule for the sequence is that each number is the position in the alphabet of the letters in the word SEQUENCE. S is the 19th letter, E is the 5th letter, Q is the 17th letter, and so on.

SMALL BUT POWERFUL

If a number is both a perfect square and a perfect cube, then it is a perfect sixth power. The next sixth power after $1^6 = 1$ is $2^6 = 64$, which is both 8^2 and 4^3. The next sixth power is $3^6 = 729$, which is both 27^2 and 9^3.

BE PERFECTLY FRANK

Five hot dogs (intermission) plus four hot dogs (left over) equals just one-eighth of his original supply, because we know that a total of seven-eighths was sold during the game itself. That means the vendor must have started the soccer game with $9 \times 8 = 72$ hot dogs.

MAKING THE GRADE

In order for everything to work out in whole numbers, we must have 24 students in the class, because 24 is the only common multiple of 3, 4, 6, and 8 that is less than 30. Adding the fractions gives us $1/3 + 1/4 + 1/6 + 1/8 = {}^{8+6+4+3}/_{24} = {}^{21}/_{24}$, so 21 students have been accounted for with grades "B" or lower. That means 3 students must have received an "A" on the test.

Page 53   The straight is more probable. To select the four of a kind, you need to select "one card out of five cards" four times: $\frac{1}{5} \times \frac{1}{5} \times \frac{1}{5} \times \frac{1}{5}$, or 1 out of 625.

For the straight, the first card can be any card. Then, you'll need to select "one card out of five cards" three times: $\frac{1}{5} \times \frac{1}{5} \times \frac{1}{5}$, or 1 out of 125—a better probability.

Page 54   The sun would now appear to rise in the west and set in the east. This change is caused by the switch in rotation spin. The switch in revolution does not affect the direction of the apparent sunrise or sunset.

Page 55   Twenty balls arranged in four levels.

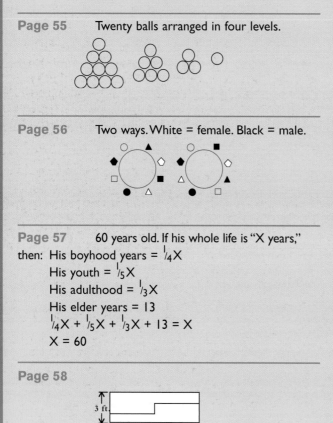

Page 56   Two ways. White = female. Black = male.

Page 57   60 years old. If his whole life is "X years," then: His boyhood years = $\frac{1}{4}X$

His youth = $\frac{1}{5}X$

His adulthood = $\frac{1}{3}X$

His elder years = 13

$\frac{1}{4}X + \frac{1}{5}X + \frac{1}{3}X + 13 = X$

X = 60

Page 58

Page 59   Although all four dice have the same relative orientation of spots, the three spots on the last die tilt from the lower left corner to the upper right corner.

When the other dice are rotated to this position, their three spots tilt from the upper left to the lower right corner.

Page 60   Anthony. The actual period is 1 second less than the time given. Emily completes ten clicks in 9 seconds. Buzzy completes twenty clicks in 19 seconds. Anthony completes five clicks in 4 seconds. This gives us the approximate rates: Emily = 1.1 clicks/second, Buzzy = 1.05 clicks/second, Anthony = 1.25 clicks/second.

Page 61   X=22; Y=25. Each circle equals 1, each square equals 5, each triangle equals 10, and the pentagon equals 2. The numbers represent the sums of the values in each row or column.

Page 66   The threads of screw A form a spiral that would "go into" the wood block. In contrast, the opposite spiral of screw B would result in this screw moving out of the wooden block.

Page 67   150 miles long. In order to complete 30 miles of distance, the faster cyclist requires 1 hour of time while the slower cyclist needs 1.20 hours. Therefore, the time difference per 30 miles of travel is .20 hours. In order to increase the difference to 1 hour, multiply the 30 miles by 5.

Page 68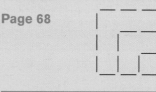

Page 69   The computer weighs 16 pounds and its monitor weighs 32 pounds.

Page 70 Forty-eight gumballs. Since two guesses were off by seven and no guesses were repeated, these values had to refer to numbers at the opposite extremes of the spread. The two extremes are 41 and 55. If you add 7 to one and take 7 away from the other, you arrive at the middle number of 48.

Page 71

Page 72 First you'll need to find out what each section needs to add up to. To get this number, add up every number on the clock's face (1 + 2 + 3 + 4 + 5 + 6 + 7 + 8 + 9 + 10 + 11 + 12 = 78). Divide 78 by 3 and you'll get 26—the sum that each section must add to. The next part is relatively easy, since the numbers are already laid out in a ready-to-add pattern.

Page 73 The direction of the look is based upon the number of neighboring eyes that are in contact with the eye's circumference. Eyes that "touch" three other circles (such as the circle in question) have a pupil that points to the right.
b.

Page 74 Thirteen squares.

Page 75 No. Six cuts are the fewest needed to produce the twenty-seven smaller cubes. Stacking doesn't result in fewer cuts. Think of it this way: the innermost cube of the twenty-seven must be formed by a cut on each of its six sides.

Page 76

Page 77 Since the four wheels share the journey equally, simply divide 50,000 by four and you'll get 12,500 miles per tire.

Page 90 1. There are ten possible combinations: BBGGG, BGBGG, BGGBG, BGGGB, GBBGG, GBGBG, GBGGB, GGBBG, GGBGB, GGGBB.

   2. The chances of two boys being on the ends are 1 in 10.

   3. The chances of two girls being on the ends are 3 in 10.

Page 91 Although this type of problem is perfect for algebra, let's do it visually. If all of the thirty heads belonged to two-legged birds, then there'd be only sixty legs. If one of the animals has four legs, then there'd be sixty-two legs. If two animals are four-legged, there'd be sixty-four legs.

   By continuing in this pattern until we reach seventy legs, we will get a combination of twenty-five birds and five lizards.

Page 92

Page 93 Nine centimeters. One basic pattern is illustrated below. Although there are other turns, they cover the same total length.

Page 94 Five girls and two boys. First, subtract the coach's 9 cups from the total amount. Therefore, the boys and the girls together drank 34 cups. The winning combination is five girls (who together drink 20 cups) and two boys (who together drink 14 cups). 20 + 14 = 34 cups.

Page 95 The symbols are the mirror images of the numbers 1 to 4 rotated on their side. The next image is a 5, modified in the same way.

Page 96 The trick to this challenge is that the line can go out of the grid. Otherwise, it is impossible to complete.

Page 97 Position the mirrors so that they are arranged like an opened book. The right side of your face will reflect on the right side of the mirror. This image does not reflect back to that eye. Instead, it bounces to the other mirror. From there, the image is reflected back to the other eye.

Page 98 Nine pounds. Examine the objects on the right side of the balance. If we looked at the balance pan containing the two bars, we'd see that one-tenth of the gold bar is absent. In its place we have nine-tenths of a pound. From this we can infer that one-tenth of a gold bar weighs nine-tenths of a pound. Therefore, a complete gold bar would weigh ten times as much. 9/10 pound × 10 = 90/10, or 9 pounds.

Page 99 Two arrows struck the 8 region (16 points) and seven of them struck the 12 region (84 points). Total: 16 + 84 = 100 points.

Page 100 They can never cast shadows of equal size. Any difference in their altitude would be negligible compared with their distance to the sun. It's those 93,000,000 miles from our planet to the sun that affect the shadows' size much more than their puny distances apart.

Page 101 At that time of day, the shadow is two-fifths of the object's height. If the tree's shadow (two-fifths of the unknown height) is 25 feet, then the height of the tree is $62\frac{1}{2}$ feet.

Page 136 120 pounds. If she needs to add "half of her weight" to get her full weight, then the weight that she does tell (60 pounds) must be half of her total. Therefore, 60 pounds is half of her weight. 60 + 60 = 120 pounds. If this doesn't seem right, just work it backwards starting with the 120 pounds.

Page 137 Make three cuts that divide the cube into eight smaller but equal cubes. Each of these eight cubes has a side length of 1 inch to produce a surface area of 6 square inches. The sum of the eight cube surface areas is 48 square inches.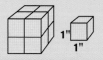

Page 138 The number of beetles captured on each successive night were 8, 14, 20, 26, and 32.

Page 139 The trains will be tied 3 hours after the faster train (or $4\frac{1}{2}$ hours after the slower train) begins the race. For example, if the trains travel 60 mph and 90 mph, the $4\frac{1}{2}$-hour journey for the slower train covers 270 miles, while the 3-hour journey for the faster train also covers 270 miles.

Page 140 Young Ed. The car that travels along the curved slope accelerates faster. This extra speed results from the quick drop in the path that allows the car to quickly pick up speed. The car moving down the straight slope accelerates at a slower and more uniform rate.

Page 141 The level of water will not change. Although the top of the cube floats above the surface of the water, the amount of water in the entire ice cube can fill a space equal to the dimensions occupied by the part of the cube that is under the water's surface. In other words, as the ice cube turns to water, it produces the same amount of water as the space occupied by the submerged part of the cube.

Page 142

Page 143

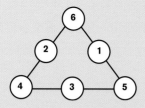

Page 144 Both the crate and the chimp go up.

Page 145 It doesn't matter which mountain you climb. All three paths will be the same length. The length of the path is not determined by the shape of the mountain but the slope of the road.

  Since all three mountain paths have the same slope, you'd have to walk the same distance in order to climb each 10,000-foot summit.

Page 146 This is simpler than it may seem. Since the mold doubles in size every day, it covered half as much area one day before!

Page 147 White. The bear must be a polar bear. To conform to the given pattern, the hiker must begin the trek at the North Pole.

Page 148 There are several ways to divide the juice. Here's one of the quickest:

Vessel size (oz.)	24	13	11	5
To start	24	0	0	0
First	8	0	11	5
Second	8	13	3	0
Third	8	8	3	5
Fourth	8	8	8	0

Page 149 There are a total of 27 cubes. There are six cubes with one grey side, twelve cubes with two grey sides, eight cubes with three grey sides, and one cube with no grey sides.

Agent Brown's Shining Moment

When Agent Brown got into the Cadillac, he had to adjust the rearview mirror. This meant that the previous driver had been significantly different in height. Since the shorter mobster was close to Brown's own height, he knew the taller man had to be the driver. Therefore, the shorter man was the shooter.

Super Bowl Madness

The poison couldn't have been in the communal snack food. It must have been in the victim's drink. But Sonny tasted his father's highball right before the game and showed no ill effects.

The only possibility left was the ice. Marie had added poisoned ice cubes to her husband's glass. The fast-acting poison melted as he drank, killing him almost a half-hour after his wife had mixed the deadly highball. While Vince lay gasping for air, his wife was in the kitchen, cleaning the glass of any telltale residue.

Death of a Deceiver

The naked body on the autopsy table held the pivotal clue. On Jerry Fisher's ring finger was a tan line, just where his wedding ring had been.

Lieutenant Miller pointed it out. "When Jerry went over to Gail's apartment, he naturally removed his wedding ring. Unfortunately, he forgot about the tan line. It's winter here, so he never had to deal with this problem before. There's no way Gail could have spent the afternoon with him and not noticed that line."

His partner nodded. "Let's go back and talk to Ms. Lowenski."

The Party's Over

The captain noticed that Fernando's balloons had been on the lawn, indicating that they had been blown up with regular air, not helium. And yet, on a windless day, there was one balloon stuck high in a tree. The captain could only conclude that Fernando had planted it there. When Fernando climbed the tree and glanced over the fence, he saw no evidence of a robbery. He actually committed the crime later, while his friend went down the street to place the 911 call.

The Smuggler and the Clever Wife

The guard's wife caught the one discrepancy no one else did. The Mercedes woman had used a different-colored car, not black this time, but dark blue. Could the woman be driving a different car on each trip across the border? It was worth checking out.

Late that same afternoon, when passport control stopped the woman from re-entering the U.S., they found her dressed much more casually. They also found her taking the bus. It was so simple that no one had seen it. The woman was smuggling cars—a whole fleet of stolen Mercedes.

The Suicidal House Guest

When Officer Warren counted off all the electronic or battery-powered devices, the one that he did not find was a T.V. remote control. It would have been impossible for a bedridden man to operate a ceiling-mounted T.V. without a remote control.

The last person claiming to see the victim alive was Dr. Yancy. Officer Warren theorized that the doctor killed his uncle before exiting the bedroom. He then took the remote control, left the house, and sneaked around to Uncle Ben's window. By using the remote from outside the locked window, Dr. Yancy was able to give the impression that Uncle Ben was still alive.

Long-Distance Murder

The homicide captain was struck by the fact that the study extension phone held no fingerprints, even though the victim had used the instrument just minutes before. The only reason the killer would wipe off the telephone was if he or she had used it. This led to the arrest of Jim and Melba Cord.

Jim Cord wasn't at home 30 miles away. He was right inside the family mansion, strangling his father. When his wife shouted for him to pick up the phone, Jim heard her voice over the nurse's speakerphone. He picked up the extension in the mansion study, thereby establishing his alibi. Afterwards, he wiped off the phone and left by the French doors, the same way he'd entered.

The Queen Glendora Photos

The row of scalloped cuts on the empty envelope indicated a pair of nail scissors. Since the thief cut open the envelope before leaving the office building, this clue pointed to the only person to carry such scissors as part of her regular equipment: the manicurist.

Dodo was arrested along with her boyfriend Bart, who had arranged the sale to True Gossip Monthly.

The Dirty Cop

Officer Brady had observed his suspects well. Marjorie, for example, was right-handed, as indicated by the watch on her left wrist. Adam's use of his right hand to zip up his trousers indicated the same thing. On the other hand—literally—was Charlie Salt, who had been writing with his left.

Since a left-handed person naturally tears off matches from the left side of a matchbook, Officer Brady knew that Charlie was his dirty cop.

The Stolen Cleopatra

The fact that both men wanted to be searched meant that the thief no longer had the coin on him. Since neither man had left the Marsh premises after the theft, the coin must still be there, hidden somewhere.

The patrolman noticed that the plants had not been watered. He also noticed that the potted plant was leaning toward the darkened living room instead of the sunny kitchen windows. Since plants naturally lean toward sunlight, the patrolman knew that someone had recently moved it. Sure enough, the ancient coin was hidden under the pot. The patrolman took Kenny Johnson in for questioning.

In Kenny's statement, he said that Digby was holding the coin after leaving the house. This was obviously a lie.

Archie's Christmas Surprise

Gene Granger supposedly did not hear about the suicide until he arrived on the nineteenth floor. And yet, when Granger unlocked the door to his conference room, there was no Christmas present waiting under the tree for Archie. Granger had personally selected presents for all of his employees—all except the man he killed, the man he knew would be dead. There was no other way to explain the oversight.

Hank notified the police, who soon uncovered Granger's massive embezzlement.

Postgraduate Murder

The noise that Glen heard out back supports Sonny's story of coming home a few minutes before the murder and tripping over something. The torn-out extension cord and the bent prong also support Sonny's story. But, if Sonny's fall pulled the cord out of the outlet, then Bill Mayer would have found himself suddenly in the dark.

Why didn't Bill mention the failure of his work light?

Simple—he didn't know about it. At that moment, he was already sneaking upstairs, intent on shooting Harry Harris, the friend who had seduced his girl.

The Last Poker Hand

Had Bugsy, with his dying efforts, been trying to identify his attacker? If his killer had been the Reverend King, he might have picked a king from the scattered cards. Holding a jack would have fingered Jack Lawrence. Any spade would have identified Alan Spade. And all the dying man had to do to identify Joseph Blush was to grab the empty bottle of Blush gin. Instead of any of these clues, however, the victim was holding five diamonds, otherwise known as a flush.

When Jack Lawrence mentioned the other players, he got one name wrong. Instantly, the sergeant knew the truth. Jack had killed Bugsy, then placed the cards in his hand, hoping to frame the man he had mistakenly known as "Joe Flush."

Eye Spy

It's a cold winter's day, and Lu Ching's apartment is almost as chilly. So, why is the desk fan whirling? And in an empty apartment?

Julia turned off the fan and found the eight negatives. They were taped to the four fan blades, one on each side of each blade. The speed of the fan's rotation had rendered them invisible to the naked eye.

The Piney Bluffers

Although two of the stories may sound suspicious, they are really perfectly plausible. Al Fishburn's story, however, contained a definite falsehood. Al said that he and his partner had set up their tent in the morning. And yet, the ground inside the tent was wet, indicating that they had set it up either during the rainstorm or after. The officer detained them for further questioning.

The Vandalizing Visitor

The officer was struck by the fact that the second suspect, Mr. Brier, had used a pay phone to call his room instead of one of the courtesy phones. When a service technician from the telephone company opened the phone's coin box, he found a rare old quarter. Mr. Brier had stolen the quarter from the display case. Using the pay phone was the only way he could think of to get rid of the incriminating coin.

An Attack of Gas

The dead flies on the windowsill were solid evidence that Gerald Espy's room had been gassed after sunrise. If it had been done during the dark of night, the flies would not have congregated by the light of the east-facing window.

Only one of the suspects has a morning alibi—Frank Townly, who had been locked inside the tavern. That means it was Melvin who had sneaked into his father's room that morning and committed the murderous act.

The Convent Mystery

Since nothing was ever missing, the inspector theorized that the intruder might be trying to remove something that arrived over the weekend. The only thing that regularly arrived over the weekend was the mail. His theory was bolstered by the fact that the Saturday mail was the only delivery personally handled by Mother Superior—each Monday morning.

The one woman who might benefit from intercepting the mail was Barbara, who had lied on her application. She had never worked for an Alaskan convent. During the week, Barbara screened the letters, looking for an Alaskan postmark. Then every Saturday, she broke in shortly after the mail delivery and checked again.

The Shortcut Robbery

Mary Ramsey testified that she saw her assailant only from the rear. And yet she stated categorically that he had been wearing a cardigan, a sweater that buttons up the front. There was no way she could have known from the rear if the sweater was a pullover or a cardigan. Mary was lying.

The police soon discovered that she faked her own attack in order to steal the jewelry store's receipts.

The Locked Room

Sheila testified that Jack looked through the keyhole. According to Jack, however, he made the suggestion but didn't have a chance to act on it before his brothers started ramming the door. Sheila may have been in a position to hear Jack talk about keyhole spying, but she didn't actually see him do it.

The most likely place for Sheila to have heard Jack was from inside the bedroom itself. Sheila killed her mother, set up the suicide, then hid behind the door. After the boys broke it in, she emerged from hiding, making it look as if she'd just arrived.

A Chinese Lie Detector

At dawn the next day, the emperor's court returned to the public garden and were amazed to find that not one but two of the bamboo stalks were higher. "Were there two thieves?" the captain wondered out loud.

"No, just one" the wizard replied. "Arrest the man with the short stalk. He was the only one with a reason to fear my magic. Thinking that his own stalk would grow, he sneaked back here in the middle of the night and cut it a finger joint shorter."

The Brothers Ilirium

The choir testified that Mike had been thrown before impact. And yet blood had been found in the car, indicating that Mike had been dead or injured before being thrown. The only person who testified to having actually seen Mike drive off was Roger, making him the prime suspect.

"We had a fight out in the garage," Roger confessed. "I knocked him down and he hit his head. It was an accident, but I was scared. I put the body in the convertible and drove down to the first sharp turn and stopped the car. Then I put a rock on the gas pedal and switched it into gear. I didn't worry about the blood because I didn't think he'd be thrown."

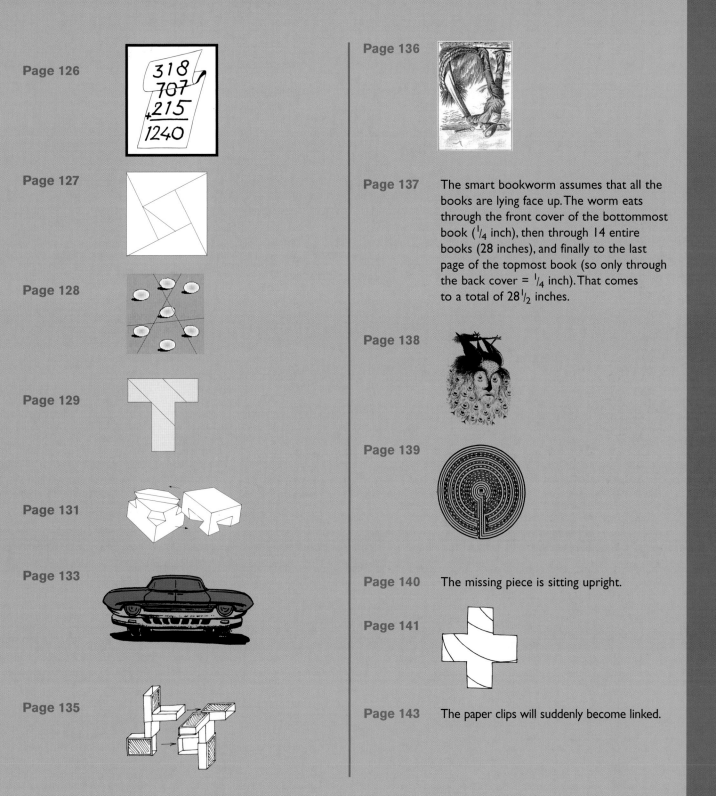

Page 126

Page 127

Page 128

Page 129

Page 131

Page 133

Page 135

Page 136

Page 137 The smart bookworm assumes that all the books are lying face up. The worm eats through the front cover of the bottommost book ($1/4$ inch), then through 14 entire books (28 inches), and finally to the last page of the topmost book (so only through the back cover = $1/4$ inch). That comes to a total of $28\frac{1}{2}$ inches.

Page 138

Page 139

Page 140 The missing piece is sitting upright.

Page 141

Page 143 The paper clips will suddenly become linked.

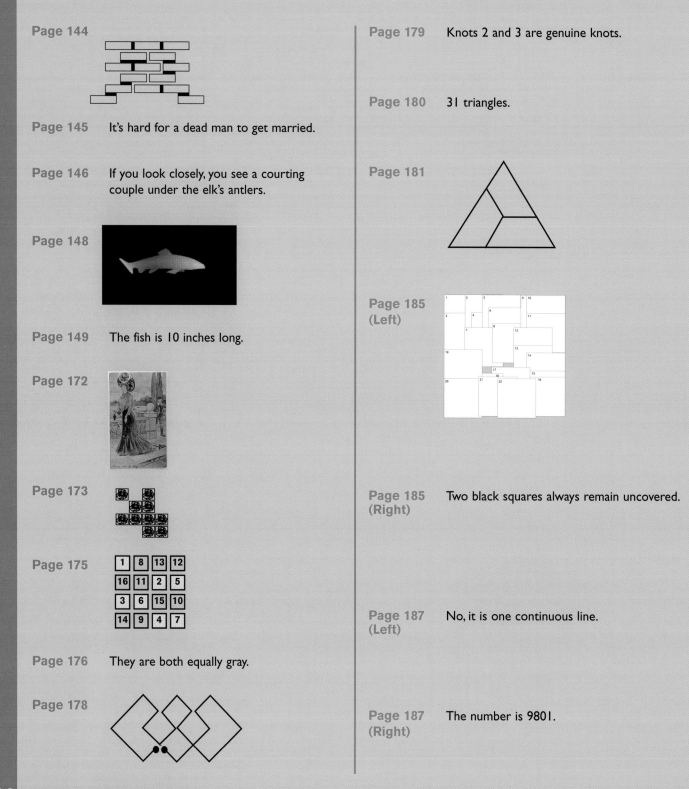

TRICKY PUZZLE ANSWERS

Page 144

Page 145 It's hard for a dead man to get married.

Page 146 If you look closely, you see a courting couple under the elk's antlers.

Page 148

Page 149 The fish is 10 inches long.

Page 172

Page 173

Page 175

1	8	13	12
16	11	2	5
3	6	15	10
14	9	4	7

Page 176 They are both equally gray.

Page 178

Page 179 Knots 2 and 3 are genuine knots.

Page 180 31 triangles.

Page 181

Page 185 (Left)

Page 185 (Right) Two black squares always remain uncovered.

Page 187 (Left) No, it is one continuous line.

Page 187 (Right) The number is 9801.

Page 75

Silicon Sally is a computer program.

In recent years, gangs of cyber terrorists have extorted between $400 million and $800 million around the world. With a customized office management system costing as much as $125 million, financial houses in both New York and London have paid ransoms rather than have their computers crash. These orchestrated crashes are caused by information warfare devices such as high-emission radio-frequency guns, capable of blowing a devastating electronic storm through the system.

Page 76

There couldn't be a grand staircase in a bungalow.

Page 77

Dr. Probe simply replaced the hamster.

Page 78

As you can see, the trick is to make the three knives interlock while resting on the glasses.

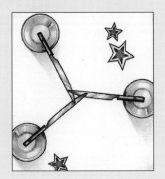

Page 79

Small house flies do not grow up to be big house flies; they're born full size, just like bees and butterflies. Larger flies are more likely to have been in the chrysalis longer and therefore are generally seen later in the year.

Page 84

There's no such language as Belgian. Languages spoken in Belgium include Dutch, French, Flemish, and Walloon.

Page 85

All bananas are picked while green, not yellow. Wild bananas in particular are both seedy and inedible. If a banana is picked when yellow, the starch will not turn to sugar, causing the banana to be tasteless. Further, should a banana be picked after it has ripened, the skin will usually break open, allowing bacteria to invade and cause it to rot.

Page 86

Although more than 50,000 pigeons were used as communication couriers in World War II, carrier or homing pigeons are strictly one-way birds. A pigeon is not able to take a message anywhere and then return home with an answer. The pigeon is taken along until a message needs to be sent back to the base—in this case, the bird's home. The message is then attached to the pigeon and the bird is released.

Page 87

Porcupines cannot shoot their quills, since they lack the necessary muscular mechanism to fire them. A porcupine defends itself by raising its barbed quills and thrashing its tail to drive them into an attacker.

Page 88

The barber was a woman.

Page 89

He saw the lights of the cars below. Only two European countries drive on the left side of the road—Britain and Finland. Since it was a very large city he saw, and they were destined for Greece, Snorri knew it could only be London.

Page 182

If Clem's musty old house had been boarded up for 7 years, the sterling silver cutlery would have been badly tarnished and not shiny. It was an obvious plant by the master of scams—Sam Sham.

Page 184

When Shadow crossed the room to close the window, he noted the heavy candle drippings facing the window. With a steady breeze blowing through the window, the wax drippings would have formed on the opposite side. Shadow knew that Shady had tampered with the scene and had carelessly misplaced the candle.

Page 186

Mike Peters was a 6-month-old baby.

Page 188

Shady, who had the only key, said that neither he nor anyone else had been in the room for a week. If this was true, the leaves of the plant would have been leaning toward the window, not away from it.

Page 190

Art Bragg would have suffocated in less than 2 minutes. By breathing through a 6-foot-long tube, he would be breathing the same air he expelled, rapidly reducing his oxygen level to zero.

Page 192

It is impossible to maintain one's balance in this manner. As any gymnastics teacher would know, if your feet are in contact with a wall and you attempt to bend over without bending your knees, your center of gravity will no longer be over your feet, which will cause you to fall forward.

Page 194

Professor Quantum flipped on the first switch and waited a couple of minutes. He then shut the first switch off, flipped on the second switch, and proceeded to go to the storage room. Once there, if the light was on, Quantum would obviously know that the second switch was the correct one. If it was still dark, Quantum would feel the lightbulb to see if it was warm. If so, the first switch was the correct one. If the bulb was both cold and dark, the correct switch would have to be the third one.

Monte Carlo

He lost. Every time that Hystrix wins, his money increases 1.5 times (with $100, he bets $50 and if he wins, he has $150). When he loses, his money is reduced by half. So a win-loss combination results in a loss of one quarter of his money. The more he plays, the more money he loses, even though he wins the same number of times as he loses.

The Harem

There were seven locks. Let's name the locks A, B, C, D, E, F, and G. The vizier had keys for A, B, C, D, E, and F. One of the slaves had the keys for A, B, C, and G. Another one, for A, D, E, and G. Another, for B, D, F, and G. And the last, for C, E, F, and G. With seven locks, the Great Tamerlan's system works—but not with fewer locks.

The Dividing End

The number is 381654729.

If the number is ABCDEFGHI, B, D, F, and H are even numbers. The rest are odd numbers. ABCDE can be divided evenly by 5, thus E = 5.

ABCD can be divided evenly by 4. Therefore, CD can also be divided evenly by 4, and since C is an odd number, D can only be 2 or 6.

ABCDEF can be divided evenly by 6 (by 2 and by 3). Since ABC can be divided by 3, DEF can be also. Consequently, DEF is 258 or 654.

You can deduce the rest from here.

The Island and the Englishmen

Six Englishmen. Let's draw four circles representing the clubs. Every two clubs have one member in common, so we draw a line from each circle to one point (an Englishman). Each dot is connected to two lines. This is the situation in the illustration, indicating six Englishmen.

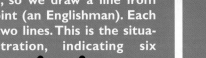

A Warm Farewell

10 men and 6 women. The number of handshakes and kisses adds up to 55. Each Porter said good-bye to each Robinson. If we multiply the number of members of both families, the result should be 55. There are two possibilities: 55 = 11 × 5 (one family with 11 members and the other one with 5), or 55 = 55 × 1 (which could not be possible, since a family is not formed by only one person).

We now analyze the handshakes following the same procedure. There are two possibilities: 21 = 7 x 3 (7 men in one family and 3 in the other) or 21 = 21 x 1 (which could not be possible, because none of these families has so many members, as seen above). Therefore, one family is formed by 7 men and 4 women, and the other by 3 men and 2 women.

The Ant and the Clock

The ant walked 54 minutes. From the first meeting to the second, the minute hand traveled 45 minutes and the ant a distance in minute marks of 105 minutes (45 + a complete 60-minute lap). The illustration below shows the path followed by the ant. The speed ratio is 45/105 = 3/7. From the start to the first meeting, the minute hand traveled a distance X and the ant (30 − X). Using the speed ratio, this would be X/(30 − X) = 3/7. X = 9 minutes. If we add these to the 45 minutes that it took the ant to get to the second meeting, we come to 54 minutes for the ant's trip.

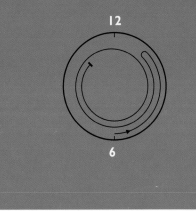

Mister Digit Face

The 9 must be inside the circle, because no product can be 9_ or _9. The 1, 2, and 5 must be outside the circle. From here on you can find the solution. (Other answers can be made by flipping or rotating the circle.)

Digit Tree

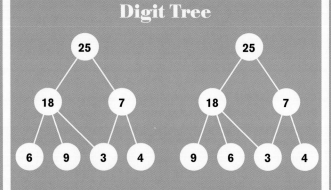

New Race

One car goes twice as fast as the other. The first crossing took place at point A. Consider A as a new starting point. Do the same for every crossing point. Since they drove at consistent speeds, the distances from A to B, B to C, and C to A are the same. After point A, one car must have driven twice the distance as the other to reach B at the same time. Therefore, one goes twice as fast as the other.

Logic Apples

Alonso 1, Bertrand 2, George 3, and Kurt 5.

Alonso could not have eaten 5 or more. Bertrand could not have eaten only 1 or he would have known that he hadn't eaten more than Alonso. Neither could he have eaten 5 or more. He could have eaten 2, 3, or 4. George figures this out, although he still doesn't know if he ate more than Bertrand. This means that George

must have eaten 3 or 4. Kurt can only deduce the other amounts if he ate 5. And the rest, in order to add up to 11, must have eaten 1, 2, and 3.

Added Corners

The 8 cannot be in a corner, so we have to put it in a square. The 7 must go in a square too. This makes it easy to figure out the rest.

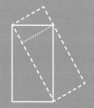

Rectangles

Both rectangles have the same area, 40 square inches. If you draw the dotted line you will see that the solid line divides the inclined figure into two equal pairs of triangles on both sides.

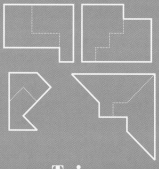

Figures to Cut in Two

Twins

I spoke to Peter. If a person always lies or alternately, always tells the truth, he cannot admit that he is lying (if this person were a liar, he would be telling the truth, and if this person were honest, he would be lying). Therefore, Paul could not have answered my question. Peter could answer about Paul without contradicting himself. What we don't know is who the liar is.

Twin Statistics

More than 3% of the population are twins. Out of 100 births, 97 are single and 3 are twins. That's 103 babies in total, six of which are twins, which represents 5.8% of the population.

The Professor and His Friend

Professor Zizoloziz wins. Every player takes an odd number of matches per play. After the first player goes, there will always be an odd number of matches left. After the second player goes, there will always be an even number of matches left. Therefore, the second player is the winner.

Economical Progression

1, 6, 11, 16, 21, 26. Other solutions are also possible.

Up and Down

22 steps. While Zizoloziz goes up the entire staircase, I descend the staircase except for 11 steps (7 at the top + 4 at the bottom). Since he goes twice as fast as me, the entire staircase is 2 × 11 steps.

What Month–I

February of a leap year. If a month starts and ends with the same day of the week, it must have a complete number of weeks plus one more day. The only possible month is a 29-day February.

What Month–II

August. In order to add up to 38, it can only be the highest possible number for the last Monday of a month (31) and the highest for the first Thursday of a month (7). Therefore, both last month and the current month ust have 31 days. The only two 31-day months in a row in the same calendar year are July and August.

Soccer Scores–I

The Eagles had 5 points. There were 10 matches in the tournament with a total of 20 points to be won by the teams. The table already has 15 points assigned. Therefore, the remaining 5 points must belong to the Eagles.

Soccer Scores–II

Lions 0, Tigers 0. Lions 1, Bears 0. Tigers 1, Bears 1. The Lions could only win 3 points by winning one match and tying another. Since they only scored one goal, the results must be 1-0 and 0-0. The Bears tied one and lost the other match. The scores must have been 1-1 and 0-1. Their tied game must have been against the Tigers. So the Lions beat the Bears 1-0, and the Lions tied the Tigers 0-0.

What Time Is It–I

5:00. From here, the minute hand will take 30 minutes to reach 6, and the hour hand will take an entire hour.

What Time Is It–II

There are two possible times in this situation: 5:15 (the minute hand takes 15 minutes to reach 6 and the hour hand takes 45) and 3:45 (the minute hand takes 45 minutes to reach 6 and the hour hand takes 2 hours and 15 minutes, which is 135 minutes).

What Time Is It–III

2:12. The hour hand is at the first minute mark after 2, and the minute hand is on the next minute mark.

What Time Is It–IV

9:48. The minute hand is on 48 minutes and the hour hand is on the next minute mark.

Prohibited Connection

Each middle digit (2, 3, 4, and 5) can only be connected to three others (for example, 2 can only be connected to 4, 5, and 6). There are two circles with four connections. We can only put 1 and 6 in them. Once you insert these, the rest is easy to figure out. Another solution exists where the order of the numbers is switched, so 1 and 6 switch, as do 2 and 5, and 3 and 4.

Concentric

30 square inches. We turn the small square as shown in the picture on the next page. We can see that it is half the size of the big one, as indicated by the dotted lines. These dotted lines divide the large square into 8 triangles, and the small square into 4 triangles.

Hidden Word–I

SOB

Hidden Word–II

PITHY

Hound–I

20	13	12	11	⑩
19	14	⑤	6	9
18	⑮	4	7	8
17	16	3	2	1

Hound–II

25	26	27	㉘	29	30	31
24	15	⑭	㉟	34	33	32
23	16	13	12	11	8	⑦
22	17	18	1	10	9	6
㉑	20	19	2	3	4	5

Hound–III

2	1	9	10	11
3	8	16	15	12
4	7	17	14	13
5	6	18	19	20
25	24	23	22	21

Hound–IV

25	16	15	12	11
24	17	14	13	10
23	22	21	20	9
2	3	18	19	8
1	4	5	6	7

Broken M

Skin and Shoes

It is enough to look at only one shoe. If, for example, the white man's right shoe is red, the left one has to be black. This means that the black man will have one left red shoe and one right white shoe, and so on.

Fort Knox Jumping Frogs–I

Move 5 onto 2, 3 onto 7, 4 onto 13, 6 onto 1, 12 onto 9, 11 onto 14, and 10 onto 8.

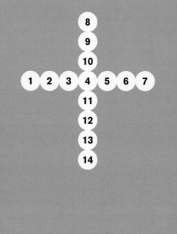

Fort Knox Jumping Frogs—II

Move 5 onto 12, 6 onto 4, 10 onto 11, 8 onto 1, 3 onto 2, and 9 onto 7.

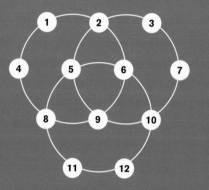

Irregular Circuit

300 yards from point A. The first passing point can be considered as a new starting point. Therefore, the new passing point will be 150 yards away.

Place Your Cards

From left to right: queen of spades, six of diamonds, and ace of hearts.

Nice Discounts

You first buy books for $80 and, the next day, for $70, which represents a discount of $70 × .08 = $5.60. (It will be the same result by inverting the order of the purchases—first the $70 purchase and the next day the $80 one.)

Enigmatic Fares

98999 and 99000. The tickets are consecutive in number. If the professor had answered "yes" to the question about the five digits of one ticket adding up to 35, the friend could not have figured out the numbers. There would have been several possibilities (78659 and 78660, 36989 and 36990, etc.), so the professor must have answered that indeed neither of the tickets added up to 35.

Both tickets add up to 62 (an even number), which means that the first one must end in a 9. If it ended in only one 9, one ticket would add up to 35. Let's call the first ticket ABCD9 and the second one ABC(D + 1)0. The sum is A + B + C + D + 9 + A + B + C + D + 1 = 62, meaning that A + B + C + D + 9 = 35. If it ended in two 9s, the sum of both tickets would give us an odd number.

Therefore, the ticket must end in three 9s and no more than three, or the sum wouldn't be 62. We can call the tickets AB999 and A(B+1)000, where B is not 9. The sum of both is 2 × (A + B) + 28 = 62. Therefore, A = 9 and B = 8.

Eve's Enigma

Thursday. The snake is lying, because it says that today is Saturday and tomorrow is Wednesday. Therefore, today is one of the days when the snake lies (Tuesday, Thursday, and Saturday). It cannot be Saturday or else the snake would not be lying in one statement. Nor can it be Tuesday, for the same reason. It can only be Thursday.

John Cash

The reward was 125 dollars. If you erase 1, you have 25 left, which is one fifth the original amount. If you erase 2, you have 5 left, which is one fifth of this amount.

To get 125, find a two-digit number in which you can take the first digit off and the result is one fifth of the number. The only possible number is 25:

$$25 \times 5 = 125.$$

Russian Roulette

The arsenic is in the jar labeled "SUGAR." We know that the snuff is above the salt. They cannot be on the right side, because then the salt would be in the jar labeled "SALT." They cannot be in the center either, because then the second answer would not be true since the coffee and sugar would not be next to each other. Therefore, they are on the left. So the coffee and sugar are in the jars marked "TEA" and "SALT," respectively, leaving arsenic for either the jar marked "ARSENIC" or "SUGAR." Since it's not in the correctly labeled jar, it must be in the jar marked "SUGAR," and the tea is in the jar marked "ARSENIC."

The Calculator Keys

There are two possibilities:
1. Exchange the 4 with the 5 and the 2 with the 8. 729 – 546 = 183.
2. Exchange the 3 with the 9 and the 4 with the 6. 783 – 654 = 129.

Strangers in the Night

The blonde woman killed Mr. Farnanski. There are only four true statements. Only one person is guilty. Therefore, three of the "I'm innocent" statements are true. Only one more statement can be true, and this must be the one made by the man in the dark suit or by the blonde woman. Therefore, "The brunette killed him" and "One of the men killed him" are false statements, so the blonde woman is the killer.

The Foreigners and the Menu

They could have ordered ABCDD their first night (finding out what D is), AEFGG the second night (finding out what G is and what A is, since they had ordered it the previous night, too), and BEHII the third night, (finding out what I, B, and E are). This leaves C, F, and H out, and since they had ordered these dishes once and each came on a different night, they should know what they are.

INDEX

BRAINTEASERS

10, 11, 12, 13, 14, 15, 16, 17, 18, 19, 20, 21, 22, 23, 24, 25, 26, 27, 28, 40, 41, 42, 43, 44, 45, 46, 47, 48, 49, 50, 51, 52, 136, 137, 138, 139, 140, 141, 142, 143, 144, 145, 146, 147, 148, 149

CLEVER MIND

A&P 82
All in the Neighborhood 76
Be Perfectly Frank 88
Don't Leave Me Out 73
Fill in the Blanks 70
Full of Hot Air 80
Head Start 78
How Far? 71
Lazy Days of Summer 66
Look Before You Leap 85
Making the Grade 89
Missed One! 83
My Three Sons 81
On All Fours 72
Pieces of Eight 67
Playing the Triangle 79
Seeing Spots 69
Six-Shooter 84
Small But Powerful 87
So Far, Yet So Close 74
Something is Missing 68
Strange Sequence 86
Through the Looking Glass 77
Wagering Above Board 75

CRITICAL THINKING

53, 54, 55, 56, 57, 58, 59, 60, 61, 66, 67, 68, 69, 70, 71, 72, 73, 74, 75, 76, 77, 90, 91, 92, 93, 94, 95, 96, 97, 98, 99, 100, 101, 136, 137, 138, 139, 140, 141, 142, 143, 144, 145, 146, 147, 148, 149

EYE-POPPERS

114, 115, 116, 117, 118, 119, 120, 121, 122, 123, 124, 125, 172, 173, 174, 175, 176, 177, 278, 179, 180, 181

IMPOSSIBLE OBJECTS

Ambiguous Stepped Pyramid 170
Cubes in Limbo, 82
Diamond Crossover 164
Dowel Block 161
Escalating Cube, 80
Ethereal Hexagon 167
Four-Seven Stick Stack 169
Incongruous Stepped Wall 171
Integral Cubicle, 81
Mental Blocks 163
Rectangular Trihedron 168
Space Fork 165
Tri-Domino 160
Triple-Warped Tribar 158
Truncated Tribar 162
Twelve-Cube Triangle 159
Two-Story Cube, 83
Warped Tribar Truncate 166

LATERAL THINKING

Alex Ferguson 24
Another Landlubber 22
Bertha's Travels 10
Chimney Problem 23
Co-Lateral Damage 17
Criminal Assistance 13
Dali's Brother 26
Deadly Dresser 20
Denise and Harry 16
Engraving 25
Flipping Pages 21
Golf Bag 20
Half for Me and Half for You 26
In the Middle of the Night 12

Inheritance 19
Landlubber 21
Legal Relief 28
Lifesaver 18
Material Witness 13
Mechanical Advantage 17
Nonconventional 28
Not Eating? 23
Office Job 16
One Mile 25
Plain and Simple 14
Rush Job 15
Shell Shock 14
Sick Leave 11
Single Word 18
Superior Knowledge 24
Test 22
Top at Last 12
Tracks of My Tires 10
Unfinished Business 19
Upset Woman 11
Who Did It? 27
Window Pain 27
Wonderful Weather 15

MIND-BENDERS

40, 41, 42, 43, 44, 45, 46, 47, 48, 49, 50, 51, 52, 53, 54, 55, 56, 57, 58, 59, 60, 61, 62, 63, 64, 65, 78, 79, 80, 81, 82, 83, 90, 91, 92, 93, 94, 95, 96, 97, 98, 99, 100, 101, 172, 173, 174, 175, 176, 177, 178, 179, 180, 181, 183, 184, 185, 186, 187, 188, 190, 192, 194

MINDTRAPS

75, 76, 77, 78, 79, 84, 85, 86, 87, 88, 89, 182, 184, 186, 188, 190, 192, 194

INDEX

OPTICAL ILLUSIONS
10, 11, 12, 13, 14, 15, 16, 17, 18, 19, 20, 21, 22, 23, 24, 25, 26, 27, 28, 40, 41, 42, 43, 44, 45, 46, 47, 48, 49, 50, 51, 52, 53, 54, 55, 56, 57, 58, 59, 60, 61, 62, 63, 64, 65, 66, 67, 68, 69, 70, 90, 91, 92, 93, 94, 95, 96, 97, 98, 99, 100, 101

SELF-SCORING IQ TESTS
Test 1 29–39
Test 2 102–113

SHREWD CHALLENGES
A Warm Farewell 66
Added Corners 72
Ant and the Clock, The 67
Broken M 132
Calculator Keys 191
Concentric 101
Digit Tree 69
Dividing End, The 64
Economical Progression 93
Enigmatic Fares 187
Eve's Enigma 189
Figures to Cut in Two 74
Foreigners and the Menu 193
Fort Knox Jumping Frogs—I 134
Fort Knox Jumping Frogs—II 135
Harem, The 63
Hidden Word—I 126
Hidden Word—II 127
Hound—I 128
Hound—II 129
Hound—III 130
Hound—IV 131
Irregular Circuit 184
Island and the Englishmen, The 65
John Cash 189
Logic Apples 71
Mister Digit Face 68
Monte Carlo 62

New Race 70
Nice Discounts 186
Place Your Cards 185
Professor and His Friend 92
Prohibited Connection 100
Rectangles 73
Russian Roulette 191
Skin and Shoes 133
Soccer Scores I 96
Soccer Scores II 97
Strangers in the Night 193
Twin Statistics 91
Twins 90
Up and Down 94
What Month I & II 95
What Time Is It I & II 98
What Time Is It III & IV 99

SNEAKY THINKING
150, 151, 152, 153, 154, 155, 156, 157, 158, 159, 160, 161, 162, 163, 164, 165, 166, 167, 168, 169, 170, 171

TRICKY PUZZLES
126, 127, 128, 129, 130, 131, 132, 133, 134, 135, 136, 137, 138, 139, 140, 141, 142, 143, 144, 145, 146, 147, 148, 149, 172, 173, 174, 175, 176, 177, 178, 179, 180, 181, 182, 185, 187

TRIVIA
History & Science 114, 115, 116, 117, 118, 119, 120, 121, 122, 123, 124, 125
Movies & Television 40, 41, 42, 43, 44, 45, 46, 47, 48, 49, 50, 51, 52

Music, Arts & Letters 53, 54, 55, 56, 57, 58, 59, 60, 61, 62, 63, 64, 65
Travel & Geography 84, 85, 86, 87, 88, 89

TRULY BAFFLING ILLUSIONS
Christmas Tree 152
Dark Diamonds 150
Floating Diamonds 154
Italics 156
Long Long Lizard 153
Luminous Illusion 151
Perpetual Motion 157
Visual Turbine 155

WHODUNITS
Agent Brown's Shining Moment 114
An Attack of Gas 130
Archie's Christmas Surprise 124
Brothers Ilirium 135
Chinese Lie Detector 134
Convent Mystery 131
Death of a Deceiver 116
Dirty Cop 122
Eye Spy 127
Last Poker Hand 126
Locked Room 133
Long-Distance Murder 120
Party's Over 117
Piney Bluffers 128
Postgraduate Murder 125
Queen Glendora Photos 121
Shortcut Robbery 132
Smuggler and the Clever Wife 118
Stolen Cleopatra 123
Suicidal House Guest 119
Super Bowl Madness 115
Vandalizing Visitor 129